The Uriah Factor

A novel by
D. Charles King

Name: D. Charles King
Title: The Uriah Factor
By D. Charles King
ISBN:
978-1-963611-19-9 (paperback)
978-1-963611-21-2 (ebook)

Subjects: 1. Literature & Fiction>Religious & Inspirational Fiction>Christian>Romance>Contemporary
2. Literature & Fiction>Religious & Inspirational Fiction>Christian>Romance>Mystery & Suspense
3. Mystery, Thriller & Suspense>Thrillers>Historical

Cover Design: Robin Black
Cover photo credits: Female Runner iStock-Maridav; war background WWII_iStock-Zeferli

Unless otherwise noted, all scriptures are from the KING JAMES VERSION, public domain.

Published by EA Books Publishing, a division of Living Parables of Central Florida, Inc. a 501c3

EABooksPublishing.com

DEDICATION

In memory of Sgt. Charles N. King, I Company, 379th Regiment, 95th Infantry Division, 3rd Army, who died as a result of wounds received at the Saar River crossing December 1944.

And David wrote in the letter, saying, "Set ye Uriah in the forefront of the battle, and retire ye from him, that he may be smitten, and die." — *II* Samuel 11:15, KJV

ONE

THE CLASSROOM WAS an anachronism—but then, Dr. Warren Emerson, who taught the class, often felt like an anachronism himself.

The classroom, designated Hilliard 100, in one of the older buildings on the campus of Duke University, was a semi-circular auditorium comprised of nearly one hundred desks, all bolted to the floor and all varnished to a high gloss, each row of desks banked toward the entry door in the back, like a series of concentric C's—each row two steps above and slightly wider than the previous row. Hilliard 100 had no windows. The desks, the paneled walls, and the floor were stained the identical color (it could have been called a dark honey) and it seemed as if the maintenance department, having found an approved color—rather than risk a departure from the scheme—had painted everything with the honey stain. The color extended to the stage which ran the width of the front of the room. The monochromatic wooden motif extended to the huge podium in the middle of the stage. Spotlights were oriented toward the podium, which accentuated its gloss. That additional luster made the podium look like it was encased in a cloudy glass shell.

Dr. Emerson, who sat on the right edge of the stage, looked at the podium. *How many layers of varnish are there? Does maintenance add a layer each year?*

The only departure from the honey color theme in Hilliard 100 was the chair on the stage in which Dr. Emerson sat. That chair was not wooden; it was aluminum and plastic—blue plastic—obviously originating from a later era than the desks in the lecture hall. In fact, Dr. Emerson had borrowed it from across the hall. He was positioned at the edge of the broad stage where he could see both the podium and the classroom. A well-worn leather valise lay against the side of the chair.

Warren Emerson, B.A Western Illinois; M.A. Purdue; Ph.D. Columbia, was 61 years old and although he had an alert countenance and a cheerful disposition, looked somewhat older. Years of bending over books had curled his posture somewhat—and while he always intended to maintain an exercise program, he rarely persisted more than a few weeks at a time. Warren Emerson read profusely—on a wide variety of subjects—and often late at night he was prone to interrupt his reading to check the refrigerator for left-over lemon squares, for which his wife was famous among the students who were frequently in their home. That tendency accounted for the pudge which protruded over his belt, which he often patted absentmindedly, as if his subconscious mind was reminding himself of his lack of discipline. *As soon as this term is over, I will adopt an exercise program,* he told himself. It was the same promise he had made nearly every year of the twenty-two years he had been at Duke.

He looked at the lecture hall. Fewer than twenty of the one hundred desks were occupied by students. Dr. Emerson did not ordinarily conduct *HI422, Concepts in History* in Hilliard 100. Ordinarily the class met on the third floor—in a more conventional classroom. However, at the end of the term, when it was time for student reports, he preferred to move the class to the lecture hall. With its stage and podium, it seemed more appropriate for oral reports. However, as he looked at the room, he realized it was an appropriate metaphor for himself—fixed, monochromatic, and encased in the past. *If I'm here next year, I will not use this room for reports,* he told himself.

If I'm here next year ... Dr. Emerson had been giving a great deal of thought to the idea that he would *not* be here next year—that he might actually retire. Retirement held obvious attractions to him—less pressure for class preparation, more time with Rachel, his wife, and the opportunity to travel. *Would my retirement package be adequate to cover our travel? Supplemental income will be necessary, no doubt.* Two years earlier he had written to a few American schools in Europe about part-time teaching positions, and the responses had been encouraging. Rachel had encouraged him to take the step. He drafted a

3

resignation letter to the Duke administration—but that letter, two years later, still lay in the drawer of his desk.

The reason that letter still lay in his desk had to do with one particular student. That student, two years earlier, had reignited the energy for teaching Warren Emerson had felt when he first started his career. That student held an affinity for one of his personal strong interests—ancient Greek history, and that student was about to graduate *magna cum laude* in a few weeks. That student had become a regular visitor in his home and he—as well as his wife—had developed a strong attachment to that student.

That student was currently sitting on the front row of the desks in Hilliard 100. Her name was Jamie Patterson; she was listening carefully to the student on the stage who was delivering his oral report. She twisted her pencil as she listened. Dr. Emerson recognized the habit. Jamie always twisted her pencil when in thought.

He could not, however, give the rest of the class any credit for thinking—or even for paying attention. Some of the male members of the class—who had deliberately positioned themselves near the front, along the edges of the concentric desks—were not watching the presenter; they were watching Jamie Patterson. Hers had already been one of the most famous female faces on campus even before the *Sports Illustrated* article had come out a few weeks earlier. Her face on the front of a national magazine had inspired a strange pride among her classmates. "Yeah, I've got History with her. She's a fox all right," Dr. Emerson heard one of his students say. He was not entirely sure he understood all the current slang, but he understood the context and tone of voice behind the description "fox".

Her uncommon good looks had always gained attention and during her sophomore year, as Jamie had distinguished herself in the classroom some male students had referred to her as "The Face … The Brain..." but when she won the conference championship in the 800 meters, the appellation was amended to "The Face … The Brain … The Legs." More than once Dr. Emerson had seen a pair of male students meet Jamie on the campus sidewalks, and in passing they would smile, and one would whisper: "The Face … The Brain …" and the other would rejoin with "… the Legs."

But he noted with some amusement that these young men, although they often talked *about* Jamie, they never seemed to talk *to* her.

Dr. Emerson mentioned that fact to his wife one evening. "The boys are all intimidated by her," she responded. (Rachel Emerson always referred to the male students as "boys", never "men.")

"The smart ones," she continued, "the intellectuals, are intimidated by her looks and the social ones are intimidated by her intellect."

Warren Emerson considered his wife's analysis and nodded in agreement. "However," he responded, "I'm not sure but that the 'smart ones', as you call them, are not also intimidated by her intellect. She's certainly smarter than any of those who have been in my classes recently." He paused for a moment before going on. "The interesting thing is that I don't think Jamie has any idea she is intimidating." What Dr. Emerson said about Jamie was accurate. She seemed completely unaware that she was intimidating. She dressed conservatively, wore little jewelry except gold loop earrings—a gift from her father—almost no makeup, and she took little pains with her hair, which today, as it was almost every day, was pulled into a ponytail.

Many of the students who sat behind Jamie and were not afforded a view of her now famous face, were looking at the walls—as if they were imaginary windows—perhaps imagining how the morning sunshine looked on the jonquils and irises blooming along the edges of the sidewalks as spring came to the North Carolina landscape. A few feigned interest in the report emanating from the podium, but one student near the back had given up all pretense of paying attention, and had put his head on his desk. His eyes were closed, and a little drool had formed out of the corner of his mouth, which glistened on the varnished desktop. Others fidgeted in their seats. One of the few female students worked assiduously on her fingernails with an emery board.

Dr. Emerson did not fault any of these students for failing to listen to this particular report from this particular student. Lance Snelling was the student, and, as Dr. Emerson would report later to his associates in the History Department, "Mr. Snelling apparently misunderstood the assignment; he thought it was for a student *harangue* rather than a student *report*."

"Obscene amounts of money are misdirected …!" Lance Snelling shouted from the podium, temporarily awakening the student in the back, who raised his head slightly, then put it back down again.

Dr. Emerson looked at his students. Several of them, he knew, would be entering law school in the fall. When he had begun teaching, more than two decades earlier, a higher percentage of his seniors sought careers in teaching, but that tendency had changed. Now a higher percentage planned careers in law. The only question for undergraduates was: Which undergraduate degree will I seek prior to law school— Political Science, English, or History? Fewer chose History than the other two, but many of those who did, sat in this class.

One of the debates among professors on campus was whether abrasiveness among pre-law students was an inherited or learned characteristic—and although there was no consensus on that issue, it was generally held that those future lawyers who chose history as their avenue to law school were on the lower end of the abrasiveness spectrum, and for that Dr. Emerson kept reminding himself he should be grateful. "Sometimes I wonder," one of his colleagues from the English department said, "whether some of these students love law—or whether they love money."

Dr. Emerson could offer no reply to that concern, but he certainly did not love law or money. He loved *ideas*—particularly ideas rooted in history, the great ideas and events and concepts and inventions that shaped the world. To these ideas and themes he was as addicted as any addict to his heroin. He read about these ideas; he thought about these ideas; he talked about these ideas, and he instructed his students (or at least, tried to instruct them) concerning these ideas. He was not consistently convinced that he was effective in communicating his passion for *ideas*. However, Jamie Patterson, he realized, was different from the great majority of his students. Because of her enchantment with the great ideas, he had become enchanted with her. She seemed to be the first student in many years who shared his passion for the great themes of the humanities. *If only I could persuade her to seek a career in teaching.*

Dr. Emerson looked at the class again as Lance Snelling continued, "... irresponsible, misguided and reprehensible policies of the administration ...!" he shouted. The girl filing her nails stopped briefly, rolled her eyes, and went back to her efforts. It was understandable that these students were generally inattentive to the student reports—the weather was warm, graduation was imminent—and most of the reports were boring. The only real exception to the class's inattentiveness regarding the student reports had occurred the day before when Jamie Patterson gave her report. It compared citizen participation in modern

American democracy to participation in the ancient Greek democracy. It was a brilliant paper, but Dr. Emerson knew it was Jamie Patterson's appearance—not the content of the report—that created the interest. After that report, all others were bound to be anti-climactic.

Jamie twisted her pencil. She was listening to the report. Dr. Emerson was glad *someone* was listening. He saw her jot a note on her pad.

Lance Snelling was dressed completely in black—black pants, black collarless shirt, a black jacket over that, black socks, black shoes. His hair was dyed black and his goatee—had it been thicker—would have been black also.

He delivered his report with great intensity, but his eyes were riveted on his notes. He never looked up. He alternately gripped and struck the podium, rocking his thin body and arms back and forth in time with his sentences. His tone was condescending—as if he were explaining his points to a child. "There is no excuse for the inexcusable behavior of this administration ..." Dr. Emerson shook his head. *No excuse for the inexcusable ... Should I count off for redundancy?*

Jamie made another note in her pad. She was not unfamiliar with Lance Snelling. They had entered Duke the same year. Lance had started in Political Science, but he flunked PS94 *Contemporary Political Ideologies* the first semester and then transferred to the History department, where he and Jamie had had several classes together for the last seven semesters.

Lance Snelling was well known at the university as the most energetic campus activist that had come through since the '60s. Over the course of his Duke career, he had been the outspoken advocate of several issues. Elimination of the grading system had been one of his early topics. "If I had his grades," one professor noted, "I also would suggest the elimination of the grading system." His advocacy for free tuition for all students (along with room and board and a monthly stipend) followed soon after. More recently, he had advocated for free condom distribution at the campus health clinic. "Does anyone really believe," one campus wag had posted on a campus bulletin board, "that Lance Snelling will save money when condoms are free?"

Lance Snelling's most recent cause—and the one that was the subject of the report he was delivering was "A Call for the Elimination of College Athletics".

"Obscene amounts of money are invested for purposes not essential to the mission of the university…" he ranted.

The topic was not appropriate for this class, but Dr. Emerson, like the rest of the faculty, had taken the position that it was easier to placate Lance Snelling than to argue with him.

Dr. Emerson recalled a comment from a colleague, "For Lance Snelling, every conversation is an argument—an argument that must be conveyed in the harshest possible terms."

He kept his face down as he read the hand-written text from ruled notebook paper. His hair was long in front, which obscured his face, and the forelock flopped in emphasis when he came on a point of particular anger, "... gladiator-athletes who stir blood-thirsty crowds to greater and greater frenzy ..." His forelock flopped violently when he hit the podium with his open palm. The noise woke the sleeping student again, who raised up, looked around briefly, wiped the slobber from his cheek and put his head down again.

Lance Snelling continued with mounting energy: "If this were truly an *academic* institution, as it purports to be, then it would do away with athletics altogether. An *academic* institution has no place fostering, encouraging, or promoting an athletic program—an *academic* institution should promote *academics* and nothing else." Each time he said "academics" he flopped his hair for emphasis. "This institution needs to return to its intellectual roots; it needs to shed itself of all extraneous baggage that hinders it from its core mission—which is to be the best *academic* institution it can be. *Athletics* (he pronounced the word as if it were an obscenity), which has no place in any enlightened society, certainly has no place in an *academic* society." His voice rose to a shout. "The sooner this university's athletic program is divorced from its academic program, the better the university—and society will be!"

Lance Snelling, for the first time, looked up at his audience. His report was concluded. The expression on his face was anticipatory—as if he expected tumultuous applause, or to be carried on his listeners' shoulders to the president's office, where papers would be signed, and notices given that the university had abolished the athletic department—making the world a better place. He stood like a liberator—a messiah.

However—in the classroom itself—such a response did not seem imminent; his audience did not seem to be immediately ready to carry the champion anywhere. Lance Snelling, when he looked up at his classmates, found his would-be disciples, rather than animated by his charge to them, rather than energized by his entreaties—to be in some sort of stupor. A few looked at their watches, calculating how much longer it would be until the bell rang. Others looked around absent-mindedly. The girl with the fingernail file put it away in her purse, snapped the purse closed and put it in her lap.

Dr. Emerson picked up his valise and walked over to the podium. "We have a few minutes." He spoke slowly and calmly. He hoped the timbre of his voice might mitigate the tone of the just-concluded presentation. "Does anyone have any questions or comments related to Mr. Snelling's report?"

No one responded.

Dr. Emerson surveyed the class. "Are there any questions or comments?" The student who had slept through the class wiped the drool from his cheek and adopted a studious expression—as if he were contemplating a penetrating question, but that question remained unasked.

"Anyone? A question or comment?"

Still no response.

"Miss Patterson, I think you took some notes."

The class turned their attention toward Jamie.

"Miss Patterson?"

Jamie put her glasses on. The tortoise-shell frames highlighted her sun-streaked brown hair. "There are two points in Mr. Snelling's argument that should be addressed," she said clearly. "First, the paper contends that the athletic program is a financial drain on the university. That is an undocumented assertion. He cites the amount of money that is expended in an athletic program—for scholarships, for salaries, for administration, for facilities and maintenance; however, the paper did not cite any revenues. Athletic departments receive revenues from ticket sales, from media contracts and from donations. The failure to cite these revenues flaws the argument of the paper."

Jamie paused for a moment. Lance Snelling shifted his weight from side to side and straightened the papers in his hands. Dr. Emerson motioned for Jamie to continue.

"If the revenues I mentioned were considered, I believe adequate data is available to refute the general argument that an athletic program is a financial drain on a university—at least at a university with a successful athletic program. A great deal of data suggests that a university with a successful athletic program enhances the overall financial status of that university. Besides the obvious benefits of increased ticket sales and increased media revenues, general student enrollment has been shown to be linked to the athletic success of the university. In other words, a high school senior is more likely to enroll at a college that had a successful athletic program during the student's senior year in high school. This additional tuition, of course, raises the general income of the institution. In a similar vein, it has been demonstrated that alumni donations, a major source of funding for most universities, is correlated to athletic success. A doctoral thesis on this subject, submitted recently by a Florida State physical education major, who included Duke University in his study, found that alumni donations closely tracked athletic success—a pattern he found at all the universities cited in his study."

Lance Snelling rolled his tongue over his lips as Jamie looked down at her notes. Dr. Emerson nodded for her to go on.

She seemed reluctant but continued. "In addition to the interpretative flaw I see in the paper, there is, I believe, a logical flaw as well. The paper calls for, and I think I am quoting correctly: '… a return to the purely *academic* role of the institution.' The reasoning here seems flawed in the etymological usage of 'academic'. That word is derived from a particular school in Athens—The Academy. If we were to check the curriculum of The Academy, we would find that it put a much greater emphasis on athletics than do modern institutions. A greater portion of the day—for students at The Academy was spent in wrestling and track and field events while a lesser portion of the day was devoted to logic, rhetoric and philosophy and participation in the athletic events was not limited to a few—it was required of all."

Jamie looked reluctant to continue, but Dr. Emerson nodded for her to go on.

Jamie looked at her notes again. "And I think the founder of The Academy, from which we derive the word *academics*, would find it odd that athletics be excluded from the curriculum, for Plato—who founded the school—had been a wrestler and an Olympian long before he became a teacher."

The class went quiet.

Two of the young men looked at each other, smiling, and mouthed silently in perfect unison: "The Face, The Brain."

Lance Snelling, still beside the podium, pointed his finger weakly as if he were going to make a rebuttal—a rebuttal, it seemed, that would not form on his lips. He narrowed his eyes, and a little guttural sound came from his mouth as he cleared his throat, but that was the only response he could muster. Then, at that moment—as if the gods of academia wanted to spare Lance Snelling any further embarrassment—the bell rang, and class was over.

TWO

"LADIES AND GENTLEMEN..." The speaker wore a Veterans of Foreign Wars cap and a blue-fringed gold-colored VFW vest. He stood on a platform inside the University of Kansas football stadium. Behind him, in blue and red, painted in the endzone was: "Jayhawks". The field was filled with several thousand people, most seated in folding chairs, some still milling around the edges of the seating area. Much of the lower level of the stadium seating was full as well. Signs were scattered throughout the stadium. "Henninger for President", or "Harrison Henninger" or "Harrison 'Hell-No' Henninger", but most said just "Hell No!" and most of them had a handgun pictured prominently. Stretched across the goalposts behind the platform hung a banner "Veterans of Foreign Wars—Kansas" Another banner below it said, "THE WAR ON WASHINGTON".

"... allow me to introduce ..." the speaker paused for effect, "... one of us, a true American, a true patriot, a warrior for our nation—" Cheering from the crowd began to swell as they raised their signs in the air. A few hundred red, white, and blue balloons were released. "... the one who will lead us on our war on Washington ..." he pointed to the man on the platform who was rising from his chair. "Ladies and gentlemen, help me welcome Harrison 'Hell-No' Henninger! The noise that erupted at that moment rivaled any such cheer for a game-winning touchdown.

As Harrison Henninger shook the hand of the man who had just introduced him, the crowd waved their signs and chanted in unison, "Henninger … Henninger … Henninger". He stepped to the podium and the cheers swelled.

He took the podium with both arms. The California billionaire was not a tall man nor broad-shouldered, but his bearing, as he held the podium, emanated strength and confidence. He wore an unbuttoned VFW vest over an open-collared blue shirt. He narrowed his eyes and looked at the throng below. Flash cameras around the edge of the stage threw their light against his face in machine-gun fashion. It was a stern face. It was a face whose image had appeared on the cover of all the major news magazines during the past few months as Harrison Henninger had become the most amazing U.S. political phenomenon in decades.

The face that the flash cameras illuminated was a steely, unrelenting face. None of the photos on the covers of the magazines had shown Harrison Henninger smiling—and none of the ones taken at this occasion would either. His hair was a flat gray, like the color of an old Navy vessel, thinning slightly and combed back from his forehead. Those eyes were gray, matching his hair and there was a cool intensity in his visage as he surveyed the crowd below him. He was not unaccustomed to this spectacle. It was a scene he had witnessed almost daily for the last two weeks. He referred to his campaign as "The War on Washington" and he was in the final week of a two-week campaign that began in California, headed east, with stops planned in a dozen cities across the country, with the intention of concluding in Washington, D.C. Most of the events were planned in football stadiums because few indoor facilities could accommodate the crowds that Henninger attracted.

The cheering continued. For thirty seconds or more he nodded his head in approval of the adulation. Finally, he raised his arms to quiet the crowd. Even as the noise subsided there were punctuated exclamations of "Give 'em hell, Harrison!"

The noise became a low buzz. Henninger looked at the crowd with his gray eyes. He nodded his head more vigorously. The buzz became louder in anticipation of Henninger's next move. They knew what to expect. Henninger reached toward his pocket as a crescendo of cheers arose. He slowly pulled a handgun from his pocket and held it up for all to see. The crowd roared.

"This gun ..." he said as he wrapped his fingers around the handle, sliding his trigger finger into the slot, turning it back and forth "... is a U.S. Army standard-issue Colt M1908 38 caliber hammerless handgun, manufactured in the United States of America and designed to eradicate the enemies of the

United States—and this gun is loaded!" This was Henninger's trademark opening to his speeches. It never varied. Every speech began with that introduction. "But it is more than that. It is a symbol—a symbol for all who want to confront our enemies again. This gun went with me across Europe, and it fired on our enemies. It is a symbol that we are ready to fight again!" The crowd erupted in applause.

"In Washington, D.C., that cesspool of professional politicians, they know we have declared war … and they know we are coming—and that's why they are afraid."

His detractors, and there were many, accused him of building a campaign on resentment—a charge he did not deny. "Of course, there is resentment," he told the press in Denver two days before, "We resent those idiots in Washington who are giving our country away. When we started this campaign a few months ago, it was in response to your complaints—complaints about taxes, complaints about corrupt politicians, complaints about unfair competition for jobs, complaints about the inaccessibility of markets and complaints that no one cared for the common people anymore. Well, we have heard those complaints, and we are taking those complaints to Washington."

Henninger paused when the crowd cheered. "No offense to the gentleman who introduced me, but I have not said I was a candidate for president of the United States—not yet. But you might be surprised how many contacts we get from the professional politicians—

those guys in Washington. Yeah, they call us. And you know what they want to know?" He looked over the audience. "They want to know *what I want.* They sound like a defeated enemy ready to discuss terms of surrender. They want to know my terms."

He held up the gun again. "Now when I carried this gun across Europe, we did not offer any terms to Adolph Hitler. He was told to admit to unconditional surrender. And what did he do? When he was not offered terms, he blew his brains out. We didn't offer any terms to the Japs either. Unconditional surrender was the only option."

The "Henninger Phenomenon", as it was called, had baffled politicians and political pundits. One editorial said this:

Harrison Henninger is not the first politician to tap into voter resentment—but he has proven to be the best at it and the best at reaching a wider range of political convictions. His message—though some deem it as crass—has resounded with a significant number of American voters. And although Harrison Henninger has no political experience and although he has not officially committed to offer himself as a presidential candidate— whether he does so or not—he has made himself a significant factor in the race.

It was true that Henninger had no political experience, and it was also true that he did not have a traditional campaign organization—facts that further confounded the professional politicians.

Harrison Henninger's political organization had its beginning, shortly after the last presidential election. He had contributed heavily to several congressmen, several senators and especially to the sitting president, Wilson Cavanaugh. To all these politicians he made it abundantly clear that he wanted new tariff legislation passed—legislation he claimed was necessary to protect U.S. industries, but which his critics said was simply to provide a monopoly for Henninger Industries. When the legislation he wanted was not passed—and had not been strongly supported by the White House—Henninger began to put together an "exploratory committee" to determine the feasibility of his running for president himself. The question was—and the political pundits asked it often: "Does Harrison Henninger want to be president … or does he just want to become richer?" It was a question Harrison Henninger would not answer. However, he always answered the equally frequent question: "When will you make an official announcement concerning your candidacy?" The answer always came quickly: "As soon as I'm damned ready."

Anger was the impetus that provoked Harrison Henninger to develop a political organization and anger seemed to sustain it.

Harrison Henninger employed the same attitude in his campaign as he had in his business—blunt, aggressive, and hard-nosed. Henninger Industries, the west-coast company he had founded shortly after World War II, owned a series of electronic, agricultural, textile, and manufacturing interests throughout the west coast—from San Diego to Seattle, and it held shipping and mining interests throughout the west and also in South America. In recent years the company had begun to add real estate and agricultural holdings in the eastern U.S.

Henninger Industries had donated hundreds of thousands of dollars to U.S. politicians—in the hope of keeping foreign products out of the U.S. Japanese, Chinese and German products came into the country much too easily, Henninger told the politicians. And South American cheap labor was taking jobs from Americans, he complained.

His complaints found sympathetic ears among a wide variety of Americans. It appealed to business owners because they agreed with Henninger's assessment of unfair competition. It appealed to union workers—black and white—for they saw their jobs going to workers in other countries. It appealed to farmers, for they saw an opportunity to open overseas markets for their goods. Henninger's message, in fact, seemed to appeal to everyone. The polls showed Henninger—although he had not announced his candidacy—making impressive progress each week. His claim—that the politicians were scared—was not an exaggeration. The president's advisors were working overtime in an effort to blunt Henninger's momentum. In the president's most recent press conferences he had mentioned "unfair competition" and "foreign governments dumping their products in America" to help mitigate Henninger's appeal. He said he would ask Congress to provide legislation that would "ensure every American citizen has an equal opportunity in the world marketplace".

"Yeah, now, all of a sudden they hear us," he told the crowd in Denver. "They hear us because we're shouting so loud, but as soon as we quit shouting, do you think they will hear us?"

"Hell no!" came the thunderous response.

"The professional politicians want to know what I want. They sound like a defeated army ready to discuss conditions of surrender." He held the gun so the crowd could see it. "Remember what I said. When I carried this gun across Europe, we did not offer any conditions to Adolph Hitler—and he blew his own brains out. Same thing in Japan. Unconditional surrender was what we demanded, and those generals slit their own bellies. My message to Washington is: *Learn something from history!*" A great roar went up from the crowd.

"Make no mistake. We are under attack again. The Germans are attacking us with their cars and their technology. The Japanese are attacking us with their cars and stereos and computers. The Chinese are attacking us with their textiles. The Middle East is attacking us with their overpriced oil. The Mexicans are attacking us with their cheap labor. The world is attacking the United States of America … and what are those people in Washington doing to defend us? Nothing!"

He paused while the crowd cheered again. "Now I want to ask you a question—" The audience hung on his words. They knew how Henninger closed his speeches. "I want to ask you a question," he repeated. *"Are you going to take this anymore?"*

"Hell no!" came the response.

Henninger cupped his hand around his ear, *"I couldn't hear you."*

"Hell no!" the crowd responded even louder.

"What is my name?"

"Harrison ... hell, no ... Henninger!" reverberated through the stadium as Henninger held his hands in the air—his right hand holding his U.S. Army standard issue Colt 38 handgun—before departing the stage.

THREE

"I AM NOW certain I have grown old."

Patrick McCullough, Provost for Academic Affairs for Duke University, stood at the third-story window of his office, hands behind his back, looking out at the campus below. The window casements were thrown open, and from his vantage point, looking down on the central campus lawn, he could see a scene worthy of a postcard. Below him lay English gothic buildings, constructed from blue-gray and russet igneous stone—those buildings connected by an intersecting maze of sidewalks, with dozens of blossoming dogwoods throwing pink and white flowers on the grass with each puff of breeze. Students, laden with back-packs, walked briskly on the crisscrossed sidewalks, the geometry of those sidewalks softened by the filigree of oak leaves hanging over them.

During the earlier part of the academic year, Dr. McCullough could look on the stately spires of the Duke Chapel and see the statue of the university's benefactor, James B. Duke—cane in one hand, cigar in the other—but on this day in mid-May, the fresh growth on the oaks outside his window had obscured his view in that direction.

"And how have you come to this recent certitude, Patrick?" Dr. Emerson asked without looking up from the book *In Defense of Sanity,* by G.K. Chesterton, that he was perusing. He turned it over in his hand and replaced it among the hundreds of other leather-bound volumes on the shelves—shelves that ran to the ceiling. The provost's office was expansive. One section was the working section where the provost had his desk and the other, with an array of wingback chairs and a small couch around a low ebony table, was designed to accommodate a small gathering. The couch and chairs were brown leather with tufted buttons and bronze lions' paws on the legs. Bronze lamps sat on the ebony end tables between the couch and the chairs. The interior wall of that section—like the other area—was covered by the bookshelves, which were filled with brown and black and maroon leather-bound tomes, held in place by heavy bronze bookends. Interspersed among the books were several marble busts of some of the world's great thinkers. When Dr. Emerson looked at these bookshelves—and this office—he thought of how disorganized his own bookshelves and office were in comparison, but he knew these books and this office served a different function. These books were not for reading. These books were for intimidation.

Dr. McCullough often had the unpleasant duty of meeting with a student and parents in this room to discuss the student's "lack of academic progress", the conventional euphemism used to describe the particular student's failing grades. Dr. McCullough, in these instances, would sometimes suggest that it might be wise for the student in question to continue his or her education at another institution. During these appointments, Dr. McCullough sat in the chair with its back to the bookshelves and busts. The parents and student facing Dr. McCullough had to look—against the backdrop of several hundred classic editions—at the serious faces of Cicero, of Beethoven, of Jefferson, of Shakespeare and of Seneca. Psychologically, as the student and parents looked over Dr. McCullough's shoulders, it seemed as if the geniuses of the past were in agreement with the provost—as if they had come to the meeting to corroborate Dr. McCullough's recommendation—and who could argue with such a committee?

"The reason I am certain I am getting old," Dr. McCullough continued, "is because an attractive young woman is walking across the campus lawn—and rather than watching her, I am watching all the young men watching her."

"It comes from all that training in sociology," Dr. Emerson said, replacing *The City of God* on the shelf. "You sociologists have an inordinate concern about what others are thinking—but then, I must also be getting old myself, for I am unwilling to come to the window to assess the facts."

"You won't need to. The one creating the attention, I am certain, is Miss Patterson, your prize student, the one with whom we have the 2:00 appointment."

Jamie looked at her watch. It was a runner's watch, a gift from her father, a digital Casio with the capacity to time her splits, but at this moment she just needed to know the time. It was 1:52.

I think I know the question I will be asked in this meeting—but I don't have an answer.

She walked briskly across the campus lawn. Dr. Emerson had promised her the meeting would take only thirty minutes, which would allow her enough time to get to the track for 3:00 practice. Nonetheless she had taken the precaution of dressing for practice. She wore a shiny dark blue wind suit, the jacket unzipped and a fanny pack across her waist. She walked quickly across the sidewalk. Her ponytail, brown but sun-streaked, protruded from her baseball cap. She was known for her graceful stride as a runner, and her practiced pace showed in her walking as well. One sportswriter had written: "Jamie Patterson, in her running, melds natural grace with uncommon speed." Another said, "The fluidity of her stride makes it seem that she has made some accommodation with the natural forces which impede the rest of us."

If Jamie noticed those watching her, she did not show it. She was a few minutes behind her planned schedule, and she did not want to be late for the appointment. She was certain the meeting would have something to do with the recent magazine article.

Who would have thought that my picture would be on the cover of Sports Illustrated?

She checked her watch again as she entered the administration building. 1:54.

I have enough time to freshen up a little.

She went into the ladies room and unzipped her fanny pack, put her baseball cap inside and took out a hairbrush, making several quick strokes through her hair before replacing it and rezipping the pack. She looked at herself in the mirror, and then, as a second thought, she reopened the pack, dug down and found a tube of lipstick and a blush stick. She rarely wore any make-up, but she remembered what her father had said: "No reason you can't be a Southern lady as well as a track star."

Dabbing the lipstick on her lips, she smiled at the remembrance of her father. Her mother had died when Jamie was fourteen and her father did not often give "motherly" advice.

Jamie looked at her face again. Her cheeks were tanned by all the hours on the track, so she put the blush stick away. She looked at herself in the mirror. She remembered when, as a sophomore, one of the campus organizations called her and asked her to enter the Miss Duke University pageant. She had laughed so spontaneously that she had to apologize to the caller. The idea seemed so funny to her. Her image of herself—part nerdy intellectual who spent too much time in the books, part tomboy who could outrun all the boys in her high school—would not allow her to see herself parading across a stage in a pageant dress.

She closed the pack again and checked her watch again. 1:58. She exited the ladies' room, walked up the two flights of stairs, pausing for a moment to look out the gothic arched windows at the campus scene below. The stone buildings, the giant oaks, the sidewalks and the grass gave her an odd emotion.

I am about to graduate! How is that possible? I am going to miss this place.

As if on cue, the campus chimes sounded two deep notes as she entered the doors to the administration offices. Before the receptionist could call Dr. McCullough, he opened the heavy wooden door that led to his office.

"Please come in, Miss Patterson. And thank you for coming at such short notice."

"Thank you, Dr. McCullough."

"I don't think it is necessary to introduce you to Dr. Emerson, but you should understand," he said with a wry smile," we in the administration do not, on the university level, ordinarily condone such things, but it has been reported you might qualify as a 'teacher's pet' in Dr. Emerson's classes."

"If I am the teacher's pet, it is because I have shamelessly campaigned for the position."

"Please, Miss Patterson, have a seat." As they sat, the receptionist brought a silver tray with a tea setting. "I hope you will have some tea."

"One sugar, no cream," she replied. "And please accept my apologies for wearing my training suit to this appointment. I feel poorly dressed in this environment." She looked around at the imposing bookshelves.

"No apology is necessary, Miss Patterson. I understand perfectly." Dr. McCullough took a sip of his tea. "It may surprise you to learn that I have some track experience myself. I represented Princeton in the 1953 Penn Relays."

"I did not know that. What was your event?"

"The 440—as it was called in those days—but that is the extent of the questions I will allow," he laughed. "Please—no inquiries about the place of my finish—or my time. My athletic achievements, I'm afraid, unlike yours, were not impressive."

Jamie smiled and sipped her tea.

"Your best event, I believe, is the 800 meters," the provost continued.

"My father was my high school track coach. He encouraged me to concentrate on that event. It is not the most glamorous event; other venues get more attention—but my dad knew I didn't have the natural speed for the shorter events, so he advised me—if I had ambitions for national competition, I should choose the 800. I can compete in the 400—and the 1500—but the 800 is where I give my focus."

"Ah—focus ..." Dr. McCullough put his tea cup on the tray. "A perfect lead-in for me to provide an explanation as to why we have asked you here this afternoon—an explanation you have been too polite to request. But a young woman of your grace and abilities should not have to squander a spring afternoon with two old fogies such as we, so let me get to the point." Dr. Emerson nodded in agreement.

Dr. McCullough stood and went to his desk and picked up two manila folders, which he placed on the table. These two folders contain the records for two Duke students. One is a *summa cum laude* student in the upcoming graduating class; the other is a world-class athlete. Duke University, of course, each year, produces young men and women of unusual academic achievement and the school likewise often matriculates athletes who go on to compete on the highest levels. All to say, neither of these files, alone—is radically unusual. However—" he looked over to Dr. Emerson who smiled.

"However," he continued, "what is unusual is this: both these files belong to the same person, Miss Patterson. *You* are both students. *That* is unusual."

He handed the folders to Dr. Emerson. "I have asked Dr. Emerson to read a synopsis of each file."

Dr. Emerson took his glasses from his coat, nodded to Jamie and smiled. "Where should I begin? High school valedictorian … President's List every semester while at Duke … Phi Beta Kappa … various departmental honors—I will not cite them … an article published in Historical Review, the first by an undergraduate at Duke … and if you will excuse me for 'spilling the beans' you will receive notification tomorrow that you are the recipient of the Beeson Award, given annually to the senior athlete with the highest grade-point average."

Dr. Emerson took the other folder. "Duke University school record in the 800 meters, set as a sophomore, broken twice as a junior and then twice again as a senior … Atlantic Coast Conference 800 meters record, set as a junior, then broken again earlier this year … All-conference selection for three consecutive years and all-American as a junior and as a senior. And then, of course there is this:" he held up a copy of *Sports Illustrated*. Jamie's picture was on the front. Emblazoned across the photos was "FAST ANGEL IN BLUE DEVIL COUNTRY".

"Oh, please, not that article again," Jamie groaned.

"I'm sorry," Dr. McCullough said. "I know this has been an intrusion into your privacy, but the university will, no doubt, gain some benefit from this attention."

He put the folders neatly on the coffee table. "But let me get to the matter that led me to ask for this meeting. You are a candidate for a Rhodes scholarship, and if I were to be allowed to use terminology that would never be used in the formal confines of the Rhodes committee—I think 'shoo-in' would be appropriate."

Dr. Emerson smiled and nodded in agreement.

"However, I also know you are a candidate for the U.S. Olympic team. The process for that eligibility does not run through my office, so I have no official information; however, like many others, I read the newspapers and there is general unanimity among the media experts that your achievements warrant inclusion on the U.S. team."

Dr. McCullough paused for a moment to collect his thoughts. "Given these two opportunities and given the reality that the calendar might not allow for both—creates a dilemma—but it is the best dilemma I can imagine. Either of the choices available to you will bring great credit to the university, and I have no intention of trying to influence your decision. However, if you were to determine that you should accept the offer to join the U.S. Olympic team and that opportunity precluded the acceptance of the Rhodes offer, the university would like to be able to respond appropriately to the Rhodes committee. Do you understand my situation?"

"Yes, Dr. McCullough, "I do. And I genuinely appreciate your kind words. If I had an answer for you, I would give it today. I do not want to put the university in a difficult position. However, I need to discuss this with my father, but with the conference championships coming up soon and the NCAA championships the week after, I will not have that opportunity for two weeks."

"If you can provide an answer in two weeks, that will be fine." He stood and extended his hand. "Miss Patterson, it has been a pleasure to have these moments together. I'm sorry that you will be leaving the university, but we will be proud to share you with the world."

She shook hands with Dr. Emerson as she dismissed herself.

The two men stood quietly for a moment after Jamie left. Dr. McCullough broke the silence. "She is as delightful as you said, Warren."

"Yes, she is. Did you know she spent last summer on a church mission project—helping build a medical clinic in Mexico?"

Dr. McCullough shook his head. "A beautiful young woman … a world class athlete … a nationally recognized scholar—and devoted to her faith." He shook his head again. "She's too good to be true. Do you think there were such young women when we were students, Warren?"

Dr. Emerson had a mischievous smile. "If there were, Patrick—they would not have dated us."

FOUR

HENRY PURSLEY RECLINED his seat in the first-class cabin—although the message light above him had not yet granted him that permission. It was out of character for Henry Purlsey to violate a rule. He was not a man ordinarily disposed to defiance—but the events of the last few months had changed him drastically. The 737 pulled alongside the runway of Dulles International Airport, waiting for final clearance. Henry Pursley did not look out the window, but if he had, he would have seen that an early evening fog and mist obscured his view. The blinking lights on the wing reflected against the glasses on Henry Pursley's face. Behind those glasses was a worried face. *They can add 'failure to observe airline message instruction' to the other charges,* he thought, as he pushed his seat back. *That shouldn't add a great deal of time to the sentence.* He smiled at his own joke—gallows humor.

Henry Pursley had reasons for his worry. He was convinced he was going to prison. He was involved in events over which he had no control—events he sensed were going to be disastrous to a number of people, including himself. *I'm way in over my head.* He knew he was culpable. What he didn't know was how to extricate himself from his culpability—even though he thought about that every moment.

I wonder how Myra will take it. How will she feel about her husband being in prison? And what about the girls? How will they explain that to their friends?

He stretched his bad shoulder—which he often did when he was worried. The year before they moved to Washington, Henry had taken Myra and the girls skiing at Tahoe the week after Christmas. Amy, the older daughter, a fairly accomplished skier, had somehow enticed him to take the lift to one of the black diamond slopes. As Henry was riding up the lift, he sensed he was making a mistake, and had a premonition that nothing good was going to come of this decision. As he exited the lift, and looked down the steep slope, he was certain it was a mistake—but, once on the top of the mountain, what alternative did he have? He made it down the first few hundred yards by traversing slowly across the hill from side to side, then his skis got pointed down the hill—and before he could realize his predicament, he was flying straight down the slope. *How do I stop?!* His mind raced as he gained velocity with every second. He felt paralyzed. *What can I do?* Faster and faster he went—a grove of trees directly ahead of him. The sharp sting of the pine branch was the first sensation, and then he heard the awful "thump" as his body hit the tree trunk.

His left shoulder—the first part of his body to impact the tree—suffered the worst injury. His face was scratched, and he had multiple bruises on his legs and hips, but all of that healed. Amy cried interminably, saying it was all her fault, but he had tried to console her—telling her it was no one's fault. The shoulder, however, bothered him severely for several months, and even now, gave him some discomfort. It seemed to be aggravated by the early morning, or by cold weather ... or by worry.

And Henry Pursley was worried. He had the same feeling—the same apprehension—as he had had careening down the ski slope at Tahoe. *I'm building speed. I'm out of control. A crash is inevitable. But there will be more than a shoulder damaged when this crash occurs.*

Eight months earlier Henry Pursley would never have considered reclining his seat before take-off. He had always been a rule-follower; he paid his taxes on time; he never set the cruise control more than four miles per hour above the speed limit; he maintained the lawn at their house in Sacramento meticulously and never failed to win the neighborhood Yard of the Month award at least once each year. The papers on his desk lay in neat piles and he never failed to return phone calls promptly. Henry Pursley was a conscientious and dependable man who was a capable administrator. But there were some things that Henry Pursley was not—he was not a politician, as he had come to discover, although he now found himself in that role.

I had no business on a black diamond slope at Tahoe and I have no business in politics in Washington, D.C.

Henry was not ordinarily a rule-breaker, but his daughters had teased him recently when he parked in the handicap parking as he picked them up at the mall. He explained, somewhat defensively, that he had been in the slot less than five minutes, and had not left the car, and there were six other unoccupied handicapped slots nearby; nevertheless, the girls laughed about it when they reported it to their mother. And he had to admit, it probably wasn't something he would have done a year earlier but *What the heck! I'm going to prison anyway.*

Henry was certain he was going to prison. His only question was the length of the sentence. Maybe if they give me credit for being cooperative, my sentence will be reduced. Cooperative!? I will be the most cooperative witness in the history of federal court.

The plane started down the runway. Henry pushed the seat back one more notch—all the way back. No one was behind him. In fact, there were only two others in the first class cabin and they were on the opposite side of the aisle. *If the stewardess says anything to me, maybe I will show her my new business card.* He chuckled to himself at the thought of the new business card. *What a joke!* Under his name it said: Special Advisor for Economic Policy to the President of the United States. Two lines were required to get all that on the card, which Henry thought awkward, but it didn't bother Brent Arens, who created the position as well as the card. The card had barely enough room for the embossed presidential seal, which Arens thought essential. *I wonder if Brent Arens will go to prison too. No. Brent Arens will never go to prison. He's too smart to get convicted.*

Brent Arens was the president's advisor, and he was the one who was responsible for most of the initiatives, which Henry was sure, were illegal. His reputation for ruthlessness and cleverness were not unearned, and Henry often wondered if the man had made some arrangement to protect himself from implication—once these activities were revealed.

People like Brent Arens—and he had met several since he had been in Washington for eight months—fascinated Henry, men whose ambition, like their ruthlessness, seemed unlimited. After only a couple of weeks around Brent Arens, Henry realized the man organized people into two categories—those who were friends of the president and those who were enemies of the president, with each category deserving treatment according to that assessment. Friends of the president were granted favors and encouragement and concessions and opportunities. The others … well, they were treated like enemies.

As the plane began to accelerate, Henry had a second thought, punched the button on the armrest and straightened the chair back. He reached for the black leather valise on the floor and placed it on his lap—with the embossed presidential seal face down. *No need to bring undue attention to what I'm carrying.* He punched the seat button again and pushed all the way back, holding the valise with both hands as he settled back and tried to go to sleep.

The thrust of the engines pushed him into the cushioned seat as it accelerated. Henry had to acknowledge that first class seats were certainly a lot more comfortable than coach. It was a relatively new experience for him. Until he had taken the position in Washington, he had not flown regularly—and never first class. Now he found himself jetting around the country each week—and always in first class. *How long has it been? How long have I had this job? Eight months? It seems like an eternity. I don't belong here. I should have stayed in California at the Commerce Office. I could have retired in a few years, and Myra and I could have bought that beach house we talked about. Now, I may spend my retirement at a federal prison. Why didn't I stay in the Commerce Department? I guess the offer by the sitting president went to my head. If the president of the United States tells you he needs you, you can't turn that down, can you?*

Henry adjusted his pillow, but he realized he wasn't sleepy. He was still agitated over the meeting a few hours earlier in the room off the Oval Office. The memory of that meeting came back afresh. *Was it a tragedy or a comedy? Perhaps a tragicomedy. He remembered it clearly ...*

"He's pretty good," the president said in admiration, as Brent Arens clicked the remote control, and the screen went blank. Wilson Cavanaugh looked like a man you could trust—in fact, that is why some political analysts thought he got elected—simply because he looked like a man to be trusted. The wavy, gray streak of hair that ran over each ear framed a gentle face, which almost always carried a calm demeanor. It was often said that Wilson Cavanaugh resembled Jimmy Stewart and some critics said that he had begun to talk like Jimmy Stewart in an effort to enhance his likeability.

The four men in the room—in addition to President Cavanaugh, Henry, Brent Arens and James Olmstead—had been watching a tape of Harrison Henninger's latest speech, the one in Louisville. The last image on the screen had been of Henninger holding his gun above his head, accepting the applause of his audience at the conclusion of the speech. "I'm not getting that kind of applause for my speeches these days. Why do you think that is, Brent?"

Brent Arens said something unintelligible as he flipped on a switch of a lamp. He seemed exasperated, but Henry thought he always seemed either exasperated or angry—or both. He stood by the lamp, drumming his fingers on the table, a red flush on his neck around his heavily starched white shirt. His jacket was hung on the coat-rack, next to the president's. Both suits were silk, probably Italian, although Henry realized he didn't' know much about Italian silk suits.

Brent Arens wore dark-rimmed glasses, which moved up and down with his head when he was thinking—as he was at that moment. His sleeves were rolled up on his forearms. Henry had noticed that Arens, when he removed his jacket, always rolled the sleeve up very precisely—always two folds. He must, Henry thought, request extra starch at the cleaners, because his white shirts always seemed stiff—and they bellowed up around his mid-section when he walked. His tie was a subdued shade of vermillion, but the suspenders, for which he was famous, were the color of blood.

Arens took a deep breath. "Why anyone would vote for this gun-waving huckster is beyond me." He shook his head. Henninger's showing in the polls was a genuine irritation to Brent Arens because his job was to get the president reelected in November. That reelection had been a foregone conclusion until Henninger came on the scene only a few months earlier. All of Arens' machinations and careful orchestration—including the denigration of the opponent in the other major party—had been upset by this maverick billionaire from California.

James Olmstead, whose seat was closest to the president's, switched on the lamp next to his chair. Olmstead was a little older than Arens. In fact, he was the same age as the president, the two of them having formed a friendship in college. He had been the president's advisor, in some capacity or another, more than thirty years—beginning when the president had won his first election as a state senator. Henry watched

Olmstead squint as the lamp came on. Henry thought Olmstead seemed always on the verge of being overcome by weariness, as if he had seen too much—and endured too much—in his years in Washington to ever have energy again. He sat holding his glasses in his hand. Henry noticed the bags under his eyes, as if the cares and worries of advising the president had become a residue and collected there. His shirt, which was blue, in contrast to Arens' white, appeared as if it had never had any starch in it and the wrinkles seemed to complement the bags under his eyes. He looked up at Arens and in a deep, sonorous voice, the timbre matching his countenance, asked, "Who was it, Brent, who said that we should never overestimate the intelligence of the American voters?"

Arens clinched his teeth in irritation. "Overestimate is one thing, but what Henninger is saying is moronic—terminate foreign aid … close down embassies … throw up trade walls—"

"Tell them what they want to hear," Olmstead interrupted. "Isn't that what you have advised? 'Tickle their ears if necessary'. Isn't that your quote?" He turned his head at an angle as he waited for Arens' response. "Could it be," he egged him on in his deep voice, "that we have discovered someone who is just as proficient at your strategies as you are?"

"That's enough—" Arens shouted.

"Now, now," the president said, raising his hands in a calming gesture. "Am I going to have to separate you boys again?"

Henry had come to expect these scenes during the past few weeks. Arens and Olmstead were the president's two closest advisors, and their individual job descriptions were technically clear-cut: Olmstead had the job of advising the president on day-to-day operations. Arens' job was to get the president reelected. Each despised the other.

"Mr. Henninger seems to think that we failed to live up to some promises we made," Olmstead went on.

"Well," Arens answered, "some of the things he requested were absurd."

"Perhaps so, but he told Henry he wasted two million dollars in contributions to our campaign. Isn't that true, Henry?"

Henry nodded. "According to our records, Mr. Henninger contributed slightly more than two million dollars to the previous campaign."

"And he also told Henry," Arens went on, "and I will omit the expletives—that, if we want his endorsement for this upcoming election, he will get his assurances in writing this time."

"I can't imagine," the president said, "any circumstances in which I would sign such an agreement with Henninger."

"Perhaps not," Arens replied, "but neither could we imagine any circumstances in which Henninger had this much support, could we?"

The president did not answer.

The airplane leveled off and the stewardess asked Henry if he would like something to drink. He declined. "Would you like for me to put your briefcase in the overhead container?" she asked.

"Oh, no," he said, realizing he was holding the valise with both hands—more tightly than was necessary. The stewardess gave him an odd look, but he just smiled. Six hours later, the plane landed in San Francisco. Henry gathered his carry-on bag and deplaned, again holding the valise tightly.

Tomorrow morning, he said to himself, *I will meet with Harrison Henninger. When I do, I will further incriminate myself. I'm going to prison. I know I am.*

FIVE

THE GEARS ON Jamie's bike whirred metallically as she coasted into the driveway alongside the house—a white frame structure with a narrow driveway, leading to a single-car garage. The house, like the entire neighborhood, was built during the post-war building boom, all with two bedrooms and one bathroom, each house slightly individualized by paint color, trim, and shutters. Her car, a Honda Civic with a bad paint job was parked inside the garage. The car got little use except for the occasional trips back home to South Carolina. Jamie ordinarily commuted to campus on her bicycle, only a few blocks away. She chained the bike, came out of the garage, and called to her neighbor, Mrs. Fletcher, who was watering her flowers on the other side of a chain-link fence. "The azaleas look great, Mrs. Fletcher."

Mrs. Fletcher nodded. "Water and fertilizer, that's all it takes. Well, some fungicide occasionally, but mostly it's just water and fertilizer—and some compost. I try to work in some compost every year."

Jamie smiled. Mrs. Fletcher was in her late sixties, which Jamie calculated was about the median age for the neighborhood. Some of the neighbors had built these houses shortly after getting married and had

47

subsequently celebrated their 40th anniversaries in them. She had first leased the house, within easy bicycle distance of the campus, after her sophomore year, two years earlier. She had had a roommate until this previous semester, but Sissy had graduated and gone to medical school. Jamie had looked for another roommate, but when no one on her short list worked out, her father said he would foot the extra expense for her final semester.

A large calico cat came trotting from under a bush and plopped at Jamie's feet, begging for a rub. Jamie obliged. The cat's white belly contrasted with the caramel and black splotches on its side. "Aspie, you're pathetic. You're always begging for attention. Come on, let's get you something to eat." The cat scrambled to its feet and trotted beside Jamie through the back door of the little house. The cat had shown up at the house shortly after Jamie and Sissy had moved in, and when all efforts to find her owner failed, she and Sissy had adopted it. Jamie named the cat Aspasia, after the scandalous figure of Greece's golden age, a name that was most often reduced to "Aspie".

"A little patience, please," Jamie chided as the cat meowed while she was scooping a cup of dry cat food into the bowl. "Hey, don't give me that look. You know the rules. Only one can of the good stuff a week. That's all we can afford."

The cat, as if she understood the reprimand, began crunching the cat food. Jamie grabbed a bag of pretzels and went into the living room, clicking on the television as she went by it to the front door to pick up her newspaper on the porch.

The headlines said:

Henninger Will Speak at Duke.

Harrison Henninger, the controversial multi-millionaire turned politician, has just confirmed that he will speak at Awards Day at Duke this Saturday. This is a last-minute addition to Mr. Henninger's schedule, and there is speculation that Mr. Henninger intends to endow a Chair of American Enterprise at the university.

Jamie sat down to read the rest of the article when she realized Henninger was on television. She turned up the volume. Henninger was answering a question from the host of the talk show: "Hell, the first time I was accused of *xenophobia*," he pronounced the word slowly, "I thought it might be a sexual disease." The studio audience laughed. It was an audience of Henninger supporters. They had heard the joke many times, but they exaggerated their laughter for the benefit of the television audience.

"Your critics," the host said, "accuse you of having a simplistic foreign policy. What do you say to them?"

Henninger leaned toward the host and pointed his finger. "Let me tell you something about simplistic. When Adolph Hitler began running his armies all over Europe, there were hundreds of diplomats in dozens of countries trying to appease him. Until we, in this country, said 'Hell no' to Adolph Hitler, did anything happen. We kicked his rear end back across Europe until he blew his brains out. Now ..." Henninger paused, "was that 'simplistic'? Maybe so, but it got the job done. I want to bring that same sort of simplistic 'get the job done' approach to all our issues in this country. We're still in a war, but it's an economic war now. Am I going to let the Japs—the Japanese—dump their radios and stereos, products subsidized by their governments, into our markets? Am I going to let the Krauts—the Germans—negotiate away their tax liability so they can sell their cars in our country? The answer to that is 'Hell no!'"

The audience cheered loudly, and the program went to commercial.

Jamie turned off the television and picked up the phone and punched in some numbers. "Jamie?" her father answered. "I didn't expect a call from you this evening—but I'm glad to hear from you. And I want to tell you again I'm sorry I won't be there for the conference championships. You know I would like to be there."

"I know Dad and I understand."

Both Jamie and her father knew that he planned to come to the NCAA championships a little later, but her father had been her coach during high school and he had always been a proponent of the "one game at a time ... never look beyond the next event ... never underestimate an opponent" philosophy, and although Jamie was expected to breeze through the conference championships, it would have been presumptuous for him to acknowledge he planned to be at the NCAA championships.

"Dad, I have a question."

"What is it?"

"It concerns Harrison Henninger. I just learned he's coming to Duke. He's scheduled to speak at the award ceremony. Before I go to the ceremony, I want to get the story straight. Isn't he the one who was the survivor of the battle when my grandfather was killed?"

"Yes. The only survivor. The others in my father's platoon were all killed."

"I'm trying to recall the conversation we had about this."

"For many years," Jamie's father started, "I was under the impression that there were no survivors of the event, but only two or three years ago, there was a news story about Harrison Henninger and the fact that he managed to survive the battle. The story was about a big financial deal in California. Henninger's company lost a contract to a Japanese conglomerate, and the issue of Japan having been our enemy during World War II came up, which led to a discussion of Henninger's service in the war. A short description of the counter-offensive was mentioned—the battle in which my father and his platoon were killed. Henninger was not actually a member of the platoon. He was a communications officer delivering a message to the platoon when the tragedy occurred. Apparently, he had been too modest to mention his service until then."

"And you tried to contact him, if I remember correctly."

"I did try. I wrote a letter, but I never got a reply. I guess billionaires don't read a lot of personal mail—or maybe he just didn't want to be reminded of the incident."

"He seems to be reminding everyone of it now."

"Politics, I suppose. Since he came on the national scene last year, he has talked a great deal about his military service. I'm glad he's coming to the award ceremony. Maybe you will get a chance to speak to him … but be careful," he laughed. "When Henninger finds out you are the granddaughter of one of his army associates, he may try to recruit you for his campaign."

"That's not likely—" Jamie paused for a moment. "But you and I need to have a discussion about the future—after graduation."

"Yes, we do. Let's plan that discussion soon. I'll be glad to talk with you, and I will help you think through your options, but in the end, it will be your decision."

"I love you, Dad."

"And I love you. And don't forget to tell Mr. Henninger that you are the granddaughter of one of the members of 2nd platoon of K Company of the 108th Infantry Division. Your grandfather, James Patterson, was the platoon leader, so the name should mean something to him."

"Yes, I will."

"I'm praying for you," her father said.

Jamie hung up the phone. Her father always signed off their phone conversations with "I'm praying for you." She sighed. She wished she could talk with her dad about the Rhodes scholarship and about the Olympic team, but neither opportunity was official yet. "Never presume on the future" was one of his most common quotes. He had had some painful experiences that had made that adage personal. He also had been an outstanding runner and his strict training, and his doggedness had made him an outstanding miler at Clemson in the '60s, but an ankle injury kept him from qualifying for the Olympics. And Jamie knew, when her father said "Never presume on the future" he perhaps unconsciously was also referring to the death of her mother. It had been nearly eight years since her death and Jame knew her father had probably assumed that her mother would have been alive those eight years. Jamie knew much about her father—and much of what she understood was not necessarily spoken. Their relationship was as strong as a father's and a daughter's could be, because he had raised her alone since she was fourteen.

I wish you were here right now to talk with me. I could use your advice.

SIX

HENRY PURSLEY WAITED.

The waiting did not surprise him. He knew he would have to wait. He expected it. For his previous appointment with Henninger, he had waited two hours. For this appointment he expected he would wait at least that long—and probably longer. He looked at his watch. 3:20. The appointment, ostensibly, had been set for 2:00. *He will probably make me wait until the office closes.*

"Mr. Henninger," the receptionist had told him in a surly tone, as if it were an imposition that Henry was in the office, "returned from St. Louis last night."

Henry looked around him. He sat in the lobby of the corporate headquarters of Harrison Henninger Industries. A huge **HHI** logo was fixed above the receptionist's counter—a sleek, curved, chrome-and-wood piece, high enough that only the forehead and topknot of hair of the receptionist were now visible to Henry. Around him were a dozen huge black-and-white renderings of the various sectors of Harrison Henninger Industries—mining, communication, transportation, hotels, others. He realized there was nothing in the room with any color—every item was black and white. The half-dozen chairs in the room—

all empty except for his—had square metal arms and black vinyl seats. *This room is not designed for hospitality; this room is designed for intimidation.*

Henry shifted his weight in the plastic chair, trying to find a more comfortable position. He noticed the ache in his shoulder as he moved. *The previous meeting with Henninger had been humiliating. This one will probably be worse.* His mind wandered. *Why am I sitting in the office of Harrison Henninger? How did I get here? How did I ever get in this position?* His mind went back a few years ...

Five years earlier Henry Pursley had been Deputy Director of the Treasury Department for the state of California, a position he had held for six years, after working his way up the ranks—with nearly seventeen years in total in that office. Counting the three years he worked at the California Department of Transportation immediately after graduation from Stanford, he had twenty years as an employee of the State of California.

I wonder if a prison term affects one's pension status. Surely not—but I had better look into that.

Henry had never really been interested in politics, but his boss, the Director of the Treasury Department, had approached him. "Henry, I need your help," he said. *That's where it all began—with "Henry, I need your help".* The director went on to explain that he had just agreed to head up the state committee supporting Senator Wilson Cavanaugh for president. "I need someone to head up the finance committee," the director explained. "You're the man for that job. You're the best man this department has ever had with dollars and numbers."

Henry wasn't really interested in the added responsibility—and in truth, he really wasn't committed to voting for Senator Cavanaugh; however, he *was* interested in becoming the Director of the Treasury Department when his current boss retired. The director's position would bring a substantial increase in salary—but he realized, if he turned down this request, he would have no chance of getting the director's endorsement when he retired.

So, Henry took the job, and, as everyone expected, he was good at it. "Attaboys" came frequently from the political operatives, and he had to admit, using his accounting and finance background—he really did do a good job. He was able to explain the numbers— outlays, projected income and actual income—to the campaign people in such a way they could understand them—and use those funds in a timely way to maximize their advertising. When Cavanaugh carried the state by a small margin, the political powers were quick to praise Henry for his contribution.

He received a lot of congratulatory letters—one from the president himself. "Is that really the president's signature?" Amy asked. He told her he couldn't be sure; it might only be a copy of his signature, but that did not keep her from telling all her friends that "the president wrote my daddy a personal letter".

A nice article in the Sacramento Bee complimented Henry. The article had his picture with Myra and the girls and several political big-whigs provided gracious quotes. The accolades and furor had wound down by mid-December when he got a call at home from his boss. "Henry, listen to me carefully. I'm going to Washington, and I want you to go with me."

"Pardon me."

"I just got off the phone with Bret Arens, the president's advisor. I should say 'president-to-be' I suppose. It's a few weeks until the inauguration. Anyhow, they have offered me the job as Under-Secretary for the Commerce department in the new administration. I want you to go with me as Director of Finance. I've already cleared it with Arens."

"Well—"

"Henry, this is a great opportunity. The president needs you."

"I don't know if—"

"Listen, Henry. Don't give me an answer now. We can talk about it in the office tomorrow. In the meantime, talk to Myra. See what she thinks. We'll talk tomorrow."

Henry put down the phone. He didn't think the job offer was a good idea for a number of reasons. He liked California better than Washington. Amy would be following in his footsteps at Stanford in two years. The job security of a political appointment (What would happen in four years?) was not attractive to him, but he had promised his boss he would talk to Myra, and he was sure she would have the same feelings.

Myra surprised him. She was genuinely interested in going to Washington. What Henry realized later about his wife—what he did not see, but what had been evident to others—was how Myra thrived during the campaign. The banquets, the rallies, getting her picture taken with the governor and with senators and congressmen—all of that brought out a dimension in his wife Henry had not seen before. She had fairly glowed during the last few days of the campaign, and she was overjoyed when Cavanaugh won. Some of the party leaders, she related to her friends, had said that, without Henry's help, Cavanaugh might not have carried California—and if he had not carried California, he would not have carried the electoral college. A string of celebratory dinners and events followed, and she showed real pride when Henry was introduced and applauded. But those events had tapered off and she recently had had an emotional letdown.

"Henry, you know I'm proud of you. I was proud of you before the campaign. I will always be proud of you. But you said the president needed you—"

"No, *I* didn't say the president needed me. That's what my boss said. And I'm not entirely certain—"

"We should consider this," Myra interrupted. "For the first time, I think you are getting the recognition you are due. Henry, you are not just some pencil-pushing state employee who keeps the ledgers balanced. There's more to Henry Pursley than that. I've known that since I married you."

His daughters also were surprisingly positive about the move. They thought it would be a great adventure. By the end of the week, Henry had agreed to take the position.

All of them attended the inauguration and Henry stayed in Washington to assume his new duties at Commerce while Myra and the girls returned to Sacramento to finish out the school year. By the third week of June the whole family was involved in the adventure of living in the nation's capital. Myra didn't get to attend as many functions as she might have liked, but she did attend a luncheon with the first lady, and she often met with other D.C. dignitaries, as she served on a committee with several congressmen's wives. Henry did well in his new position, and everything seemed to be going well …

Harrison Henninger changed everything.

Until Henninger came on the political scene, it was assumed that President Cavanaugh would be easily reelected—but now that was not certain. Ten weeks earlier Henry's boss came by his office and told him that Brent Arens wanted to talk with him.

The memory of that meeting—in Brent Arens' office in the West Wing—was still fresh in Henry's mind. It was an unsettling meeting. Brent Arens wore his customary white starched shirt, red suspenders, collar slightly loosened, and his sleeves rolled up above his wrist. He asked some perfunctory questions about

Henry's family and background but didn't really seem to pay attention to the answers. Henry had the sense that Arens had a number of things on his mind, and this was not the most important one. After only a few moments of small talk, Arens asked Henry about Harrison Henninger.

"Mr. Henninger," Henry replied, "as you know, was the largest contributor from California to the president's campaign, but I met him only twice—both times at large gatherings—and both times our conversations were barely more than handshakes."

That reply seemed to disappoint Brent Arens. He paused for a moment before he spoke again. "Henry, the president wants you to join our team in a different capacity—in a position that will better utilize your skills and talents in service to the American people."

Henry had the sense that Arens was reading from a script.

"We—that is the president and his senior advisers," Arens went on, "know that we need to do a better job in the area of economic affairs. For that reason, the president is creating a new position— Special Adviser to the President for Economic Affairs—and he wants you to fill that position."

"But I—"

Henry's objection was interrupted by the door opening into Arens' office, and President Wilson Cavanaugh stepping in.

"Henry, it's good to see you again," the president extended his hand as Henry stood.

"Thank you, Mr. President, it's an honor to see you."

"Well, it's an honor to have someone with your skills and background on our team, but I hope Brent has had the chance to tell you that we hope you will join us in this new capacity. We think you are the man for this job. We need you."

The president dismissed himself after only a few minutes; Henry and Brent Arens talked for a few minutes longer, but Henry could not remember the content of that conversation. Henry noticed that Arens looked at his watch—so Henry took that as his signal to dismiss himself.

As Henry left the White House and the grounds, he had an oddly uncomfortable feeling—an unsettled emotion that he could not explain—and he realized he was rubbing his shoulder.

Despite his own uneasiness about the appointment, when he reported it to Myra that night, she was ecstatic, "Special Adviser to the President! Henry, this is amazing. You have been asked to be the Special Adviser to the President!!"

"... for Economic Affairs," Henry added.

"And the president himself told you he needed you!"

Myra kissed her husband. "By the president himself. Oh, Henry, I always knew that the world would discover what a special person you are!"

That's when the slope got steeper.

Henry looked at the clock above the reception desk. 4:05. He took a deep breath.

The memories kept coming …

Two days earlier there had been a meeting in the Oval Office. Besides the president, Brent Arens, James Olmstead and himself, there were two other men in that Oval Office meeting. Ray Henson, who reported to Brent Arens, and who held the title of Campaign Director, was the first. With him was Elliott Congrove, a younger man than any of the others in the room. Elliott Congrove was an expert—an expert in poll data. He had written a computer program that had been spectacularly accurate during the midterm elections. No one really understood why the program had been so accurate, but no one denied its accuracy. Henson had contracted for Congrove's services shortly after those midterms. Elliott Congrove was overweight—but even so, his rumpled clothes looked like they were made for a man even larger, and it appeared he had not shaved in a few days. Henry noticed Brent Arens looking at Congrove and could see the disdain in his face.

Elliott Congrove, however, was unaware of that disdain. He was aware only of the cheese and cracker tray the Filipino steward had brought to the meeting. He put a chunk of Swiss cheese on a rye cracker while the other men talked. He consumed the cheese and cracker in one bite and looked for other selections, settling this time on cheddar on a club cracker. He nodded when he was introduced to the president but went quickly back to the cheese tray.

Arens stepped near the president's desk. He pointed to a folder on the desk. "This latest proposal should bring Henninger to our side. It's a package we have put together the last couple of days—"

Arens stopped for a moment, his train of thought interrupted. He looked at Congrove who was spinning the cheese tray to get to the selections on the opposite side. Henry saw what Arens was looking at—Congrove's pant legs were a couple of inches shorter than they should have been and the elastic on his white socks had slipped, showing his fat ankles.

Henry could read Arens' mind—White socks! … white socks in the Oval Office!

"You were saying, Brent," the president prompted.

"Yes, I was saying I worked on this proposal subsequent to Henry's meeting with Henninger … and it should meet his demands."

"Demands …" the president turned the word over. "Demands …" he shook his head. He looked over to his right. "James, have you read this?" Olmstead nodded.

"And—?"

"Might as well give Henninger the keys to the nuclear arsenal. He's getting everything else."

"Ray," the president said. "What do you have to say about this? Is Mr. Henninger in a position to make 'demands' of us?"

Ray Henson evaded the question. He scooted to the edge of his chair. "That's why I brought Elliott along today. As you know, he supervises the poll data analysis."

The eyes of all five men went to Elliott Congrove just as he popped another piece of cheese and a cracker in his mouth. He had paid no attention to the conversation, but he now realized everyone was now looking in his direction. He also now realized the cheese he had put in his mouth was jalapeno cheddar. He waved his hand in front of his mouth and blinked his eyes.

"Elliott, the president would like to know about the poll data," Ray Henson prompted.

The young man held up his hand in a "just a moment" signal while he worked the cheese and cracker around in his mouth. Henson was irritated and Arens disgusted, but both the president and Olmstead seemed amused. Congrove held up both hands as if to say "almost got it" indication, making little smacking noises with his mouth. Then he wiped his teeth with his finger. Henson turned his head, unable to watch, and a red flush grew above Arens' starched collar. Olmstead tried not to laugh, and the president looked mesmerized.

Congrove held up his empty glass and asked, "Could I get another glass of water?"

Arens groaned and went to the window, put both hands on the windowsill and dropped his head.

"Here," the president said, rising from his chair. "I haven't drunk any of my water. Take my glass." He walked around his desk and handed it to Congrove, who drained the contents washing the water around his teeth. He gave the glass back to the president. "Thank you," he said. "That cheese sticks to your teeth."

"You're welcome," the president said, going back to his desk, a smile of bemusement on his face as he looked over to James Holmstead, who had put his hand on his forehead to cover the smile on his face.

"Elliott," Ray Henson said sternly. "The president wants to know about the polls. Did you bring a report?"

"Yep."

"And ... where is it?" Henson asked.

"Right here," he replied, pointing to his head.

"Do you have a written report?"

"Don't need it," the young man said, looking around at the others with a childish grin.

Brent Arens came back to the edge of the president's desk. "You don't need it?"

"Nope, have it in my head."

"You have it in your head?" Arens repeated slowly.

"Yep."

"And ... do you think you might share this information with the rest of us?

"Sure."

No one spoke for a moment. Henry noticed Arens hands on the president's desk. His knuckles had gone white. But Congrove just sat there, like a puppy waiting for a signal to do a trick.

"Elliott," Ray Henson said firmly. "Tell the president—and the rest of us—what the polls show. What would happen if the election were held today?"

He spoke like a schoolboy giving a rote report: "If the election were held today ... actually, I should say if the election had been held yesterday—I don't have the data for today, but if the election had been held yesterday—based on the three-candidate model on which I based the data, Candidate One—" he paused to look at the president. "That's you."

The president nodded. "Oh, yes, of course. I'm Candidate One."

"Candidate One," Elliot Congrove resumed, "would have won the election with 42 percent of the vote; Candidate Two with 36 percent; the independent candidate with 20 percent; undecided 3 percent; other, 1 percent." He smiled as he concluded his report.

"Elliott," Ray Henson said, "what about trends? What does your model say about November?"

"Given current trending data, discounting any substantial political upheavals, the results would be Candidate One 38 percent; Candidate Two 36 percent; Candidate Three, 24 percent."

"So—" the president said, "I would win the election, but by only two percent?"

"If the weather's good," Congrove replied.

"Pardon me?"

"If the weather were unusually bad—say a blizzard—in the heavily populated Northeast, Candidate One would lose."

"Candidate One would lose," the president repeated slowly as if seeking confirmation. "If there were a blizzard, Candidate One would lose." His expression, Henry thought, seemed to indicate he had been thrown into a troupe of imbeciles, and he was obligated to play his part.

"Yes," Congrove answered smiling, "Candidates Two and Three have a higher loyalty factor than Candidate One. Their supporters are more likely to vote if the weather is bad."

"Candidates Two and Three—" the president repeated, nodding his head slowly, "—have a higher loyalty factor than Candidate One."

"Yessir."

"And …" the president asked, "… can your computer tell us what the weather will be on election day?"

Congrove thought for a moment, squinted his eyes, confused at the question. "No."

Arens interrupted. "These numbers don't mean anything. Henninger can't win the election. He knows that. He does not plan to run for president. He just wants to own the whole freaking world!"

He stepped in front of Elliott Congrove. "What happens if Henninger—Candidate Three—endorses one of the other two candidates?

"Landslide for Candidate One—59 percent to 40 percent—if he has the endorsement of Candidate Three. If Candidate Three endorses Candidate Two, Candidate Two would be a likely winner—51 percent to 49 percent."

No one spoke for a moment as they absorbed this information.

"All of this," Elliott Congrove added, "assumes no significant market declines, natural disasters, or war, of course."

"Of course," the President agreed. "Of course. None of that. We can't have a war."

Brent Arens nodded at Ray Henson with a slight nod. That was his sign to take Elliott Congrove and leave the meeting. Henson stood and shook the president's hand. Congrove also stood, brushing crumbs from his belly before he extended his hand to the president.

As they were going out the door, Congrove, as an afterthought, called back, "And thank you for the cheese, too."

The door closed. All but Arens broke into laughter.

"Now Brent," the president said, "show some sense of humor. He's your boy, isn't he? You hired him, didn't you?"

"And I'll fire him if I need to. If his precious computer program is one-tenth of one percent off, I'll fire his—*white socks*!"

"But this information is valuable," the president said. "It tells us—if Mr. Elliott Congrove's computer program is correct, Harrison Henninger cannot become president."

"But it also tells us," James Olmstead interrupted, "that Harrison Henninger can decide *who will be* president. Notwithstanding his social retardation, Mr. Congrove has proven very accurate in his predictions. And we have to expect that our opponent, even if he doesn't have Congrove's predictions, he has to have some similar numbers. He certainly understands that his only chance to win the election is to get Henninger's endorsement."

"Which means," Arens said, "we need to secure that endorsement before he does. As soon as he has our assurances that we will cede him those economic agreements for the Pacific Rim, he will give us that endorsement. We have the advantage of being able to put that agreement in place now. Our opponent couldn't do that for nearly a year."

The men in the room looked around at each other.

The president spoke: "Put something together, Brent. Have Henry take it to Henninger."

"Mr. Pursley," the nasal voice from behind the counter said, "Mr. Henninger will see you." Henry looked at his watch. 4:22. *Two hours and twenty-two minutes late. It could have been worse.*

SEVEN

I SHOULD BE more focused.

Jamie was on the field—at track practice—catching her breath after a 200-yard split, but her mind was not entirely on the practice session. She found herself thinking more about her grandfather than she should have been. The news about Harrison Henninger coming to Duke—and her grandfather's association with him—had triggered more interest than she expected. Her grandfather had never been a real person to her—he was just a 5x7 photograph on the mantle, but now, for some reason she found him on her mind.

Why haven't I been curious about my grandfather? Why haven't I been interested in his history? I know more about the Peloponnesian Wars than I do about World War II.

"Sixteen days," Coach Barton's voice shook Jamie out of her thoughts. "Sixteen days," she repeated, some admonition in her voice, "until the conference championship. You were more than a second off your time on that split."

"Yes, ma'am," Jamie responded.

Focus Jamie. Focus.

EIGHT

HENRY RUBBED HIS shoulder as he left the Harrison Henninger Industries office. He felt like his entire body had been bludgeoned, but it was his shoulder where the pain seemed to concentrate. The bludgeoning, of course, had not been physical—but it had been painful, nonetheless. *How much of this can I report to the president?* he asked himself. *I certainly cannot repeat all the obscenities Henninger used describing the president.*

The meeting with Henninger had lasted exactly twenty-eight minutes—a half-hour harangue by Henninger, which offered Henry little opportunity to say anything. Henninger did the talking.

"Tell that pitiful excuse for a president, pitiful excuse for a leader, pitiful excuse for a man, to clean that chair of his in the Oval Office very thoroughly when he departs. I want it scrubbed down with disinfectants. I don't want the faintest whiff of his odor left in the room when I sit down in it."

No reason to tell the president that part.

"If he wants to keep his smelly rear end in that seat, tell him he needs to keep his promises—and this time those promises will be in writing."

I can leave out the "smelly rear end" part.

More, much more, was included in the half-hour rant, often vile, always angry. The more Henninger talked, the more furious he became. Henry was grateful when he was eventually dismissed. "The next time I see you," Henninger pointed at him from his desk as Henry was leaving, "you better have those guarantees I want—and it better have that pea-brained, pitiful excuse for a president's signature at the bottom. Now get the hell out of my office. I have to go to St. Louis to speak to a bunch of dim-witted patriots who are living in the past."

As his cab approached, Henry's mind went to Cabo del Sur. He imagined the surf rolling in on the beach and the seagulls scattering back and forth as the waves came in. He imagined sitting on the little deck of the cabin with Myra, watching the girls collect seashells.

He rubbed his shoulder again. The pain would not go away.

NINE

"YOU'RE STILL OFF pace, Jamie," Coach Barton said, her stopwatch in her hand. "Both your splits were two seconds slow." She made an entry on her clipboard. Jamie had her hands on her knees, her chest heaving, bent over at the edge of the track. She nodded. She had just run a 400-meter sprint, then, after a three-minute break, ran another. It was part of the scheduled regimen.

"Two weeks from tomorrow …" Coach Barton said. "… the conference championship. Between now and then you need to find that extra gear you're famous for."

Jamie nodded, still catching her breath.

"Extra pasta tonight," Coach Barton said. "You're burning a lot of calories. Your body needs to refuel."

Jamie forked macaroni into her mouth. She finished her second plateful, sitting at the small table in the kitchen of her little house. She took a long drink of iced tea, finishing off what was left in the glass and wiped the tomato sauce from her lips. Aspie rubbed against her leg, meowed and Jamie reached down and rubbed her head. "I'm sorry, Aspie, but I am going to leave you alone for a little while tonight." The cat meowed again. "Well, since you asked... no, I do not have a date to go to a fancy restaurant or to the theater—the truth is, I'm going to the library." Another meow. "Yes, I know you worry about me and my social life and yes, you are right—only a true nerd would go to the library on Friday night... but, nevertheless that is where I'm headed. But don't worry about me. I won't be very late. The library closes early on Friday."

Jamie spun the dial on the combination lock that held her bike in the bike rack in front of the library. She went by the stone towers at the corner of the library and through the huge doors. But instead of heading upstairs to the History section—her customary destination— she headed to Current Literature/Current Periodicals. She asked the periodical librarian for copies of *Time* and *Newsweek* for the last month. While she waited, she perused a copy of *National Review*. When the librarian returned with the requested magazines, Jamie found a seat and began reading.

The magazines gave her the background information she was seeking. Her grandfather's unit— 2nd platoon, K company of the 108th Infantry Division, had captured a bridge on the Saar River, and crossed over—but before they could be reinforced, the Germans mounted a counter-offensive, and the entire platoon was wiped out. Only Harrison Henninger, who served as a communications officer with the company commander, and who was delivering a message to the platoon when he got caught in the battle, survived. He had been wounded, according to his report, but had turned down the Purple Heart, and had never mentioned the incident until recently. When he had been criticized for seeking political favor because of his war-time service, Henninger had countered, "If you think I'm going to apologize for serving with the best men this country ever produced, you've got another think coming".

The magazines offered little information about the actual details of the battle in which her grandfather died, but she knew that would require a different level of research. *How little I know about the battle in which my grandfather died!*

Jamie determined to do the research needed to know more about her grandfather's service and his death. *I need to know more. But not now. That project needs to wait. Too much going on already.*

But she was intrigued with the idea that she might get to speak with Harrison Henninger, who might have known her grandfather, and fought alongside him when he died. *What an unlikely coincidence. The man who served in World War II alongside my grandfather is making a speech tomorrow at a ceremony where I am to receive an award. Amazing!*

The librarian came by to tell her that the library would be closing in fifteen minutes. Jamie thanked her, gathered up her notes and headed back to her house.

TEN

WITH THE GATEWAY Arch as a backdrop, Harrison Henninger told a large audience in St. Louis that, although he had not announced that he was a candidate for president—if he did wake up in the White House one morning, the first thing he would do would be to stop all foreign aid payments. "Do you realize how many billions of dollars we send to all these third-rate countries around the world? Did I say 'third-rate'?" he teased the crowd. "I'm sure I meant 'third-world'." The crowd laughed then cheered.

"Now let me tell you why we are not going to pay any foreign aid. It's very simple really. You understand it and I understand it, but apparently there is something dense in the air in Washington D.C. that prevents anyone there from understanding what is not a complicated concept."

He paused for a moment. "I am going to speak very slowly when I explain this—not because *you* have difficulty understanding it—but because those bureaucrats in Washington have difficulty understanding it." He cleared his throat. "No ... foreign ... aid. Let me repeat that for the bureaucrats: No ... foreign ... aid. Would you say it with me?" The crowd picked up the chant: "No! ... foreign! ... aid! No! ... foreign! ... aid!"

"Now let me tell you why we are not going to pay any foreign aid," Henninger said, leaning on the podium. "Some of you are *former* textile workers. I emphasize the word 'former' because many of you have had to find other employment—if you found employment at all. You worked for years producing the clothes we Americans wore during the day and the sheets we slept on at night. Every week you got a paycheck for your work. Now maybe it wasn't the greatest paycheck in the world, but it put groceries on the table. If you looked close at that paycheck, you saw that some of the money you earned—you did not receive. It was *withheld*. Our great leaders in Washington believe they know better what to do with your money than you do, so they *withhold* it. Now maybe you didn't complain about that. Maybe you felt it was your patriotic duty as an American to help the government ... and you did this for years, didn't you?"

"Yes," the crowd responded.

"So you took what was remaining of your paycheck and you bought groceries for your family ... you paid your mortgage ... you made your car payment ... you bought shoes for your kids ... and you tried to save a little money for your kids to go to college—so maybe they wouldn't have to work in the textile factory. You did that, didn't you?"

"Yes we did!" the crowd yelled.

Henninger leaned forward toward the microphone and dropped his voice. "And what did the government do with that money they *withheld* from your paycheck? They put it in *foreign aid*." He stretched out the term in a whisper, like an obscenity. "Do you know how *foreign aid* works? Do you?" He rose up from his leaning position. "Here's how it works. Your ambassador, your overpaid ambassador, who might be in Uruguay or Yemen or Malaysia or Lower Slobbovia—it doesn't matter—conducts a dinner party. At that dinner party champagne is served in crystal glasses and caviar is served on expensive china. The men wear their tails and women wear evening gowns and lots of jewelry and there's a string quartet wearing tuxedos in the corner, playing Mozart. All of this, of course, has been paid for through what was *withheld* from your paycheck. Rack of lamb and lobster is offered for the main course and then Bananas Foster for dessert, and while the wait-staff is cleaning up, the big-whigs retire to the billiard room for brandy and Cuban cigars, and your ambassador says to Mr. Presidente, "Mr. Presidente, we have several million dollars in our budget that we're not sure where to spend. Do you have any suggestions?

Well, Mr. Presidente takes a big draw on his cigar, expels the smoke, nods approvingly and proceeds to tell the ambassador that, for many years, he had thought of helping the people in his home province— those people who have been so supportive of him and enabled him to become president. What those villagers in the home province really need is a textile factory.

The ambassador nods in agreement and he and Mr. Presidente clink their brandy glasses together and they shake hands. Thirty minutes later they douse their cigar butts in their leftover brandy and agree to work with haste to put together the plan they have discussed. The next morning the embassy people have put together the paperwork; two months later construction begins, and by the end of the year there is a modern textile factory operating in Mr. President's home province, and the manager is Mr. Presidente's wife's brother."

The audience laughed and shook their heads.

"We laugh, but it's true. And then what happens?" Henninger continued. He walked back and forth behind the podium. "And then what happens? I'll tell you." Those in the stadium were silent. "Here's what happens: you come to work one morning and there's a note on your locker that your supervisor needs to talk with you. You walk into the office, and you see your supervisor's face… and you know the news you are about to receive is not good. 'It's not my decision,' the supervisor says, 'but the company is struggling and there's going to be a lay-off.' You go to your locker and clean it out. You go home and give the news to your family. You find a part-time job, but it doesn't have any benefits and you're worried about medical bills. You get behind on your mortgage. You take the college funds you have set aside to get caught up— although it hurts you to do so. Christmas comes and you're determined to get your kids something, even if not as much as last year. At the department store you see a dress that your daughter would like. It looks like the kind of dress that your company used to make before you were laid off. You look at the price. It's very similar to the dresses your company used to make. You look at the tag … and what does it say? It says 'Made in El Presidente's homeland.'"

Harrison Henninger stood silently before the audience, holding an imaginary dress, turning it back and forth, testing the imaginary material, examining the imaginary tag. Ceremoniously and with finality he hung the imaginary dress on an imaginary rack.

The next day a reporter from the St. Louis Post-Dispatch would print an article. An on-site reporter wrote:

I believe at the moment Henninger hung up the imaginary dress—had he asked the crowd to follow him to City Hall—or the state capitol—or any other government building, for the purpose of burning down that building, I believe they would have followed him and any one of the crowd would have lit the first match—such was the power of his appeal at that moment.

Henninger spoke in a whisper to a silent crowd: "It's not just dresses. It's not just textiles. It's steel. It's electronics. It's automobiles. It's farm products. It's manufactured goods. It's everything we make in America."

Henninger stood beside the podium. "Let me repeat. I am not—at this moment—a candidate for the presidency of the United States. However, if I were—by some circumstances thrust into that job, do you know what I would do on the first day on the job? Here's what I would do. I would call a little meeting. All our ambassadors would be required to attend. And I would tell them to bring their ambassadors' badges. And I would have a cardboard box in the middle of the table and I would tell them all to drop their badges in it."

A cheer went up. "And I would tell them, 'No more foreign aid. No more dinner parties. No more champagne in crystal glasses. No more lobster and rack of lamb. No more brandy and cigars … no more string quartets … and no more deals for the politicians.'"

Henninger paused again. "I want to ask you a question—" The crowd began waving their signs because they knew he was bringing the speech to a close. "It's the question I always ask."

He took his gun from the podium and held it up.

"The question is: Are you going to take this anymore?"

"Hell no!"

"Tell me again," Henninger cupped his ear.

"Hell no!"

"What is my name?" he shouted.

"Harrison Hell No Henninger!"

Henninger held his arms in the air, his right hand clutching the gun, his teeth clenched in a tight smile as the final roar came.

ELEVEN

SATURDAY, MAY 5, 1:30 P.M.

WHAT A PITIFUL wardrobe!

Jamie ran her fingers through the hangers in the tiny closet. *Three dresses! I own three dresses!*

In the closet there was no shortage of running suits along with a few slack suits, but only three dresses to choose from. Jamie always meant to do some shopping—to add a few things that would enhance her wardrobe, and her dad had sent her a check a month earlier for that purpose. The check was still uncashed. The last time she had been in a clothing store was the end of the previous semester, when she helped Sissy find some things she would need as she went to medical school. Jamie couldn't seem to find the time to make a shopping trip for herself.

"Aspie, I'm pathetic. I attend classes. I write papers. I run track. That's all I do." The cat meowed as if she agreed. Jamie looked at the closet again and then looked at her watch. It was a little after one o'clock.

I wish I could wear a tracksuit, she thought, but the instructions for the ceremony were clear—sport coat and ties for the gentlemen and dresses for the ladies. *You need to hurry Jamie. The event starts in an hour and a half.*

She ran her hands through the closet again, jingling the hangers. "Oh Aspie, I wish Sissy were here. She could help me." She pulled out the three dresses. One was winter wool, so she hung it back up. Of the remaining two choices, one was a spring dress, lemon-colored with three-quarter sleeves. The other was the summer dress, bright blue and sleeveless, which she had worn only once, the previous summer at an outdoor afternoon reception at the president's house. Jamie looked outside. The sun was shining. She held the dress up to her body. "What do you think, Aspie? Sissy said the blue dress looked good on me. Do you agree?" The cat meowed. "Okay. Decision made."

Forty-five minutes later, Jamie stood near the temporary stage that had been erected on the campus lawn. *The other dress would have been a better choice. This dress is a little tighter than I recalled.*

She stood near one of the giant oaks adjacent to the chapel. A series of those oaks framed the lawn soaking up the May sunshine. Birds flittered energetically among the trees, seeking food for their chicks. A breeze ran through the trees, giving a tremor to the leaves and giving Jamie goose bumps on her bare arms. *I really should have worn the dress with the longer sleeves.*

Three other students—also due to receive honors—stood near the outdoor stage, a raised platform with a hanging skirt and a few potted plants around it. The towering chapel, a gray stone edifice, provided the backdrop and gave the site the appropriate solemnity. However, the numerous media trucks parked nearby marred that solemnity.

Jamie checked her watch. 1:40. She had come early with the hope she might meet Harrison Henninger and ask him about her grandfather. But Henninger's party had not yet arrived. And she found herself concerned about the blue dress. Workers were laying cables from the media trucks and as they did, Jamie felt their eyes on her. *Have I gained weight? This dress is definitely tighter than I remember.* She moved closer to the trunk of the tree for shelter.

Clusters of people were scattered around the lawn, mostly faculty and families, the men in sport coats and blazers, the women in spring dresses. The women carried on animated conversations, but some of the men looked at the clear blue sky above them and checked their watches, probably wondering if they were going to be able to make their tee-time that afternoon. A few children, sentenced to wear their Sunday clothes on Saturday, played chase—despite the admonishments of their mothers. One boy, perhaps six years old, his tie loose, his shirttail hanging out of his pants, chased a girl a year or two older. She wore a frilly pink dress, the sash untied and trailing behind as she ran, squealing, across the expanse of lawn.

The event was invitation only. The guest list included faculty members and administration, significant donors, and a few key political figures. All those in attendance expected an announcement by

Harrison Henninger that he would endow a Chair of American Enterprise for the university. A few of the faculty members were cynical about taking funds from a politician, but the administration and the board of trustees showed no such reluctance. They were always receptive to donations.

The chancellor moved among the clusters of people, shaking every hand in each group, smiling and making pleasantries. On the edge of the lawn several media trucks pointed their dishes through the trees toward an unseen satellite (perhaps one that Henninger owned). Strings of heavy cable snaked across the lawn disappearing in the potted plants around the stage. Cameramen and other media people hustled to get equipment in place.

The chancellor looked at his watch. Jamie also looked at her watch. 1:47 and there was no sign of Henninger. *No chance to talk before the ceremony—maybe after ...*

A man in a black suit and dark sunglasses came to the chancellor and whispered something. The chancellor nodded and then began to encourage everyone to take their seats. She and the other honorees were directed to take their places on the stage. When Jamie took her seat, and tugged at the hem of her dress, she realized again the blue dress was a mistake. *Bad decision—I should have chosen the other dress.* The metal folding chair was cold against her legs. *I will be glad to get back in my tracksuit.*

She smiled at the Asian girl next to her. *Music? Science? Maybe Math? Probably Music. Those are the hands of a musician.* Next to her was a young man with a thin mustache, wearing a turtleneck under a sport coat with elbow patches. *Writing award, no doubt.* Next to him was a guy with a ponytail, wearing complete black. *Art, definitely Art.*

Dr. Emerson and Mrs. Emerson arrived and waved at Jamie as they took their seats.

A limousine came into view. It turned up the boulevard adjacent to the campus lawn, paused for a moment, then pulled over the curb, across the lawn to a spot beside the stage. The huge black machine, made sinister by the darkened windows, seemed oddly out of place. The lawn had been softened by recent rain and the vehicle left deep ruts in the grass. *Maybe the first part of Henninger's endowment can be used to repair the lawn.*

The chancellor came over to the limousine. A huge man emerged from the vehicle, which from his overly serious expression and efficient manner, Jamie guessed to be a security guard of some kind. Jamie remembered a Henninger commercial: "I do not need any Secret Service protection. The government has not protected its citizens for the last 40 years! Why should I trust them to protect me now? I will provide my own protection!"

It made a great sound bite and seemed to strike a chord with the anti-government sentiments of U.S. citizens. And she had to admit, the guy who got out of the limo looked like he could protect anyone or anything. His head was huge with short-trimmed bleached-blond hair and his neck seemed larger than his head. He wore a tie, but the collar of his shirt was unbuttoned to accommodate the thick neck. His suit coat was pulled tightly across massive shoulders. A matching bleached-blonde goatee swiveled from side to side as the giant surveyed the surroundings. The chancellor made an effort to greet the huge man, but was ignored. The man took a flip-phone from his pocket and carried on a hushed conversation. All conversations among the guests had gone quiet. Even the children, who somehow sensed a change of mood, gathered near their mothers. After a moment, apparently satisfied with the situation, the muscle man tapped on the side of the car.

The man that emerged was smaller than Jamie expected—and made smaller by the massive black vehicle and the bleached-blonde giant who protected him. Henninger looked a little older in person than on television, but still younger than his actual age. His relative youthfulness was, according to the rumors, due in part to a surgeon's skill. His uniform gray hair was combed back from the peak of his forehead. The effect of his combed-back hair, together with his ears, which were set tight against his head, gave him a streamlined, almost aerodynamic look, which accentuated his personality. He looked like a man in motion (or wanted to be in motion) even when he stood still. His eyes were gray to match his hair ("soulless" eyes, one writer had called them). He carried his chin in such a way that his mouth was always slightly open, his jaw jutted like a prizefighter's. He shook the chancellor's hand perfunctorily and without coming to a complete stop, started around the stage toward the assembled guests— the chancellor a step behind, trying to catch up. Henninger had the air of a man in a hurry—a man with something to get accomplished.

A line of special guests had gathered to greet Henninger. He put on a smile and shook their hands but did not let the chancellor complete the introductions. Henninger was not a man who was concerned that so-and-so owned one of the largest manufacturing plants in the mid-Atlantic, or that so-and-so was president of a regional bank—these were men Henninger could buy and sell by the dozens, and their credentials were of no importance to him.

"Blondie"—the name that Jamie had unconsciously given to the security man, began an inspection of the stage. He tilted the potted plants to look under them and Jamie wondered if the shoulder seams of his jacket might split. Jamie wanted to lean over and say to the Asian girl, "Thank goodness there are no bombs under the ficus or peace lilies," but the nervous expression on the girl's face made Jamie realize this was no time for a joke.

Blondie continued his inspection, stepping up the short stairs to the stage. The stage oscillated with the weight of each step. The man's arms hung at an odd angle from his body, and he moved in a ponderous way—the mass of his body an impediment to his movement. He peered over his sunglasses at the students who were on the left side of the stage. His expression was contemptuous as he went from Artist to Writer to Musician … and then he looked at Jamie—a long, leering look, while he worked on his chewing gum. Jamie turned away. The big man moved slowly toward the podium, still looking over his shoulder at Jamie. He continued to look at Jamie as he moved the podium. One of the media men, standing just below the podium, concerned about the cables, muttered a "Hey" to the big man above him. The butch-cut giant stepped to the edge of the stage, cocked his head to the side in a defiant manner, and glared at the worker below him. The media man, with short reflection, thought better of pursuing the matter, and went about his business among the cables. The big man half-heartedly began checking the potted plants on the stage, all the while looking back at Jamie.

He made a pretense of checking the plants beside the podium, then stepped back toward the honorees, the stage creaking with each step. The Artist and the Writer were talking with each other, but they stopped when the big man came near them. He stood over them, saying nothing, working his gum around his teeth. The two young men appeared nervous—which seemed to be the big man's intent—and he moved away, nearer the oriental girl. She kept her head down as he stood above her, his legs spread. The girl fidgeted, and Jamie heard the big man mumble, "Chink."

A fury rose in Jamie, but she wasn't sure what to do. *Do not create a scene. This is not the time.*

Jamie locked her eyes on the big man, her face defiant, as the big man took a step toward her. He tapped the leg of her metal chair with his foot, as if testing it and pulled down his sunglasses on his nose. "Now, you're not hiding a weapon somewhere in that little blue dress, are you?" She kept her eyes directly on his, keeping her rage under control. He ran his eyes all over her. "No, I guess not," he said, showing his gum between his teeth. *Do not show your anger, Jamie. Do not give him the satisfaction.*

The big man nodded his head and stepped away, leaving the stage. Jamie looked over at the Asian girl. Her hands were trembling, and a tear ran down her cheek.

At that moment, the chancellor and Henninger came onto the platform. Jamie and the other honorees stood. "Mr. Henninger," the chancellor said, "let me introduce you to those receiving awards today."

Jamie looked at Harrison Henninger. His countenance betrayed his disinterest, but he nodded. The chancellor introduced the Writer first. Henninger quickly shook his hand and moved to the Artist before the first introduction concluded. He then moved to the Musician and shook her hand before the chancellor could introduce either of them. Jamie was next. The chancellor quickly said, "The recipient of the McKenzie award—"

Jamie took Henninger's hand. He tried to pull it away, but Jamie held it for a moment. "Mr. Henninger, it is possible you may have known my grandfather. He served in the same unit as yours in World War II. I am named after him. He was James Patterson, Sergeant James Patterson—"

Henninger's hand quivered!

It was noticeable. The tremor in his hand was distinct. He tried to pull his hand away but Jamie held it for a moment longer before releasing it. She looked at the man. His face changed. The smugness in his countenance faded. His eyes went wide. *Is he sick?*

Henninger stepped away quickly. He turned his face away from Jamie. He took his seat by the podium. Jamie looked at him carefully. He was on the opposite side of the stage, but she could see him clearly. *Why did he react in that way? Why did his hand quiver? Why did his face change?* She looked at him again. He kept his face turned away, but his knee vibrated nervously as the chancellor began the ceremony.

When Jamie came to the podium to receive her award, Henninger did not look up. Holding her plaque she thanked the university for the award and her father for his direction and encouragement—and she gave a special thanks to Dr. and Mrs. Emerson "... for whom teaching, learning, and encouragement is a way of life. Thank you Dr. and Mrs. Emerson for teaching me, for encouraging me, and for allowing me to witness your love of learning." She asked them to rise and be recognized and there was a round of applause for them.

Another round of applause followed her when she left the podium—but Harrison Henninger kept his hands on his knees.

Henninger himself was introduced shortly thereafter. His speech, as the newspapers would report the next day, was considerably shorter than normal—and lacking the customary fire. And there was an awkward moment at the end of the speech, when Henninger left the podium and the chancellor had to remind him to announce that yes, his company was providing an endowment for a Chair of American Enterprise to the university.

Jamie heard little of the speech. She was still wondering about Henninger's strange reaction when she introduced herself. *What caused him to react so oddly? Maybe I just imagined it. No, it was real she told herself.*

She came out of her thoughts as she realized the ceremony concluded. Henninger was leaving the stage. She went down the stairs and around the platform in the opposite direction, hoping to catch him before he got in the limo. Questions had welled up in her mind—questions she wanted to ask Henninger before he got away. A few of the guests said "Congratulations, Jamie" as she went down the stairs, but she did not stop. *Maybe I can catch him before he gets into—*

The jolt in her arm surprised her. The plaque fell onto the grass. Blondie! The giant held her arm firmly, restraining her. She tried to pull away, but it was hopeless. She saw Henninger on the opposite side of the limo, hardly thirty feet away. He had paused before getting into the limo and looked directly at her over the top of the vehicle.

She tried to pull her arm away. "I want to—"

"Mr. Henninger won't be signing any autographs today, little missy," the big man said.

"But—"

"Here, let me get your little trophy for you." He released his grip and knelt slowly beside her, running his eyes all over her. *Do not kick him! She told herself. Do not!*

He was close enough to kick and he deserved it, but she fought the impulse. He picked up the plaque and, still kneeling, began very ceremoniously to clean the grass from it, all the while running his eyes all over Jamie's body. She wanted to scream. She wanted to knee this cretin in the face. *Do not give him the satisfaction of a response.*

He rose slowly, still running his eyes over her. "Well, I think our little trophy is going to be okay." He blew his breath on it and made a show of polishing it with his forearm. His face was so close Jamie could smell the sticky sweetness of his chewing gum. "Yeah, I think it's going to be just fine. Maybe I could come over and help you hang this on your wall—"

The limo's horn blew. "Well," he said, "I'm going to have to go. I guess we will have to pick up our conversation later." He held out the plaque, but when Jamie tried to take it, he kept in his grasp for a moment. Jamie kept her eyes directly on his face, determined that she would show no emotion. He rolled the gum in his teeth. The horn blew again. "Yeah, maybe later," he said as he released the plaque. He went toward the limo, turned and gave Jamie a wave, a smirk on his face. She stood there without moving until the limo sped away, tearing more trenches in the soft lawn.

"Jamie—" it was Mrs. Emerson who called to her. Dr. Emerson was beside her. "Jamie, are you okay?"

Jamie turned toward them. "Yes, I'm fine," she said, realizing she was lying. She was not fine. All sorts of emotions were going through her at that moment—anger, disgust, fear, frustration, bewilderment—but there was no reason to dump all that on the Emersons.

"Congratulations," Dr. Emerson said. "And thank you for your kind words for us."

"You're welcome. I meant those words sincerely."

"Are you sure you're okay?" Mrs. Emerson said. "You seem a little subdued."

"Just fatigued, I think—and maybe a little cool."

"Well," Mrs. Emerson said, "you look stunning in that dress, but I don't think it will keep you warm. Why don't you come over to the house for some soup?"

"Oh, thank you, but I think I just need to go home and crash."

"Well, okay, but Wednesday night at the regular time," Mrs. Emerson persisted. "After all, we won't have too many more of those regular Wednesday night sessions before you graduate."

"Agreed. Wednesday night. I'll be there"

"Congratulations again." Dr. Emerson said as he and Mrs. Emerson walked away. "You are most deserving of the award."

Back at her house, she put the plaque on the kitchen counter, quickly poured Aspie a bowl of cat food and went to her bedroom. She unzipped the blue dress, pulled it off and threw it over the chair by her bed. She found her terry-cloth bathrobe and cinched it tightly around her waist and fell on her bed. The emotions of an hour before—the degradation before the muscle man, the anger and frustration—swelled up inside her. She heard herself growl between clenched teeth. She surprised herself when she started crying. The frustration and degradation at the ceremony found expression in her sobbing. *This is not like me! I'm not a crier!* But her mind went back to the behemoth and his leering eyes and his mocking expression as he polished the plaque with his forearm. She unconsciously reached for her wrist—the place where he had grabbed her. She felt dirty. She broke into sobs again. She was angry with herself for her reaction, but she couldn't stop.

After a moment she found her composure. Aspie jumped on the bed and nuzzled beside her, purring. The timbre of her purring increased as Jamie stroked her.

And what about Henninger? Why did he react as he did? I'm certain—or at least I think I am—that his hand quivered when I mentioned my grandfather's name. Why?

To her frustration and anger was now added confusion. *Why would Henninger react like he did?*

She blew out a big breath and then sat up on the bed, still rubbing Aspie, who moved into Jamie's lap, sinking into the terrycloth. Jamie stroked the cat absent-mindedly, trying to recall the interaction with Harrison Henninger. *His eyes! His eyes changed when I mentioned my grandfather! The smugness, the haughtiness, all drained away. Or did I imagine that? No, I did not imagine that.*

Her mind went back to the blonde behemoth and his grip on her wrist. The loathing she had sensed came back over her again and she shivered. "Excuse me, Aspie," she said as she moved the cat out of her lap and went to the bathroom. She turned the shower on— hotter than usual—dropped the robe and got in, lathering herself vigorously as the little bathroom steamed up.

A few minutes later she was in the kitchen, back in her robe and her hair in a towel. She poked around in the refrigerator, found a Lean Cuisine and popped it in the microwave. She found some salad fixings— lettuce, carrots and tomatoes and poured some vinaigrette over them. She took her food to the living room. It was 6:00. She flipped on the local news. "Harrison Henninger ..." the reporter was saying as the camera showed the scene on the campus only a couple of hours earlier, "... has been drawing huge crowds across the country, but today's crowd was small by design—an invitation only event. The man whom many expect will soon announce his candidacy for president of the United States, visited Duke University this afternoon, where he revealed that his company, Harrison Industries, will endow—"

Jamie saw herself on the stage as the camera provided a blurb from Henninger's speech. At the edge of the stage was Blondie, looking bored. Jamie unconsciously pulled her robe tighter and turned the TV off.

She stirred the chicken breast and broccoli around her plate for a moment, but she was restless. She got up suddenly, went to her closet and found a running suit, put it on, went to the bathroom and blew her hair almost dry. "Sorry, Aspie," she said as she tied her shoes. "I'm going out for a while." She patted the cat's head. "I'll be back soon."

She left the front porch and settled into a controlled pace as she ran. *This is therapy,* she told herself. *This is not training.* This had been her pattern since high school—whenever a problem or issue came up—go for a long jog. Something about the rhythm and the solitude of a long, slow run allowed her to—if not solve the problem—at least identify the issue in her mind.

She ran through the curving streets to the edge of campus. The scent of honeysuckle hung close to the earth in the warm evening air. The campus buildings were more brightly lit than usual—as students used vacant classrooms to cram for final exams. *That's one thing you don't have to worry about, Jamie.* As a graduating senior—and the requisite grades in her classes—she would not be required to take final exams. Not all students were seeking well-lit areas—and not all were preparing for tests. Some couples had sought out dark alcoves and secluded benches to snuggle together and whisper assurances of fidelity for the next three months. Most of those assurances would probably not survive the summer's heat, but the vows seemed as much a part of the campus ritual as the final exams.

That's another worry you don't have, she reminded herself—a complicated relationship. You've never had a complicated relationship. In fact, she told herself, you've never even had a non-complicated relationship.

She thought about the past four years—a few dates, mostly for special events, but nothing that endured. "You intimidate the boys," Sissy once told her while the two of them were laughing about doing their laundry at the laundromat on a Friday night, rather than preparing for a date.

"Me? Intimidate? What have I ever done to intimidate anyone?"

"It's not what you have done," Sissy responded. "It's what you are—you're too smart—you're too good-looking, and—" she said as she plopped a stack of underwear in a bag, "… you run too fast."

Jamie pooh-poohed the whole idea although sometimes she also heard the young men whisper as she passed: "The Face … The Brain … The Legs …"

She came to the wooded area behind the chapel. She jogged up the well-worn steps beside the stained-glass windows of the chapel. The glow of the dim lights inside shaped the blue, red and gold windows against the dark walls. At the top of the steps, she stopped. As she soaked in the warm evening air, she realized how much she was going to miss the university. She was not by nature sentimental, still she realized how quickly the past four years had gone—it seemed only weeks ago that she had crossed the campus as a freshman. A sense of melancholy came over here. She tried to put the thought out of her mind. It was easier to avoid thinking about leaving. If she thought about leaving, she would have to think about the Rhodes offer … and about the Olympic team … and—

This isn't helping. You promised yourself you wouldn't think about those things until after the NCAA meet.

She quit jogging and began walking, still turning over the events of a few hours earlier. Magnolia leaves, crusty and brown, fallen from the trees flanking the chapel, rustled against the pavement under her feet as she walked. She walked by a couple on a campus bench, both hands clasped together, forehead against forehead.

She came to the campus lawn and went across to the area where the ceremony had been held. She looked at the ruts left by the limousine. The chairs, the podium and the potted plants had been removed, but the stage was still standing—presumably for the maintenance crew to disassemble in the morning.

Focus Jamie. Focus. What is it that has you in turmoil?

The memory of the behemoth's grip on her arm and his leering face, and the disgust came back to her afresh. However, she realized that was not the real reason she was in turmoil—the real reason for her turmoil was Harrison Henninger—and his strange reaction to her mention of her grandfather's name.

She stepped up on the stage and stood where she shook hands with Henninger, recalling the event. *I did not imagine his reaction. It was real. But I need to get more information.*

TWELVE

JAMIE WAS NOT as attentive during the church service as she should have been. Her mind was still replaying the events of the previous afternoon.

"Uriah," the pastor said, "was a better man drunk—than David was, when sober." The pastor was preaching from the well-known passage about King David and his sin with Bathsheba, when he tried to cover up his sin by recalling her husband to Jerusalem, plying him with wine in the effort to get him to have sexual relations with his wife. "But," the pastor said, "as the King James Version has it, 'Uriah *went not down* to his house'. Uriah refused to take comfort in his own house, with his own wife while his fellow soldiers were in the field. The Bible is not a romantic book," the pastor continued, "It never glosses over the frailties and failures of the men and women of its pages. Although David is one of the greatest figures in the Bible, his sin—his sordid behavior and his effort to cover up his sin—does not go unreported. Betrayal is an awful offense, an awful sin, and God did not allow David to escape the results of that sin. His efforts to conceal his betrayal of Uriah were not successful. David's sin was revealed, and he paid dearly for his offense."

When the service ended, Jamie shook the pastor's hand as she left. "Congratulations on the McKenzie Award," he said. "And be sure I am praying for you for the conference championships—and I will be there to cheer you on."

She thanked him, took her bicycle from the rack, and began pedaling toward her house. She went only half a block, made an abrupt U-turn, and headed toward the library. *Might as well start that research now.*

Five minutes later she chained her bike to the rack outside the library and went inside. She apologized to the librarian for needing to borrow a legal pad and pen, but the librarian provided both, saying there was no need for an apology, and congratulated her on the McKenzie Award.

She took the stairs—two at a time—up to the third floor—Social Sciences. Most of the study tables were in use, the bookstacks on the tables high enough to almost conceal the student behind them. *Hmm ... someone has put off writing that term paper until the last minute.* She found one table in the corner that was not being used and put the legal pad and pen on it and went to the card catalog.

Forty-five minutes later Jamie had amassed a respectable stack of books herself. She began writing notes on her pad. Many of the notes were bibliographic—lists of other books to look up. While the Duke library was a magnificent collection, the information she was seeking—about a specific platoon of a specific company of a specific regiment involved in a specific battle during World War II—was very specialized and no non-military university would be expected to have such information on its shelves. She found some broader treatments of the war, huge tomes like *The U.S. in World War II—European Theatre of Operations,* which covered the war in Europe in broad strokes, describing the major operations—but not the individual battles—of the conflict. She found the biography of George Patton, the famous general who commanded the 3rd Army in Europe, but it made no mention of the events at the St. Laurent bridge.

None of the other reference books made mention of that specific topic either, but she made a list from the cited books in the bibliographies. Some seemed promising—the memoirs of the colonel (later general) who commanded the 108th during the war, and a few others, while not specific to actions of the 108th, dealt with the events and locations of the regiment, but the most encouraging book in that list was *The History of the 108th Infantry Division—1918-1946*—which was the official U.S. Army record of the regiment. She put the page of notes in her pocket and returned the pad and pen to the librarian. The Inter-Library Loan desk was not open on Sunday afternoon, but Jamie purposed to be back first thing in the morning.

THIRTEEN

"WELL, THIS IS a different line of research than your usual inquiries," Mrs. Jansen, the lady in charge of Inter-library Loan, said, looking at the list Jamie had given her.

Jamie knew Mrs. Jansen well, having availed herself of I.L.L. services quite often over the past few years as she had prepared research papers—most of them related to ancient Greek history.

"And I'm surprised you are doing research this late in the term. Aren't you scheduled to graduate in just a couple of weeks?"

"Well," Jamie answered, not sure how to reply, "this is some personal research."

"Hmm—" the lady said, looking down over eyeglasses perched at the edge of her nose, held around her neck by a gold chain. "George Patton … 3rd Army … 108th Infantry Division … give me a moment."

Jamie watched the blue, flickering reflection of the computer screen on Mrs. Jansen's perched eyeglasses as the lady typed. "Hmm …" she said several times as she turned her head sideways, looking at the screen. She jotted some notes on a pad beside the computer, then clicked the mouse and the nearby printer started its "clickety-clack". Mrs. Jansen took the printout from the printer and neatly tore the perforated edges from the sides.

"I confined the search to libraries within 300 miles," she said. "I found several with all your requests. West Point, of course, has all of them, but also so does VMI, which is nearer."

"How soon do you think you can get them?"

"You know," Mrs. Jansen replied, "I have a friend at the VMI library. She heads up their I.L.L. She might do us a favor. I will give her a call."

"Oh, thank you Mrs. Jansen. I genuinely appreciate your help."

"I'm glad to be of assistance. If you come by tonight, I will leave a note here on the desk telling you what I have learned."

A little before 2:00 pm, Jamie reported to the training room for a heat treatment for her quadriceps. It had been a slight injury, weeks earlier, and in truth it had completely healed, but the trainer suggested two treatments a week as maintenance therapy. The student trainer rubbed a petroleum jelly-like substance on her upper leg and then placed the heated pad over it as Jamie lay on the table. The warm treatment, the steamy vapors in the air, the towel under her head and the soft pad were ordinarily relaxing—in fact, Jamie had dozed off the previous Friday when she got the treatment. But today she found her mind still churning. *Harrison*

Henninger. Harrison Henninger. Why can't I get him off my mind?

On the track she began her warm-up phase. She ran a slow-paced half-mile to get warmth in her muscles, then went through her stretching routine, then ran another half mile to get ready for the real work. Monday was speed day, the day she worked on her sprinting speed. Her regimen called for her to run six 100-meter dashes for time. Between each 100 meters, she jogged around the remainder of the quarter mile track, and then ran another 100. It was a grueling pattern, but she knew the regimen was necessary if she were to reach her goals. She was often reminded of the plaque above her father's desk when he coached at the junior college: **The will to win is not as important as the will to prepare to win.** Her target time for each 100-meter dash was 13 seconds. Others, she knew, were faster than she, but all-out speed was not her greatest strength in the 800—her greatest strength was establishing a grueling pace and maintaining it for the entire race. Jamie's victories in the 800 were never spectacular; she never overtook a competitor on the backstretch to win a victory. No photos showed her extending her neck at the finish line to eke out a victory. No, Jamie's strategy was to set a pace—a grueling pace—that made it impossible for her competitors to overtake her. Her competitors often led her at the 400 yard mark, and occasionally at the 600 yard mark, but the last half-lap of the race invariably belonged to Jamie as those competitors could not maintain the rigorous pace to the end.

"13.7, Jamie," Coach Barton said, looking at her stopwatch as Jamie finished her first dash. "You need to pick it up." The next time for the split was 13.3, but that was to prove her best time of the afternoon. The last segment was 13.9.

"You need to tell me," Coach Barton said as they were leaving the track, "if that quadricep is bothering you again."

"No injury, Coach Barton. I just had an off day. I'll have it back tomorrow."

The note from Mrs. Jansen was waiting for her as promised—and the news was good. The VMI librarian confirmed that all the books Jamie requested were available for inter-library loan, and that she would do what she could to expedite the process and get the books to Duke as soon as possible.

FOURTEEN

HENRY PURSLEY WATCHED a boxfish paddle around the aquarium, its dorsal fins spinning like tiny motors, barely propelling its appropriately named and clumsy-looking body through the water. A few dozen other fish, all more streamlined and more colorful than the boxfish, swam around the rocks and coral of the display, while an eel of some sort peered out from its burrow. Henry remembered the first time he brought the girls to the National Aquarium, and they had seen the odd-looking fish that was shaped like a box with almost no tail and a tiny, puckered mouth. "Oh, mother," Allison, the younger daughter had said, "it has sad eyes. Do you think it wants to go back to the ocean?" Her mother assured her that the boxfish was perfectly happy in the aquarium, and that its eyes only *looked* sad. "And it is safer in the aquarium. It's dangerous in the ocean."

The boxfish swam over to the edge of the glass as if it were looking at Henry. *Maybe Allison was right. Maybe its eyes really are sad.*

When he had come to Washington and the Commerce Department three years previously, the fact that his office was in the same building as the National Aquarium was a fascination to his daughters and they made several excursions that first summer the family was in Washington. Myra would bring sack lunches for the four of them, which they sometimes ate in Henry's office before walking over to see the fish. The two girls would walk ahead of their parents, identifying the fish as they walked. Myra would take Henry's hand as they walked. "All your hard work has paid off," she said as she squeezed his hand.

The boxfish, its curiosity apparently satisfied, swam off.

Henry looked at his watch. It was one thirty—still an hour and a half until the appointment with the president and his team. He dreaded it. The meeting with Henninger had not gone well and he was going to have to be the bearer of bad news. *Don't kill the messenger.* Wasn't that the cliché?

He remembered the first few times he had gone to the White House. Those had been heady days: Myra and the girls were fascinated when he told them about visiting the Oval Office and meeting the president. Those days were over. He now went regularly to the Oval Office—now that he was "Special Advisor," but there was no thrill left in the event. When he had been appointed to that position, Myra and the girls had experienced a fresh surge of pride—but he asked himself: *How proud will they be when I'm in a federal prison?* That question in his mind led to others: *I wonder if a prisoner can request a specific federal prison for the term of incarceration? Where is the closest federal prison to Sacramento? Will Myra and the girls even want to visit me?*

He looked at his watch again. Still more than an hour until the meeting. If this had been one of his early meetings with the president and his team, he would have already been at the White House. But he didn't go early anymore. He did not like the West Wing. The West Wing had no good place to wait. The halls were cramped and oppressive. *Cramped and oppressive! I'm going to learn what cramped and oppressive are really like.*

When he first took the job as "Special Advisor", the idea of moving along the corridors of the White House, he had to admit, was somewhat exhilarating, but his sense of self-importance was soon deflated by the scrutiny of the Secret Service men who patrolled the halls, stone-faced men with one finger on the flesh-colored devices in their ears, who never seemed to recognize him, no matter how many times he visited the West Wing.

It was not how he had envisioned the job—sitting in a cramped hallway of the West Wing, waiting for an hour for a fifteen-minute appointment with the president, scrutinized by humorless Secret Service men in black suits. So, now he waited at the aquarium. He would watch the fish until about twenty minutes before the appointment. Then he would walk the few hundred yards to the White House before entering those constricting quarters of the West Wing.

He might as well watch the fish—he had nothing to do at his desk. His job, as he soon learned, was strictly related to communicating with Harrison Henninger. Henninger called him "errand boy".

I can't dispute the cognomen. Or is it "agnomen"? Maybe I will brush up on my Latin when I'm in prison.

With no real responsibilities, Henry spent his time thinking—and worrying. He realized he did not dread incarceration as much as he dreaded embarrassment—for himself, for Myra and for the girls. Two or three years—*surely it will not be more than that*—he could endure, but the humiliation for Myra and the girls—having to live with the whispers … that would be the difficult part.

The boxfish suddenly darted across the glass with surprising speed, apparently alarmed by some movement of the eel. It settled in the corner, its little propeller-fins holding it suspended in the water, its pursed mouth as sad as ever.

Henry took a deep breath. The air in the building was thick with salt-water vapor. The aroma reminded him of the California coast. *I should have taken that job at Campo del Sur.*

Henry had inherited the beach house near Campo del Sur from his parents. It sat on a cliff above the sea on the edge of town. He, along with his parents, had spent his summers there as a boy. He had roamed in the woods and along the beach, certain every day that he would find a message in a bottle—a note from some sailor marooned on a desert island, desperate for rescue.

He never found the message in the bottle, but the place was no less magical for him. From the house, which sat on a low bluff, sandy hillocks below, when the air was clear, it seemed he could see a thousand miles out over the ocean. He wished he could stand there again, hear the waves roll and thump below him, feel the sea breeze push his pants against his legs and see that broad expanse of open ocean again.

You had your chance.

The part-time mayor of Campo del Sur, a good friend of his father's, had made the offer. "Henry, we need a city manager—there's too much going on here for an old goat like me to handle. New condos ... a shopping mall ... another golf course in the works ... our classrooms getting crowded. These are things I can't handle. I've talked to the council members. We think the revenues from all this construction would fund the salary for a city manager. It wouldn't be as much as you're making working for the state but—"

I should have taken that offer.

He and Myra talked about it. They gave it consideration. Much was attractive about the opportunity, but the bedrooms at the cottage were small; the kitchen was outdated; the plumbing needed a major overhaul; and a few more years as an employee of the state would enhance his retirement package, so he turned it down.

A group of school children—first or second graders, Henry guessed—ran by him, their shrieks bringing him out of his thoughts. They ran to the huge glass panel just beyond him and he saw the sign that explained their excitement:

Sharks are fed at 2 P.M. Mon., Wed. & Sat.

Piranha are fed at 2 P.M. Thur. & Sun.

Henry laughed under his breath. The wonderful irony of the sign had never dawned on him before— *Only the feeding times for sharks and piranha are listed! How appropriate for Washington!*

FIFTEEN

DESPITE HER ASSURANCES to her coach, Jamie did not have her form back on Tuesday. She sensed it herself. Her running seemed mechanical. Nothing was fluid. She told herself to find her stride and stay in it—but she could never find it. She was three seconds off her goal in the 600 meters she ran, and she could break 30 seconds only once in the four 200 meters she ran— nearly two seconds slower than her goal.

Coach Barton asked again, and Jamie shrugged it off again—but she herself was also beginning to have concerns about her performance.

Before going home Jamie decided to go by the library—to see if there was any news about the books she had requested. She took the familiar path behind the chapel and stopped for a moment as she passed the World War II memorial, which honored those Duke alumni who lost their lives in the conflict. A low wall ran along the left side of the sidewalk which held a series of bronze plaques, set in the beveled stone, which held the names of 236 Duke alumni who died in the war. *Two hundred thirty-six men!* Jamie thought. *Each one certainly had plans for life after the war.* She knew that more than 400,000 Americans died in combat during World War II. *My grandfather was part of that gruesome statistic. He was one of those 400,000. He, like the others, without doubt, had ambitions for a life after the war.* She ran her fingers across the names set in the beveled stone. *How many times have I walked past this memorial without an appreciation for those who died in that war? I have not adequately appreciated the magnitude of that national tragedy.*

As if to add to the somber mood, a light mist began to fall, dislodging the fragile dogwood blossoms, which fell on the plaques. Water began to collect in droplets on the bronze names of each of the alumni.

I may not be able to adequately appreciate the horror of that war, but I am determined to know more about my grandfather.

"Perhaps by tomorrow," the librarian told Jamie. "My friend put them on a Greyhound bus earlier today." She put her hand to the side of her mouth. "That's one of our interlibrary loan secrets—" she said. "—when we need to get a book in a hurry. Usually, I reserve that option only for faculty, but I'm making an exception this time. Do you promise you won't tell anyone?"

"Oh, thank you. Yes, I promise. You can be sure your secret is safe."

SIXTEEN

"HE WANTS *WHAT*?!" the president asked.

The Oval Office clock said 3:55. The meeting had started late. Henry, despite his efforts, had endured more than an hour in the claustrophobic halls of the West Wing, waiting for the appointment. Some supposed national emergency—something to do with the Cubans, according to what he overheard—had necessitated the president's attention, and the handling of that emergency had pushed back the president's schedule as he met with military advisors. James Olmstead was seated near the president's desk while Brent Arens, as was his custom, stood with his hands on his hips next to the palm in the Chinese pot, looking out the windows to the White House lawn.

Henry repeated the portion of the report he had just given: "Mr. Henninger wants the right to approve the members of the commission for their original five-year terms."

"That's absurd!" the president shouted again. "The Japanese would have a fit. The Chinese … the Koreans … even the Australians. They would all raise hell. We would have every nation in East Asia against us."

The president looked at Henry with a "kill the messenger" look.

Henry wished he were back at the aquarium looking at the boxfish. He wished he were back in Sacramento working for the state of California. He wished he were at Campo del Sur watching the waves on the beach. He wished he were anywhere except the Oval Office of the White House in Washington D.C. —giving bad news to the president of the United States. His meeting with Henninger had been humiliating— and now he had to bring bad news to the president and his advisors. *I'm in over my head.*

"I think," James Olmstead said wryly, "that Mr. Henninger is irritated with us."

"It's all because of the failure of the Etheridge Act, isn't it?" the president asked.

"The Etheridge Act was a terrible piece of legislation," Brent Arens said, without turning around.

"But as I recall," Olmstead continued, "our office gave that bill our endorsement prior to the election."

Henry knew about the Etheridge Act. It had been proposed by a new congressman from California, who reputedly had been given several hundred thousand dollars by Henninger to introduce a bill in congress creating a Pacific Rim Commission, whose recommendations would be binding for U.S. policies in the region. One portion of the commission's charter— seemingly innocuous in the first reading—was the provision that the commission would designate certain portions of the economy as "National Interest Sectors"—and would grant those industries, for up to seven years, special tax incentives and special protection from other competitors. Henninger, as the president and his advisors knew, expected his communications and shipping industries to be designated as "National Interest Sectors."

When James Olmstead first read the proposal, he had said: "I don't know why he wants seven years. With these protections—within three years—he will own every cargo ship, every satellite and every computer chip from Los Angeles, San Francisco and Seattle to Tokyo, Shanghai, Singapore and Melbourne. He will underprice all his competition and then buy them out when they can't compete."

"James," the president said, looking at Olmstead, "you must have a perverse sense of humor. You look like there is a smile on your face."

"Oh, I was just thinking of the custom of several centuries ago—when the invaders were at the gates and laying down their demands, it was not uncommon for them to include a demand for the king's wife and daughters. At least Henninger has not asked for your wife and daughters."

"My wife is 62 years old, and I don't have a daughter," the president said flatly. If he appreciated Olmstead's humor, he didn't show it.

He walked around his desk. "Every member of the commission … he wants to name every member of the commission." He turned the concept over in his mind. "He would become the virtual dictator of all trade in the Pacific Rim." He looked at Henry. "Did you get any idea if our opponent has agreed to this?"

"They are in communication—that's obvious from my conversation, but I do not know any specifics of that communication."

"What actually did Henninger say about his communication with our opponent?"

Henry paused.

"Well," the president said, "tell us, Henry. Tell us exactly what he said."

"He said," Henry began, "I'm quoting him: 'Maybe I need to get both of those boys in here at the same time and have a wrestling match to see which one I will endorse.'"

"That arrogant son-of—"

"Let's give it to him." Brent Arens interrupted the president without turning away from the window.

"Give it to him? What do you mean, Brent? Do you mean give him the right to name the members of the commission?"

"Yes," Arens answered.

"We'll have a war!"

Arens turned back to the others in the room, "Give it to him and then take it away. Create the commission now and while Henninger is beginning to name the members, we will dissolve the commission's charter— replace it with something similar—with the same name—but something we control."

No one spoke.

The president shook his head warily, "I don't know—"

"It's our best choice," Arens pressed. "You could wait a year or longer to dissolve the commission—it will take that long for the Japanese and Chinese and others to realize that Henninger is stacking the deck. We can carry Henninger along until we reconfigure the commission—or do away with it altogether."

The president turned to Olmstead. "What do you think, James?"

"I don't know anyone who has hoodwinked Henninger."

"Henninger!" the president erupted, calling the name like an obscenity. "I am so tired of hearing that name. How did this happen, James?"

"It's simple. He gave us money. He expected those contributions would gain him favorable legislation—the Etheridge Act. We didn't support the bill. That made Henninger angry. Apparently he is still angry."

"How much money did he give us, Brent?"

"More than two million—counting reported and unreported."

Henry winced when he heard "unreported". A vision kept coming into his brain—being sworn in at a Senate subcommittee hearing—*Mr. Pursley, were you aware that the offers you conferred to a private citizen were a violation of United States law?* Or, *Mr. Pursley, were you aware that the administration intended to enter into agreements that violated current international trade statutes?* Now the panel had another incriminating question to ask him: *Mr. Pursley, were you aware that the administration failed to report all campaign contributions?* Henry rubbed his shoulder.

"We need to act quickly," Arens said. "We have the advantage of incumbency. We can set up the commission right away. Our opponent can't do that. It's our best point of leverage. All other things being equal—given Henninger's acrimony toward us—if we don't do so, he will throw his support to the other side."

The president slumped into his chair. He looked at James Olmstead with an unspoken inquiry on his face. Olmstead gave a slight nod.

The decision was made. Henry knew it.

I'm going to prison. I'm sure of it.

SEVENTEEN

JAMIE SIGHED AS she closed the book—*War As I Knew It*, George Patton's autobiography. It had none of the information she was seeking. Beside it was *Patton: The Man Behind the Legend,* another biography, but likewise without any pertinent information. Neither of them had mentioned the events at St. Lautern, which discouraged Jamie. These books from VMI had come in that afternoon and Jamie picked them up immediately after track practice—when, once again, her times in the sprints were off significantly. Coach Barton questioned her again and Jamie tried again to reassure her coach that she was okay—but she, also, was beginning to wonder if she was, indeed, okay.

For the last two hours Jamie had been flipping through the books, hoping to learn more about her grandfather and his platoon—but there simply weren't any references. The two biographies of Patton failed to mention the event when her grandfather was killed and the same was true of the other books on her table. Only the official history of the 108th Infantry mentioned the events, and then only to say, "Third battalion suffered significant losses at the Saar River crossing before pushing the Germans back to the east."

"Not a lot of information," she said to Aspie, who jumped in her lap. "I had hoped to learn more," she said as she stroked the cat. "I really, really would like to know more. There must be more information than this."

Aspie meowed in agreement.

EIGHTEEN

THURSDAY, MAY 9, 5:15 P.M.

"OKAY, LADIES, LET'S stash the brushes for a minute."

Sybil Barton entered the meeting room carrying a stack of papers. The women's track coach looked as if she herself could run a marathon, which in fact, she did with regularity. Jamie and the other team members were seated in the meeting room of the Athletic Department—a theater-styled room that doubled as a physical education classroom. They had just finished their workout and had assembled for the next day's itinerary. Mirrors and brushes and other grooming paraphernalia were stacked at each desk as the team members looked into the mirrors and worked on their hair.

Coach Barton sometimes envied the coaches of the men's team. *They don't have to contend with grooming.* Only Jamie Patterson, of the girls in the room, was not working on her appearance. *Of course. The girl with the Miss America looks hasn't even combed her hair.* Jamie seemed to be deep in thought and that worried her coach.

"Okay ladies. Put the mirrors away. I need your attention for a moment. No surprises and no changes in our routine. On Saturday we will have a simulated meet. We will follow the same essential schedule next week we have followed all year—" Jamie wasn't listening. Her mind was on that brief encounter with Harrison Henninger.

Am I making something of nothing? Was he really alarmed when I gave my name or was that just my imagination? Why is this troubling me so? She replayed in her mind the encounter with Blondie, the muscle-bound moron and his not-so-subtle remarks. *No need to get angry all over again.*

The coach was talking about maintaining the same routine for the conference championship as for other meets. "I believe several of you are close to a personal best. Tomorrow will be a light workout and then on Saturday, as I said, we will conduct a mock meet. We will follow the same schedule on that day as we will the following Saturday at the conference championship. Sunday and Monday we will not practice. You will have a chance to get your legs back under you. Those muscles need to regenerate. Stay off your feet as much as possible. On Tuesday, come prepared. We will start building toward Saturday. This is a process. Every day is important. Plan to make every effort in your preparation this coming week. That preparation will put you in position to achieve your goals.

Jamie wasn't sure she heard what her coach said. *Get this Henninger out of your mind! You have a conference championship and a NCAA championship to think about. Then you have a decision to make—will it be the Olympics or Rhodes?*

"Any questions?" Her eyes scanned the room. "Okay, pick up a copy of your individualized schedule on your way out. It shows your specific practice plan for tomorrow. Get a lot of sleep. Drink a lot of water and eat a lot of carbs. You're dismissed." The rumble of moving chairs and the buzz of female voices brought Jamie out of her thoughts. "Jamie, could I see you for a moment?" the coach said, as the girls began to file out of the room.

Jamie threw her backpack on her shoulder and waited at the podium as the last few girls picked up their schedules. "Don't forget your appointment with the trainer in the morning," she said to one of the girls.

Sybil Barton looked directly at Jamie. "Is there something on your mind?"

"I guess it shows," Jamie answered.

"Jamie," Coach Barton said, adjusting her chair. "For four years I have never had to motivate you or to tell you to prepare yourself, or to push you to train harder and I can't start now. What I am saying is that I have never had to do many of the things a coach is supposed to do for an athlete. Your technique, your motivation, your practice habits—none of these things have required very much of my attention—and I hope I have been wise enough to stay out of your way. And it may be a little late—with less than two weeks left in your college career—for me to change my role, but—"

"Coach Barton, I'm sorry. I know I was distracted today."

"I don't need an apology. You have reasons to be distracted. It would be unusual if you were not distracted—I know you have the Rhodes scholarship on your mind. All I am asking is that for the next week you apply some of the iron will and determination that Jamie Patterson is known for."

"I will, Coach Barton. I will."

"Then get a good night's sleep. I will see you tomorrow."

As Jamie left the fieldhouse and walked across the campus, she saw Dr. Emerson's car in the back parking lot of the history building. She smiled as she looked into his car. It was littered with file folders and stacks of books. It was not unusual for him to be working this late into the afternoon—in fact he was often in his office until late at night. He seemed to be one of those rare individuals who conducted his life with little regard to the clock. His graduate assistants and his secretary had, as their primary responsibility, to get him to his classes and appointments. His classes were popular with students. He was known as a lively lecturer—yet who preferred a robust class discussion rather than a lecture. Although he had been at the university more than twenty years, and could have elected, given his seniority, to teach only upper-level courses, he still taught one session of Western Civilization—a freshman course. Admission to that course was difficult. It was said that the class roll was composed entirely of high school valedictorians. Jamie, in fact, had been a high school valedictorian and she had been admitted to the course and it changed her academic future.

As an entering freshman she had planned a degree in pre-Law or pre-Medicine—that was what all her high school teachers and counselors had recommended—but Dr. Emerson's class changed her direction. His class was based not so much on events, but *ideas*, the great ideas that formed the modern world. She could still remember the day Dr. Emerson said that democracy and sport both developed from Greek culture in the same era. "Does anyone think there could be a relationship?" he asked the class. No one had responded, but after the class Jamie approached Dr. Emerson about the question. "Dr. Emerson, *is there* a relationship between ancient Greek democracy and ancient Greek sport?" He did not answer the question directly, but he wrote down the names of a few books he recommended. Jamie went to the library after class, checked out the books, spent the weekend reading and re-reading them. The concept fascinated her—that somehow freedom and sport were related and that the same Greek hills that produced the first democracies produced the first athletes as well. It was an idea that she nurtured through four years of history classes and became the thesis for her senior paper.

The door to Dr. Emerson' office was open and although his desk faced the door, she could hardly see him at his desk for the stacks of books. Sheaves of papers were strewn around, some in stacks—others not. Bookshelves ran from floor to ceiling around the room and the single window in the office was half-obscured by stacks of books. Dr. Emerson, glasses on his nose, moved his head back and forth like he were at a slow-motion tennis match, looking first at the reference book on his left and then the one on his right. Jamie was struck by the caricature of the absent-minded professor and how the scene before her could have been a cartoon. She knocked on the open door. "Oh Jamie, come in," Dr. Emerson said, marking his place in a book as he got up.

"I'm sorry to disturb you."

"This is no disturbance. Please sit down." He stood and removed a stack of papers from the only other chair in the room. "Here, please have a seat."

Jamie realized that it was Dr. Emerson's cheerfulness, as much as his teaching ability, which had made him so popular on campus. She remembered some prominent alumnus presenting him with a teaching award. "It is not so much that he is *interesting*," he had said, "but that he is *interested*." Jamie realized how true that assessment was—Dr. Emerson had a great capacity for learning, but he seemed genuinely concerned about his colleagues and his students as well. He had never been an athlete himself, but he attended all the games on campus, and since Jamie's freshman year, he and his wife had not missed a home track meet and attended a few meets out of town.

"Jamie, I must tell you—you have become somewhat a hero—I should say heroine, I suppose—in the department, because of your comments in my class the other day."

"I did not intend to embarrass Mr. Snelling."

"I know you didn't—which is a reflection of your charitable nature—but you have to understand how the department views Mr. Snelling. He is, shall we say— less than endearing. Some of my associates have admitted the only thing keeping them from flunking him in their course was the prospect of having to have him return to the class the next semester."

"Still," Jamie said, "his lack of 'endearing' qualities notwithstanding, I did not intend to embarrass him."

"I think you may have taught our friend Mr. Snelling a valuable lesson. Convictions, even strongly held convictions—even strongly held convictions stridently expressed—should have a foundation of facts. The sooner Mr. Snelling can learn that, if he can learn it at all, the better he will be. Our world certainly needs idealists. Perhaps with some maturity, Mr. Snelling will be able to channel his idealism to something productive. That should be our hope and our prayer."

Jamie smiled. She looked at her mentor. He, as always, was a gracious man.

"By the way," Dr. Emerson went on, "I have a letter I want you to see." He pulled an envelope from his desk drawer. It bore a British stamp. "It's from my friend Colin Smithson, a university lecturer at Magdalen College, Oxford. As you know, I spent two consecutive summers at Oxford just a few years ago, on a research fellowship, and Colin and his wife became good friends with Margaret and me. I wrote to him—about you—a few weeks ago, and I enclosed a copy of your senior paper. His reply came just yesterday. Here's a portion of it: 'I read with interest the student paper you enclosed in your correspondence. As you requested, I am offering my opinion. My first reaction is this: the paper reveals an appalling lack of tutorial control on your behalf! Why have you allowed this young lady to produce—on an undergraduate level—a paper that would have been better suited for a doctoral thesis! It shows quite well how you chaps in the colonies fail to exercise proper control over those in your tutelage—but what can one expect from those given to unruly remonstrations (dressing up as wild Indians and the such) over minor items like a tax on tea? Besides, the theme of the paper is somewhat disturbing (democracy and its origins), for if I recall correctly, that may have been the thing (freedom and individual rights and all that stuff) that caused all that fuss a couple of centuries ago. Additionally, my distress is compounded by the realization that this young lady may study with us in Oxford next year and that we, in our department, may be expected to supervise a graduate paper expected to exceed the quality of what you have sent. It is a pressure that I do not welcome. My only consolation in this potential development is Miss Patterson's regular citations in her paper of Magdalen's College's most famous lecturer, C.S. Lewis. In that I see the imprint of your influence. I genuinely hope you and Margaret can join us here again. Your friend, Colin.'"

"Your Professor Smithson sounds like a real character," Jamie said.

"Indeed, he is. A delightful character. A brilliant man and a man of faith. If you have the opportunity to study with him, you will see for yourself. Is that why you have dropped by—to talk about that opportunity?"

"No, actually I'm looking for help with some research."

"Research? Research on what? You've completed all your courses."

"Not academic research—some personal research. My grandfather, my father's father, was killed in World War II. He served in the 108th Infantry, in the same company as Harry Henninger. Meeting Henninger the other day—if you can call shaking his hand an introduction—stirred some interest. I realized how little I knew about my grandfather … there was a picture of him in uniform that hung in the hallway at home and his medals were in a frame—and I knew he and his unit had been all killed in action, but I really knew nothing about the events themselves." Jamie started to mention Henninger's reaction at their introduction but caught herself. *Keep your paranoia to yourself.*

"Well, perhaps I can help you—or at least tell you where to go for help. Tell me what you have found so far."

"Our library has only general information. I obtained some books from VMI through Inter-Library Loan—which did not have the information I was looking for. The George Patton biographies do not mention the battle involving my grandfather's death."

"You will discover," Dr. Emerson said, looking over his glasses, "that George was quite selective about what was included in his biography. Several of his bad days did not warrant mention, I'm afraid."

"I talked with the librarian in the history area and she suggested I send a request to the National Archives, so I did that."

"Mmm … As the saying goes: 'Don't hold your breath'. When you receive your reply—and you will receive one—it will have been channeled to the Moreland Center."

"Moreland Center? What is that?"

"The military history wing of the National Archives. They operate under the charter of the National Archives, but they are concerned solely with U.S. military records. Their letter to you will request additional specific information and tell you to allow at least twelve weeks after the receipt of the information they requested to receive the information you requested."

"Twelve weeks!"

"At *least* twelve weeks. I once wrote them that several wars had been waged in less than twelve weeks—but I'm afraid my sarcasm did not earn a more prompt reply."

Rising from his chair he walked over to one of his crowded bookshelves. "But there is someone who could help. Kincaid is the man. I haven't talked with Milt in months, which I regret. This might be the time to reconnect. I wonder if he is home?" Dr. Emerson said, talking to himself. "Let me see if I can find his number." He pulled out the top drawer in his desk and stirred through piles of items—papers, paperclips, pens, and paperweights.

"Excuse me, Dr. Emerson, but who is Kincaid?"

"Milton Kincaid. Milt and I were colleagues at George Washington for a few years back. He later taught Economic History on the graduate level at Georgetown. One of his books is on the impact of World War II on the economy. He still does considerable research at the Moreland Center, and I think he is just the one to help us, but I can't find his phone number. I'm sure Margaret has it at the house. Come by the house and we will give him a call."

The front yard of the Emersons' house was a conglomeration of flowers. Hollyhocks ran up the side of the house, halfway up the windows. Day lilies, both orange and yellow, filled up much of the front yard.

Azaleas, impatiens, and several varieties of ferns bordered the porch. "My effort to create an English garden," Margaret Emerson had told Jamie once. "But my friends at Oxford would not be impressed."

Jamie decided Mrs. Emerson's interest in flowers was not unlike her husband's interest in academic topics—broad and far-reaching, but not very systematic.

Jamie announced herself as she entered. "Come in, Jamie," she heard Mrs. Emerson say from the kitchen. "Warren is in his study. He must be looking for something. I hear him going through his drawers."

"Hello, Jamie," Dr. Emerson said as he opened another drawer. "Now, where are those phone numbers? Ah! Here it is! I knew I would find it." He pulled out a small black spiral notebook. Let me see if I can reach Milt." In just a few seconds he was exchanging pleasantries over the phone. "No, the next time we go fishing, I'm sitting in the *front* of the boat and you're sitting in the back," he laughed. "Milt, let me get to the point. I wonder if I could presume on your help with a military research project. One of my students, Jamie Patterson, is here with me and she could benefit from your expertise. Here, let me have you talk with Miss Patterson yourself."

"Hello Dr. Kincaid. This is Jamie Patterson."

"I am so glad to meet you—even over the phone. I have heard Warren speak of you often."

"Thank you, Dr. Kincaid. I do not want to impose on you, but I am looking for information about my grandfather who was killed in action in Germany in 1945."

"Ah, Miss Patterson, I will be glad to help you, and I don't want to discourage you concerning your investigation into your grandfather's military records, but I must give you an honest appraisal of the difficulties you are facing. First of all, the conduct of a war—as you can imagine—requires an incredible amount of paperwork. Every decision, every staff meeting, every change of orders, every menu, every communication through the chain of command produced tons and tons of paperwork. So the question became after the war: What do we do with this paperwork? And the military does not believe in destroying paperwork—the thinking is, I suppose, that some military statistician might need to know how many cans of beans a soldier consumed during the course of the war. Almost all of that paperwork, Miss Patterson, is extant—all the ground orders, the requisition forms, the training schedules—and it's here in Washington at the Moreland Center for Military Records. And although I certainly do not want to discourage you in your effort to find your grandfather's records, I would be remiss in my responsibility if I did not appraise you of the difficulties. The problem is twofold: the information isn't properly cataloged and much of it is in poor physical condition. The sheer volume of material makes it almost impossible to catalog. The administration of the Military Records Division receives a great deal of criticism—unjustified criticism, in my opinion—about their inability to provide complete records, but there is simply too much material and much of it is damaged. And, adding to the difficulties, a fire in 1973 affected many of the records. Some were burned and many more were water-damaged. Again Miss Patterson, my intent is not to discourage you—"

"I understand," Jamie interrupted. "It sounds like a difficult process. Would it be a waste of my time to come to Washington to look at the records?"

"Let me make a suggestion. I will be at Moreland tomorrow. Let me do some preliminary investigation. I can apprise you of the condition of the records and then, depending on what I learn, you can make a determination as to whether the trip would be worth the effort."

"I don't want to cause you any trouble," Jamie said.

"It will be no trouble. Like I said, I will be at Moreland tomorrow anyway. Just give me your grandfather's name, his rank and the unit he served with, and I will find out what information is available. I will call Warren with a report. Tell him to expect my call this weekend."

"Thank you, Dr. Kincaid. I certainly appreciate your help."

"No trouble at all. I'm glad to help."

After Jamie had given Dr. Kincaid the information about her grandfather, she hung up the phone. "Dr.

Kincaid says he will call this weekend to provide a report on the condition of the records."

"That's wonderful." Dr. Emerson said.

"Soup's on!" Mrs. Emerson called from the kitchen.

Jamie had half of a second bowl of the beef stew and a second slice of cornbread but declined the lemon squares. The conversation at the table was pleasant and relaxed and ran from recollections of Dr. Emerson's last fishing trip with Dr. Kincaid to Mrs. Emerson's concern about the squirrels damaging her hollyhocks to Jamie's senior paper to what Lance Snelling's future might hold. Only when the topic went to Harrison Henninger's visit to the campus did the strange and uncomfortable feeling come back to Jamie.

"I'm sorry," Dr. Emerson said, "that you were unable to talk with Mr. Henninger about your grandfather.

"Yes," Jamie replied, shielding her emotions. "It was unfortunate."

A knock at the door interrupted Jamie's thoughts. Two students from Dr. Emerson's World History class were at the door. They needed help with a section of the textbook they didn't understand. Jamie excused herself, thanked Mrs. Emerson for the meal and hopped on her bicycle.

When Jamie turned her bicycle into her driveway, Aspie came trotting out, tail in the air and her collar bell ringing flatly. She nuzzled against Jamie's leg as Jamie propped the bike. "Just a second, Aspie. Try a little patience." She picked up the cat and heard her purr. "Let's fix you some supper," she said, putting the cat on the ground. The cat followed her through the back door. Jamie flipped on her television as she came into the house and got the cat food from the pantry. When the television came on, Harry Henninger was being interviewed. *Why does this man give me the creeps?*

"Mr. Henninger, are you too old to be president of the United States?"

"Can't you people come up with some fresh questions? For the past few weeks, the only questions I have been asked seem to be: 'Are you too old?' and 'Are your answers too simplistic?' I have given several answers to those questions the past few weeks, but from now on I am going to answer all reporters' questions using our campaign motto: 'Hell no!'"

"But surely Mr. Henninger, you have some plan for the future as to foreign affairs?"

The camera zeroed in on Henninger's face. He narrowed his eyes as he spoke. "When Adolph Hitler ran his armies all over Europe there were thousands of diplomats in dozens of countries trying to make deals with him—trying to appease him. Not until we in this country told him 'Hell no!' did anything happen. We kicked his rear end back across Europe until he blew his brains out. Now was that a simplistic approach? Maybe so, but it sure as hell got the job done. I want to bring that same sort of American 'get the job done' attitude to all issues, foreign and domestic. We're still in a war, but it's an economic war now. The biggest issues facing this country right now are economic issues. Am I going to let the Japs sell their stereos and radios through unfair trade practices? Hell no! Am I going to let the Krauts, I mean the Germans, come into this country and negotiate away their tax liability so they can build their cars here and put U. S. manufacturers out of business? Hell no!"

The TV screen went to a chart that showed Henninger's rise in the polls during the past few months. "With promises to spend fifty million dollars of his own money during the campaign," the newscaster was saying. "Harry Henninger—" the screen went to a photo of a smiling Henninger—" is making himself a very real factor in the presidential race …"

Jamie looked at the screen and then flipped the switch to turn the television off. She asked herself again: *Why does this man give me the creeps?*

NINETEEN

AT NINE O'CLOCK, a man came out of his Georgetown apartment—as he did every evening the weather permitted—with a Sheltie on a leash. A coat and an umbrella hung on his arm, but after stepping on the porch and testing the evening air, he realized the rain shower had stopped. He reopened the door, hung the coat on the rack and put the umbrella in its stand. The little dog did not understand the delay, tugged on the leash and barked a mild complaint. The man reassured the little dog, came down the stairs, adjusted the lease and patted the dog on the head again. He walked up the sidewalk for two blocks, allowing the dog to sniff at each gate. At the second block he turned across the street, as he always did, but as he entered the street, the beam of a pair of headlights came up the street at an increasing rate of speed. The man turned his head toward the headlights as they grew brighter. He squinted at the lights, doubly bright as they reflected off the wet street. He hesitated, uncertain which way to turn. The headlights came closer, increasing in speed. The man froze in his steps. At the last possible second, he released his grip on the dog's leash. A double "thud" filled the night air as the car hit the man and his body hit the street.

The little dog ran back and forth on the sidewalk yelping, trailing its leash. When the car had careened down the street and the red reflection of its taillights had disappeared, the little dog came back into the wet street, licking its master's inert face, moaning pitifully.

TWENTY

HER SHOWER WAS running, and Jamie was about to step in when the phone rang. Her first inclination was to let it ring, but a call on Saturday morning was unusual. *Probably some last-minute change in the practice schedule.* She turned off the water and put on her robe, cinching it around her waist.

"Jamie—" the voice on the line was Dr. Emerson's and from the tone, she knew something was wrong.

"Dr. Emerson, what is it?"

"I'm afraid I have bad news. Dr. Kincaid was killed in an accident last night."

"Oh, no! Not that nice man I talked with on the phone."

"I'm afraid so. I received a call just thirty minutes ago. I realize you did not actually know Dr. Kincaid, but I knew you were expecting some communication from him about your research."

"I'm so sorry to hear this news, Dr. Emerson. You have lost a friend."

"Yes, I have—and although we try to remind ourselves of the transient nature of our existence— sometimes we receive unwanted reminders of that stark fact."

"I appreciate the call, Dr. Emerson."

She put the receiver back in its cradle, but she sat on the stool by the phone for a few moments, trying to make sense of her uneasiness. Aspie nuzzled against her leg, purring, somehow sensing Jamie's emotions. Jamie reached down to rub her and as she did, she saw a copy of last week's *Newsweek* magazine. On the cover was a picture of a smiling Harrison Henninger, defiantly holding his gun across his chest. Jamie felt a shudder come over her and she pulled her robe tighter.

TWENTY-ONE

I CAN'T BELIEVE I'm doing this!

Jamie turned the steering wheel to exit Interstate 85 and join Interstate 95 northbound. The sign said "Washington, D.C. 140 Miles".

I can be there in less than three hours. Still, I can't believe I'm doing this.

Jamie adjusted the dial on her car radio. The music on the classical station didn't seem to suit her mood. She scrolled through an oldies station. Ricky Nelson was singing "Poor Little Fool." Jamie smiled at the irony. *Jamie, you are a fool. Why are you so infatuated with the idea of finding your grandfather's military records? You have never shown any previous interest. Why are you so obsessed now?* She had no answers to her own questions.

NPR was doing a report on Harrison Henninger's presidential possibilities—which she didn't want to hear but thought she should. *I can't escape the man.* She adjusted the volume. The reporter interviewed citizens from a broad spectrum of the American populace. A black construction worker from Chicago said he would vote for Henninger. "Six years until I retire. I believe Henninger will protect my job." A wheat farmer in South Dakota said, "Henninger has promised he will break down the barriers to trade—and I will get a better price for my wheat. That's good enough to get my vote." A retired restaurant owner and Korean War veteran said, "Harrison Henninger is a true patriot. He fought for this country in World War II and I believe he will fight for it again."

After the interviews the analysts made their comments. "One of the most interesting aspects of this groundswell of support for Harrison Henninger," one of the reporters said, "is the almost complete lack of criticism from either of the two traditional candidates. The two major parties, to this date, have treated Mr. Henninger very gently."

"Why is that?" another reporter asked. "Are they afraid of offending Harrison Henninger?"

"I think that is exactly the case. The quandary the two major parties find themselves in is this: they want Harrison Henninger to be disparaged, but they want the other party to provide that disparagement. If Mr. Henninger drops out of the race, his support will go to one of the other two candidates. For that reason, neither of the two major-party candidates is willing to confront Henninger directly. As a result, Henninger's ideas on several subjects: foreign policy, international trade, the economy, military preparedness—which many in mainstream America characterize as simplistic—go unchallenged. Neither of the traditional candidates is willing to say to Henninger 'These ideas will not work,' for fear of alienating his supporters and losing those voters in November."

Jamie turned the radio off. *I wish one of those analysts, in all their wisdom, could tell me this: Why did Harrison Henninger's hand tremble when he heard my grandfather's name?*

Jamie pulled into a rest stop and turned off the motor. *Should I go back home? Is this really wise? Should I abandon this wild enterprise? Think, Jamie, think!* She replayed the events of the day before …

After Dr. Emerson's phone call with the news about Dr. Kincaid's death, the day became somewhat of a fog. She went to the dressing room and put on her uniform. She attended the team meeting. She went through some warm-up laps. Coach Barton asked her something, but she couldn't remember what. She vaguely remembered taking her position on the track and her teammates beside her. She remembered the starting gun—which seemed louder than usual. She couldn't remember the race, except for the last leg. She realized there was a teammate—a sophomore—on her shoulder and closing the gap between them. Jamie rarely had a competitor this close to her with under a hundred yards remaining—and although she was not known as a runner who depended on a final kick, nevertheless she gave all her energy to that last stretch and held off the challenger by a few strides. She remembered the look on Coach Barton's face when they saw Jamie's time—two and half seconds off her best time. It was not a time that would win the conference championship and it certainly wouldn't be competitive at the NCAAs. All of that was a fog in her mind.

That evening, when she got home, she called Dr. Emerson, but he had no additional information about Dr. Kincaid's death. She had gone to bed unsettled, but she couldn't explain her emotions. She had dreams, some of them about running in deep mud—all of her competitors breezing by her on a dry track. In one of her dreams the blonde behemoth was holding her ankle as she tried to run the race.

When she woke up, she made a decision.

"Yes, yes, I know," she told Aspie, who was walking around the bed meowing as Jamie threw some clothes in a travel bag. "Yes, you're right. It does sound a little crazy, but it's less than four hours to Washington. I can be there by early afternoon, and I don't have any more classes and Coach Barton has given us the day off Monday. I can spend all day Monday in D.C. doing research and get back here in time for track practice Tuesday afternoon. Now you understand, don't you? Going to Washington, D.C. is not so crazy after all." The cat meowed—a whining meow. "Well yes," Jamie said. "Maybe you're right. Maybe it is a little bit crazy."

She called Mrs. Emerson to tell her that she would not be at church and told her no, there wasn't anything wrong—which was not entirely accurate. Then she knocked on Mrs. Fletcher's door and asked her to feed Aspie for a couple of days. She threw her bag in the car, picked up her Sunday newspaper and set out for Washington.

She continued the impulse to turn around. Every mile marker required a new commitment. *I'm nearly halfway to Washington now. Might as well go on.*

She had been on the road nearly two hours—but she still wasn't certain she was going to follow through with her plan. She came to a highway rest stop. *I will make a final decision here.* At the rest stop there were dozens of cars, vans and RV's in the parking lot. The sun filtered through high, thin clouds and a number of families availed themselves of the weather to have a roadside picnic. Children ran on the lawn, playing chase and hiding behind the tall pines. She was reminded of the previous Sunday—the award ceremony on the campus lawn. The good weather, the children at play, the trees—these pleasant memories brought back bad memories—the recollection of the blond-haired brute and the strange reaction of Henninger.

Among the concession machines was one that offered fruit drinks. She dropped her coins in the slot and selected a cranapple. She found a picnic table, its concrete warmed by the morning sun, and decided to browse the newspaper she had brought while she sipped her drink. She unrolled the newspaper and dropped the advertising section in the trashcan. As she unfolded the front page, she saw Henninger's picture.

The headline read: "Assault Nears Washington". The photo showed Henninger speaking to a group of businesspeople. His handgun lay on the podium beside him. "Final Assault Soon, Henninger Promises" the second headline read. Jamie started reading the article.

"The 'Assault on Washington' or 'War on Washington,' as Harrison Henninger calls it, which began nearly six weeks ago in California, and which has gained unprecedented momentum as it has crossed the country, is in its final stages, according to Mr. Henninger. 'You don't want to give the enemy any secret information,' he told an enthusiastic group in Boston last night, 'and make no mistake about it—those people in Washington are your enemy.' Henninger's campaign continues to baffle political analysts as he has put together a strong coalition of voters across the political spectrum. Although he has been criticized for not providing details of his political agenda, his position in the polls has steadily improved as he has 'marched' across the country.'

Jamie heard herself sighing as she folded the newspaper. Every time she heard his name, or saw his picture or heard him quoted, she had the same sense of foreboding. *How can I explain the look on his face when he heard my name? That was one week ago. Why haven't I had one settled moment since that time?* She turned to the Sports section and found the article on the track meet and began to read:

Much has been made of the decision Jamie Patterson will have to make concerning a

potential slot on the U.S. Olympic Track team, or whether she will opt to continue her studies across the pond. If yesterday's results at the simulated meet were any indicator, we can only hope Miss Patterson has kept her GPA up, because her athletic performance is slipping. Unless she shows at next week's conference championships that Saturday's time was just an off day, the decision will have been made for her, and you can expect Miss Patterson in the fall to be hitting the books in England rather than pounding the pavement in Los Angeles.

She saw a quote from her coach—something about "focus." She recalled Coach Barton had used that word with her after Saturday's simulated meet. *Why would the coach be concerned about my focus?* she asked herself, laughing at herself. *Just because on a whim of three hours ago I am now on the side of the interstate half-way between Durham and Washington, on my way to look at the military records of my grandfather, who died forty years ago—and to determine if there is any connection between him and this Henninger guy—a billionaire—who gave me a weak handshake.* She laughed at herself as she imagined trying to explain these absurdities to Coach Barton. *Why don't you go back home, Jamie? Go back to your house and your cat, push yourself really hard this week and get ready for the conference championship and the NCAA's. Spend the time you have during the week seeking advice and laying out plans for the next year. Get your head clear and get it focused. Write some letters to the military records people, if you must. Your grandfather has been dead forty years—a few weeks cannot matter much.*

Jamie took a deep breath and blew it out. She folded the newspaper and put it under her arm. She looked around her. Some children had a wiffle ball and bat and were playing as the grown-ups were laying out a picnic. A woman was walking her dog. Several people were looking at the large map on the bulletin board. One man lay on a picnic table, his cap over his eyes, asleep. Children and adults were dropping coins in the concession machines. Cars were pulling in the parking spaces at the same rate others were pulling out. The high-pitched whine of tractor-trailers filled the air as they streamed by in both directions.

With the newspaper under her arm, she walked back to the car, not sure in which direction she intended to go. She tossed the newspaper into the passenger's seat and sat down behind the wheel. She paused for a moment before she started the engine. She backed out and put her Civic in Drive.

Which way, Jamie? Which way will you go?

She found the classical station on the radio. Bach, the Brandenburg Concerto was playing—a purposeful piece, not strident, but determined and assuring. It suited her state of mind. She turned up the volume and pushed the accelerator as she pulled into the interstate traffic. She was headed north. The sign read: **Washington, D.C. 108 miles**.

TWENTY-TWO

HENRY PURSLEY SMILED at the Secret Service agents as he left the West Wing. He always smiled at them, but they never smiled back. Even so, he maintained the practice. *Are they trained to avoid smiling? Is that part of their instruction? Or, do they hire only people who are incapable of smiling?* Part of the reason he was smiling, however, was not just his effort at congeniality—he was smiling because of his amusement with Brent Arens, whose company he had just left. *Why do I get perverse pleasure from Brent Arens' frustration?*

It was Harrison Henninger's recent speech that had stirred Arens up. Henry, when asked by Arens if he had seen the speech, said "No," but that was a lie. He had, in fact, seen it but, he didn't want to get drawn into the discussion any more than necessary. *Besides, perhaps a little lying now will be good practice for later. That could be a skill I need to cultivate.*

In New York, Henninger told the crowd that, if he were sworn in as president, he was going to close the U.N. He was going to turn the building into housing for those on welfare. And he said he was going to impound every car of every diplomat until they paid their parking bills. And if they didn't pay in ninety days, he would give those cars to the citizens of the city. "The people of New York will put these cars to better use than these dingbats from Lower Slobbovia," Henninger shouted. He got a thundering ovation and he closed the speech by telling the crowd to "... come by the U.N. building to pick out a car."

That speech, plus new poll numbers from Congrove—numbers that indicated Henninger was making progress at the president's expense, had really set Arens off. He had fumed and cursed throughout the meeting. Olmstead said little and seemed more fatigued than ever and Henry wondered if Olmstead didn't feel like he did—that he wished he could just go away to a quiet and safe place.

"Do we have a deal with Henninger?" the president had asked Henry.

"Mr. Henninger would not make a commitment. He said he would be back in touch." Henry did not tell the president all that Henninger said, including Henninger's evaluation—using a great deal of profanity—that the president was a "mealy-mouthed, degenerate, pitiful excuse for a leader. I'm a better politician than he is," Henninger told Henry, "—and I've only been at it a few months while he's been doing it his entire miserable life—and you can tell him I said so."

Henry, of course, told the president no such thing. It would have served no purpose—other than making the president—and Brent Arens—angry.

How did I get myself in such a mess?

He remembered his dream last night. It was the Senate sub-committee dream. Every night it was either the Senate sub-committee meeting or the Tahoe skiing dream. Some nights it was both. Last night, he found himself sitting up in bed saying repeatedly, "Guilty, guilty, guilty." Myra put her arm on his shoulder and told him to go back to sleep, but he lay there a long time with the image of senators and aides and photographers and reporters looking at him on the witness stand. It was a nightmare that could very well come true—and he knew it. *Maybe if I cooperate I will only get six months—or a year. After that, will I be able to get a job? Maybe I could get on the lecture circuit. I could talk about power and intrigue in Washington. Who am I kidding? If I get this behind me, I never want to talk about it again.*

TWENTY-THREE

SUNDAY, MAY 13, 2:40 P.M.

JAMIE'S RESERVATION AT Holiday Inn-Arlington was waiting for her. She had chosen the hotel because the track team had stayed there during a meet at George Mason University the year before. She checked in, threw her travel bag in the room and walked toward the Metro stop. Even though she knew the Moreland Center would be closed on Sunday afternoon she wanted to be familiar with the area so she could find it easily the next morning.

At the Vienna Metro stop she looked at the confusing array of instructions for purchasing her ticket. She determined her route. She would take the Orange line to L'Enfant Plaza, which was near the Archives stop. From there she could walk to the Moreland Center. She calculated her fare, slid three one-dollar bills in the machine, which dropped her a little change and spit out her ticket. She went through the turnstile, down the escalator to the boarding platform. Only a couple of dozen people were waiting. At first she was confused as to which side of the platform she should stand to catch the train going downtown. A young black man with a Caribbean accent recognized her confusion and told her, "Vienna … end of the line. Both sides go to the city." She thanked him for the information and only a couple of minutes later the train arrived and she boarded. When the train was in motion, Jamie looked out the window as they skirted alongside the interstate, the train nearly matching the speed of the cars. She looked at her watch. 5:20. *I should have a couple of hours of daylight before I head back.*

The train abruptly dropped underground. The darkness of the tunnel and the rhythm of the train made her realize she was sleepy. She had not slept well last night, and she did not want to admit her turmoil over Henninger had kept her awake—even though she knew it was true. She settled her head against the side of the swaying compartment and dozed off, waking up and dozing off during the next few stops. The train came to the Rosslyn stop, and she roused herself. She looked at the map on the wall. This was the last stop on the west side of the Potomoc. In a few minutes they would come to the capital area.

She used the time to mentally run through her plans. She kept fighting the feeling that she had left something undone or that she had not made adequate plans. *Do I know what I am doing? If I were to admit it to myself, I would realize this is a wild-goose chase. What do I think I am going to accomplish with this wild escapade?* She ran through a mental checklist: *Mrs. Fletcher would feed Aspie; I have no classes and no track practice on Monday; I will be back in time on Tuesday for that practice. If everything is in order, why do I feel so unsettled?*

At the last minute she decided to get off at the Smithsonian exit, rather than L'Enfant Plaza. The walk would not be that much longer, and she was ready to get off the train. She came up the escalator to the open sunshine of Washington Mall. At the exit a high school group headed down the opposite escalator. Their chaperone was shouting to a straggler to hurry up. The street artists and vendors were beginning to disassemble their booths for the evening. The mall was filled with shouts of softball players and frisbee tossers. The late afternoon sun filtered through the parallel rows of fully leaved elms, throwing dappled light on the sandy walking surface. She looked down the path and saw the Capitol building at the end. She started in that direction. A few groups had laid out picnics under the elms. Much of the mall lawn was given to the softball games. Some were co-ed games, probably more social than athletic, but at other sites the teams wore t-shirts that served as uniforms, and seemed to take the competition more seriously. Some runners passed by her. As she waited for the light at the intersection, a red-haired girl at the opposite corner, jogged in place like a prizefighter, her ponytail bobbing rhythmically. *I hope I can find a track that's open tonight.*

Jamie crossed in front of the Capitol building, and took a sip of water from the fountain—not because she was thirsty, but because it looked so quaint. She fought the impulse to admire the building. This was not the time. She took the walking road that curved up and around the Capitol building and past the office buildings on her left. She realized she had misjudged the distance and her destination, the Moreland Center, was farther than she realized, so she picked up her pace. Her tourist map did not show Moreland Center, but she had the address and had marked it on the map. She looked around to get her bearings and turned the map in her hands to get oriented. The circle on the map was only about three or four blocks away. She looked at the sky and determined she had another hour of daylight. It would be wise, she knew, to be back on the train before dark.

The area turned quickly from office buildings to an area of Victorian style row houses, their small well-shaded yards full of plants—and separated from each other by a variety of styles of wrought-iron fences. A few residents were intent on their gardening and paid Jamie no attention as she passed. Maple-roots protruded through the sidewalk, as if micro-earthquakes had struck the area.

At the next block, the neighborhood made a transition; some of the row houses maintained their orderliness, but others were in disrepair, and a few were vacant. Window shutters with peeling paint dangled at odd angles. She came to a neighborhood park where derelicts were sleeping on the benches, brown paper sacks at their feet. Behind the park was a mosque that appeared to have been converted from a church.

She looked at her map while walking. It was probably best not to appear to be lost, she thought. She felt like she was on the best route. Only one more block. The yards she passed were full of weeds; the wrought iron gates rusty and the shutters on the houses were cracked and unpainted. She considered going back to the Metro station. It was growing darker. *I really wish I had gotten here thirty minutes earlier. Oh, it can't take more than five more minutes to get there and as soon as I see it I will head back to the Metro.*

She knew it was the Moreland Center before she saw the sign. The building, a three-story structure, distinctive only in its plainness, occupied a large lot with oaks and maples interspersed on the lawn. Except that the building was square, not rectangular, it looked much like a high school or grade school campus.

She saw the sign:

Moreland Center for Military Records

Division of the National Archives

Jamie walked up the steps to the entrance doors. **Open to the public 9:00am-4:30pm M-F** was stenciled on the door. *Okay. Take the train in the morning at 8 and you should be here by opening time.*

She made a quick circle of the building, but paid no attention to the black limousine or the Mercedes parked near the rear entrance. And the driver of the black limousine failed to notice the young lady walking by. He was a large man who sat with the driver's door open, his feet on the pavement, his elbow on his knee as he pulled a dumbbell back and forth to his shoulder, first with his right arm, then with his left, grunting with each repetition. The exertion turned his face red which seemed even redder in contrast to his bleached-blond hair and goatee.

When Jamie returned to the Holiday Inn, she asked the young man at the desk—his nametag said Theo—who had just come on duty and seemed eager to talk with her, if the track at George Mason was open at night. "I will be glad to check on that, Miss Patterson." He took her room number and her phone was ringing as she came into her room. "Miss Patterson, this is Theo—at the front desk. Campus security assured me the track is open and well-lit until 11 p.m. Could I call you a taxi?"

"Thank you, Theo, but I have a car."

She had changed into her track gear and a black wind suit and was down in the lobby in less than ten minutes. "I have a map for you Miss Patterson," Jamie said. He showed her a map he had highlighted. "It's only about ten minutes away. You shouldn't have any trouble finding it—but just in case, I have written the number of the hotel at the bottom of the page. I'm on duty all night. Just call me if you need anything."

"Thank you for your help, Theo."

"You're welcome. As I said, I'll be here all night," he said awkwardly. "Just let me know if you need anything."

She ran one slow lap and then began her stretches. The evening was a pleasant late-spring night with a clear sky and a mild breeze. The track was occupied by a wide variety of people. A few, who apparently were serious athletes, were running stadiums while some older couples walked around the outer edge of the track. One woman was walking her dog, and one young mother held a steady jog while pushing her baby in a three-wheeled carriage. Some students sat in the bleachers, their workout over, talking and laughing with each other, sipping from their water bottles. Their voices and laughter drifted over the track. For a moment an unusual feeling of well-being came over her. The mix of the age groups, the mix of the nationalities and races, the warm air, the clear sky gave her a sense of contentment and it made her realize how tense she had been over the last few days. *There is some good in this country.*

She ran another lap at a slightly quicker pace and then began her workout in earnest. She ran three laps— a quarter-mile each lap—at a strong pace, and then one lap just coasting. She walked a lap and then ran a series of intervals in which she would sprint a half lap and then coast a half lap. After her first sprint she had captured the attention of most of the others around the track. The other runners had all moved to the outside as a courtesy. The older couple would stop each time Jamie went into her sprint just to watch, and then pick up their walk as Jamie slowed down. In the stands the little groups would point and stare in amazement as she rounded the track, her arms pumping, her mouth forming a perfect oval, her head straight, her hands appearing to cut the air as she ran. Two young male runners laughed with each other as if to say: "No, *you* challenge her to a race."

When she had finished the intervals, she started a cool-down pace. As she came by the bleachers, there was some polite applause. She looked up and smiled at the small, but appreciative audience, realizing for the first time that she had been watched.

TWENTY-FOUR

FROM THE BREAKFAST bar in the lobby Jamie selected a couple of small yogurts and a scoop of granola. A few businessmen, some in suits cast admiring glances her way—but she did not notice. The TV was on CNN. Jamie couldn't hear the audio, but she saw they were doing a feature on Harrison Henninger and his "March on Washington". The camera came in close, and she saw Henninger's confident face as he spoke. *That was not the expression I saw on his face a week ago.*

An hour later, Jamie arrived at the Moreland Center. She stood in the same spot where she had stood the afternoon before. She looked at the sign again:

Moreland Center, Military Records
Division of the National Archives.

The building was no more impressive in the full morning light than it had been in the late afternoon light of yesterday. *No wonder the building is not on the maps. It would never qualify for an architectural walking tour.*

Jamie took a deep breath. She had the same sensation as at the rest stop the day before—the

165

inclination to quit this effort. *Why don't you just go back to campus and carry on with your life? Be sensible.*

She ignored the voice, took a breath, and went up the stairs and through the doors. She went inside and came to the receptionist's desk. "I'm sorry. I know that I am supposed to make an appointment, but I … I didn't have an opportunity." She gave the lady a pleading smile.

The receptionist looked at Jamie carefully. "That's alright. I'm sure we can work you in." She was an attractive, well-dressed middle-aged woman who wore a pearl necklace and matching pearl earrings. A gold chain held her glasses at her neck. She smiled, placed the glasses on her nose and took the letter from Jamie and looked at Jamie as if she were appraising her. She gave Jamie an encouraging smile and said: "I'm certain we have a research associate who can help you. Richard Roberts is one of our finest research associates. I'm sure he is available."

Richard Roberts had come into his office early that morning—although his office was not actually an office; it was a cubicle, surrounded by dozens of other cubicles in a large room on the second floor of the Moreland Center. Richard Roberts was twenty-four years old and had the lean looks of an athlete. He, in fact, had been a good high school basketball player in Michigan and had received a few Division II offers, but following family tradition, had enrolled at Annapolis, where he got only a little playing time as a freshman, and gave up basketball when he decided to transfer to the University of Virginia.

Richard had been working harder than usual the last few days. He was under a strict deadline to finish a project by Monday afternoon and he was determined to get it done. He had worked on it Saturday most of the day and for a couple of hours Sunday afternoon, and he was looking forward to getting Mrs. Marjorie Adams Prescott's project completed. Mrs. Prescott, an aspiring socialite of Stone Mountain, Georgia, had been rebuffed by members of the Daughters of the American Revolution for her failure to provide adequate corroboration for her claim that she was a direct descendant of John Quincy Adams. The original letter had been assigned to Richard purely by chance, as were most of the research assignments at Moreland Center— and it had proven to be a difficult assignment. He had originally replied that genealogical searches were "outside the realm of the mission of the National Archives" and had made some suggestions as to where she might continue her search. Marjorie Adams Prescott was quite upset with Richard's response and so indicated her distress to her husband, Charles W. Prescott, who owned the second largest truck leasing company in Atlanta—and who had made a sizable contribution to the congressional campaign of the sitting congressman from that district. A copy of the letter to the congressman that Mr. Prescott had dictated was soon sent over to Moreland, along with a note from the congressman himself, expressing concern about his constituent's treatment from a government agency. Richard's supervisor attached a memo to copies of these documents directing Richard to "rectify the situation". Richard had the letter from Charles Prescott to the congressman taped above his desk. Some of the phrases were committed to memory: "… stuffed-shirt bureaucrats who have forgotten who they work for …" and "… lack of any semblance of courtesy to a tax-paying American—"

"You're a masochist," one of the female researchers told him when she saw the letter taped above his desk.

His supervisor, who subsequently had taken a sabbatical, had offered no suggestions as to how to "rectify the situation," so Richard decided, since he had been accused of providing too little information, would provide Marjorie Adams Prescott with an abundance of information—perhaps more than she could possibly digest. He compiled every known reference to John Quincy Adams and put that information in a document. He was aided in his effort by his friend Dennis, a fellow graduate student at Georgetown, who worked part-time supervising the computer lab in the basement of the library. The computer lab had a scanner and they were able to scan all the information onto a disk, rather than type it. Dennis had joined in the project to inundate Marjorie Adams Prescott with the abundant information enthusiastically. "Cool," he said. "Victory through obfuscation. That's the government way."

The reply to Mrs. Prescott now ran to 316 pages and Richard had only to go over it one final time and smooth it out a bit before he sent it to Mrs. Prescott. With any luck, by the time Mrs. Prescott had worked through all the material, he would have received his doctorate from Georgetown and would have taken that teaching position at Colorado State that looked so promising.

For the last two years Richard had been working at Moreland Center full-time, taking evening classes at Georgetown in pursuit of his doctorate. Eighty percent of the personnel at Moreland were female—most of them older—and Richard was the kind of young man that older women wanted their daughters to marry. He had arresting blue eyes, good looks, educated—and polite. During the past two years he had been invited to several pot-roast dinners at the homes of these women—all of whom had a daughter, a niece, or a daughter of a friend who just happened to be at the house that evening. These events were invariably uncomfortable for him and he had learned to decline them, citing his evening class schedule and study load.

In addition to the Marjorie Adams Prescott deadline, he had a funeral to attend—the final rites for Dr. Milton Kincaid, who had been killed in an accident just three days earlier and whom Richard had gotten to know as a regular visitor at Moreland the past two years. The funeral was to be held that afternoon. For those reasons, he had come in early and although he had been working nearly an hour and a half, he had been on company time only five minutes when his phone rang.

"Roberts," he answered flatly. He listened for a moment. "No, sorry, Louise—give it to someone else. I'm covered up today."

Louise Watkins, the receptionist, covered the phone with her hand and held it under her chin. "Miss Patterson, there is an exhibit over there about the origin of the Military Records Division, that I'm sure you would find interesting."

Jamie pointed to the display to make sure of her instructions.

"Yes, right over there," Louise said, smiling. She waited until Jamie had walked off and then pulled the phone close to her mouth and covered the receiver with her hand. "Richard Roberts, I want you out here right now! This is a young lady you need to meet. She has no ring on her finger, and I will take no guff from you. Get out here immediately."

When Richard came to the lobby, he walked toward Louise with his hands up in exasperation. But she spoke first. "Oh, Richard! You look so good in that suit. Oh, I suppose you are going to the funeral. That is so sad about Dr. Kincaid."

"Louise—" Richard started, but she interrupted again. "Richard, you should wear a suit more often. You tall athletic guys always look good in a suit—and that color—is it navy? It's perfect for you. It sets off your blue eyes."

"Louise—"

"Over there—" Louise nodded toward Jamie across the lobby. who was looking at a boring exhibit of 1950's vintage black and white photographs describing the events leading to the establishment of the Military Records Division of the National Archives and the construction of the Moreland Center.

One of the photos showed an old school on the site; the next few showed the demolition of the school and then several pictured the construction of a huge pit being dug on the site. The caption read: "In order to accommodate expected volume of materials, the design committee planned a basement nearly three stories deep." The next few photos, in time-lapse fashion, showed the building coming to completion.

Richard couldn't see Jamie very well from the distance, but he could tell she was slightly taller than average, with tanned arms and legs. Her brown hair seemed especially shiny, even in the fluorescent lights of the lobby. Richard pointed his finger at Louise, as if he were going to chide her, but she interrupted before he could speak.

"Miss Patterson is her name. Jamie Patterson. And I want you to help her with her project."

Richard tightened his lip and walked one step toward Jamie and then came back to Louise and leaned over her desk. "Louise, I have enough projects already and I've told you a dozen times—you are not my mother. You are not responsible for finding me a girl friend. Why do you insist on trying to fix me up?"

"It's a female thing—we can't imagine any man could be truly happy without one of us."

Richard shook his head in exasperation, but Louise just kept smiling as he walked over to Jamie who was looking at one of the black and white photographs on the wall. "Excuse me, are you Miss Patterson?"

She turned and extended her hand. "Yes, Jamie Patterson. Are you Mister Roberts?"

He was momentarily taken by her face. It was a tanned face. It was a confident face. It was an intelligent face—and it was a *pretty* face.

"Yes. Yes, I am. Richard Roberts. Would you like to come back to my office?"

"Certainly."

"Well, it's not really an office. It's a cubicle."

"Just lead the way."

As they walked by the information desk, Louise gave Richard a mischievous "okay" sign. Richard led the way to the elevator and punched the key. "I'm on the second floor," he explained. Jamie nodded and smiled, holding her file folder across her chest. The elevator came and Richard held the door for Jamie. The door closed and Richard rubbed his hands nervously. "You brought your file, I see."

"Yes, I did," Jamie answered, smiling at Richard's discomfort.

"Here," Richard said when the door opened. "Turn right." He led her through the maze of cubicles to his own. Stacks of paper lay everywhere. He moved one of them from the chair next to his desk and motioned for Jamie to have a seat. She sat in the chair next to his desk and Richard took his seat. He put on his glasses and looked at the file. "Now Miss Patterson—" when he turned to look at her, he realized how uncomfortably close they were. He tried to roll his chair back, but the caster was wedged against a stack of file folders. He got out of the chair and moved the folders, and as he did, they slid off onto the floor just at Jamie's feet.

"Excuse me," he said as he picked up the loose papers and placed them back in the file folder. He positioned the chair again and sat down. He looked at the file again. "Now Miss Patterson, Jamie, looking at your file—you're smiling—"

"I'm sorry," she said, showing her white teeth against her tanned face. "Do you think we could start over?"

"Good idea. Let's move to the cafeteria. The U.S. government, I think, intended for its researchers to conduct their business through the mail. They really didn't provide enough space for personal interviews. How about a cup of coffee?"

"Make it iced tea and it's a deal."

The interior of the building, much like the exterior, was basic in its construction—tile floors, small windows, cheap furnishing—not a building that could be used as an example of government waste, Jamie decided. Richard led her to a table with plastic chairs with aluminum legs while he went to the cafeteria line.

One group—three middle-aged women, returning their trays—smiled and greeted Richard as he walked by.

"Did they call you Clark?" Jamie asked when he returned with a tray.

"Uhh—must have thought I was someone else. Sweetener?"

"One packet of blue stuff, please."

Richard took a sip and opened the folder. "Now, Miss—"

"It's Jamie."

"Okay Jamie. It's Richard."

"Richard it is."

"According to this file, you have requested information concerning Sergeant James H. Patterson, 3rd Army, 108th Infantry Division, 3rd Battalion, K Company, who was killed in action in Germany in 1945."

"March of 1945. He was my grandfather."

"Let me see," Richard said as he fingered through the papers. "Oh yes, I remember this file. K Company, 108th. That's Harrison Henninger's outfit, isn't it?"

"Yes. But don't think you have to act apolitical. I am not a Henninger fan, even though my grandfather may have been in the same unit."

"I'm sorry my voice betrayed my political incorrectness," Richard said. "While I'm on company time, I should keep my opinions to myself—even those betrayed by intonation. Well, whatever your opinion of Henninger, he may make your grandfather famous. He likes to tell about his attempt to rescue K Company."

The uneasiness about Henninger came over Jamie again, the remembrance of the handshake, and for a moment she thought about telling Richard about the incident but thought better of it.

"Well, maybe so. But tell me what I need to do to research my grandfather's records."

"How much time do you have?"

"I have all day today—and maybe a couple of hours in the morning."

"Mmm, not much time, but here's what we can do." He leaned toward her. I'm under deadline to complete some stuff by middle of the day, and then I have a funeral to attend—"

"Dr. Kincaid?" Jamie interrupted.

"You knew Dr. Kincaid?" Richard asked.

"No, we had one brief phone conversation." She explained how Dr. Emerson had put her in touch with Dr. Kincaid just a few days earlier. She again wanted to tell Richard about the incident with Henninger, but she again fought the impulse. She realized she wanted to tell someone—*anyone*—about the incident, but she realized how foolish it would sound if it actually came out of her mouth.

"I had a couple of days off, so I thought I would drive up and see if I could find some information on my own."

Richard watched Jamie carefully as she spoke. He hated to give Louise the satisfaction of being right, but—

"Okay," Richard said, interrupting his own thoughts. "Here's what I recommend. I can set you up in a conference room and get you started with some basic material. You can go through that material. I'll check on you in an hour or so and help point you in the right direction. Then, this afternoon, after I return from the funeral, I can help you."

"Oh, Richard. Thank you. I know this is an imposition. I really appreciate your help."

"You're welcome," Richard said, thinking to himself, Yes, the Prescott project has a deadline and yes, a couple of other projects are behind schedule—but they can wait.

Less than an hour later, Jamie sat in a conference room on the third floor of Moreland Center. The table was oval, wooden, with several spots where the veneer had pulled away. Half of the table was covered with an odd variety of papers and folders, along with several stacks of books. In the corner of the room was a computer table with a yellowish computer. A printer with a paper feed sat on an adjacent table. Wiring of various colors snarled underneath the table. Jamie looked at the stack of materials. At first she had been overwhelmed with the amount of material, but Richard assured her she could sort through it. He recommended looking at the books first for the historical background and then look for the specifics of K Company. "A little advice," he said. "Note anything concerning the Third Battalion of the 108th Infantry Regiment—K Company would have been in the Third Battalion. Only rarely will a specific company be mentioned in these broader treatments." She made a note at the top of her legal pad—3rd Battalion, 108th Infantry Division.

"And I do not want to discourage you, but it is difficult to find the records of an individual soldier. At best, most of these records deal with the company level, and occasionally the platoon level, but rarely on the level of the individual level."

"Whatever information you can help me find will be more than I have now."

"I'll check on you a little later," he said as he closed the door.

"Thanks," she answered, blowing out a big breath as she looked at the pile of documents.

She looked at some of the titles: Seven volumes of *The European Theatre of Operations.* Little of the material in the books had anything to do with the information she was looking for, but she found herself fascinated by the photographs. She went through the maps and strategies and the reports quickly, but the photographs of the soldiers pulled her in. Wounded men, fatigued men, men eating, men marching and men fighting—these had a greater reality than all the text and maps.

She took notes as she methodically went through the stacks of papers Richard had brought from the files in the basement. Their age was apparent—yellow or brown, or something between yellow and brown. Some were brittle and others seemed to be water-damaged. Some were on official letterhead and others were hand-written on notepaper. An amazing amalgam of governmental and war documents lay before her—everything from the program of a regimental dinner dance prior to deployment to a table of casualties after deployment. *I wonder how many of those at the dinner dance are also on the casualty list.*

Some of the documents were little more than propaganda, produced for the public, photographs showing the regiment in training, on parade, and arriving in France—French women and children waving in ecstasy. That was the picture that was painted for the general population, but some of the photographs in the files were not for public consumption—dozens of photographs showing the dead and wounded, awful wounds of an awful conflict, the images Americans during the war would not have seen. Jamie again found herself attracted to the photographs more than the written records—the vacant stare of a hollow-eyed GI told more about shell-shock than medical reports; the pictures of a bombed-out city told more about the destruction than bombing reports; the posed pictures of GIs with arms around necks told more about morale than staff reports, and the collective image of all told more about the war than all the books.

She looked among the photographs for a figure that would be her grandfather. She knew what he looked like. His picture in his uniform had been on the mantle above the fireplace at her house all her life. She thought for a moment she recognized her grandfather, and then changed her mind. It was a shot of a group of soldiers on bivouac—tents and jeeps in the background. The weather, apparently, was warm. Several of the soldiers were shirtless. It had to be France, the summer of 1944. They had not entered the line yet. The war would become worse as they reached Germany in the fall and winter that was approaching. Several of the soldiers were hamming it up for the camera. One of the shirtless soldiers, cigarette in his mouth, seemed to be pleading *"Hey buddy, take our picture!"*

Off to the edge of the picture was a young man, just a few years older than the 19 and 20-year-olds mugging for the picture. He seemed a little more reserved, a little more sober. He had turned back to the group being photographed. His face carried an almost fatherly expression. *Could that be my grandfather?* She couldn't be sure. *He would have been about 25. Only a few years older than I am now.*

She did some calculations in her mind. If that photo had been taken in 1944, her father would have been four years old. He would never see his father again. In just a few months all those in this photograph, and all the others in the platoon would be dead—only a few days after crossing into Germany. A sudden feeling of overwhelming loss came over her. She held the pictures in her hands. All these exuberant young men were about to die—die violent deaths—and it was more horrible because they had so much to live for.

She was lost in thought when Richard opened the door. "How's it going?"

"Slowly. I didn't realize how much material there was."

"It will go more quickly when you get down the specific materials. I need to leave for the funeral. I will be back around 2:30. Will you be okay?"

"I'll be fine. You've given me enough material to keep me busy for days."

"I'll check on you when I get back. You know where the cafeteria is if you get hungry."

"I'll be fine. Thank you."

It was 2:40 when Richard returned. "How's it going? Are you making progress?"

Jamie straightened up in her chair. She had a dozen or so stacks of materials on the table. "I'm not sure. I've taken a few notes, but I'm not sure I have found anything". She rocked back in the chair and stretched.

"The photographs got to you, didn't they?" Richard asked.

"Does it show in my face?"

"They get to me too and I've looked at thousands of them. It's difficult to keep from turning melancholy when you look at those pictures."

"I think I have a major case of melancholy right now," Jamie said.

"Understandable. Listen, I need another hour or so to finish my project," Richard said. "Then I can help you."

When Richard left, Jamie continued her reading, jotting down notes, but she kept returning to the photographs. Many of them depicted fighting in the bitter cold of the winter of 1944-45. She tried to comprehend the hardships that these men—including her grandfather—had endured. Suddenly a deep sense of melancholy came over her—and with it, a sense of resignation. *Go home, Jamie,* she told herself. *This is going nowhere. Give up on this wild idea!*

Richard tapped on the door and came in with a large cardboard box in his hands. "I've been in the basement," he said. "A great deal of uncataloged material is down there—stuff that is not referenced in regular searches. I brought some up."

"Thank you, Richard, but honestly—I have to tell you—I've lost heart. Maybe I will get back to this project sometime, but I should go back to school and take care of my responsibilities. I genuinely appreciate your help, but—"

"Before you give up, let me tell you—here are some records for Sergeant James T. Patterson. I wasn't sure I could find the personal records, but here they are."

Jamie looked at the box but could not say anything for a moment. "My grandfather's records—I don't know what to say. I'm—"

Richard slid her a box of tissues that were at the end of the table. She wiped her eyes.

"Richard, I am so sorry. I'm not a crier—ordinarily."

"Jamie, I would like to say I understand, but in reality, I don't. I have never had the experience of finding the records of my father or grandfather, but this is not the first time I have brought a box of records to a family member in this room—and it tends to be an emotional moment. That's why we keep the tissues handy."

Jamie dabbed her eyes again. "Okay, thank you."

Richard nodded. "Shall we look at the records?"

Jamie took a deep breath and nodded. "Yes, let's look at the records."

"Inducted June 15, 1942," Richard said as he opened a file from the box.

"Dad told me about that. His mother and father had gotten married the summer before. My grandfather wanted to become a preacher. He was taking classes through a correspondence school. They learned my grandmother was pregnant the day before Pearl Harbor. According to my dad, my grandfather waited until he was born and then he went to the recruiting station."

'Impressive," Richard said, looking at the records, "an AAM in basic training."

"Excuse me—"

"An AAM is an Army Achievement Medal. Those are rare in basic training—but as I look further, I see why. James Patterson had the highest test scores of all those in basic training—*and* the highest score in physical training. He was the champion of the mile run. And he was nominated for OCS."

"What is OCS?"

"Officer Candidate School. That doesn't surprise me that he was nominated—given these scores—but he must have turned down the offer. According to the records he was also nominated for a battlefield commission in early 1945, but before the paperwork could go through—"

Jamie finished the thought, "He died. According to my father, he was promoted posthumously."

"Yes," Richard said. "I'm sorry."

"Here's the folder with the stateside training program for the 108th," Richard said. Jamie opened the folder. The two of them followed the training program of the 108th Infantry after basic training. Texas, then Louisiana, then California, then Pennsylvania and finally New York before being transported to England. In all those places Pfc. Patterson, then Corporal Patterson, then Sergeant Patterson, distinguished himself in the training. They found several letters of commendation from his superior officers.

"Your grandfather may have wanted to be a preacher," Richard said, "but he managed to turn himself into one heck of a soldier."

"I did not realize the training was so extensive. What happened after all the training?" Jamie asked.

"Right after the Normandy invasion—June 1944—the 108th shipped to England and then to France. When they landed at Normandy, 3rd Army had pushed the Germans back across a good portion of France—so the 108th troops were initially unable to join the fight because the front had been pushed back to the west more than a hundred miles."

"Oh, I think that is when my grandfather drove a supply truck."

"The Red Ball Express—a brilliant ad hoc strategy. Volunteers drove supply trucks filled with gasoline, ammunition, and medical supplies to the front lines. It was a dangerous assignment, often driving all night on bad roads with no headlights, carrying fuel or ammunition, often drawing fire from the Germans. The effort only lasted a few weeks, but it was a profound success. Patton's push slowed down, however, when gasoline supplies were diverted to other operations. Patton was furious—and some military historians will say he had adequate reason for his fury, but Red Ball Express was no longer needed. Soon the 108th was moved up to 'the line', which at the time was only 30 or 40 miles from the German border."

Richard pulled out another folder. "I'm looking for copies of AARs," he said.

"Excuse me," Jamie asked, "but what is an AAR?"

"After Action Report. Every engagement with the enemy required a write-up. The army was very demanding of its officers and non-com that they complete their AARs. Let me quote the U.S. Army manual on the topic: 'An After Action Report documents a unit's action for historical purposes and provides key observations and lessons learned'. Ah, here's the AAR for the battle at Metz."

Jamie took a sheet from the folder and looked at it for some moments. "I think I'm going to need another tissue."

"What is it?"

Jamie pointed to the document. "Look." She pointed to the bottom of a document. It's my grandfather's signature." She took a tissue from the box and dabbed her eyes.

Richard looked at the document. It was a recommendation for a bronze star for a Pfc. E.W. Johnson. "How about that—and this is the original. This is not a copy. It is signed by Sergeant James T. Patterson." Richard began reading:

After Action Report and Medal Recommendation.

On March 4, 1945, Private E.W. Johnson, 13125934. distinguished himself in combat action at Salins, France. Several units of K Company were pinned down inside a residential building in the village, unable to move forward because of intense machine-gun fire from a nearby building. Our platoon was also taking heavy fire from a bazooka from an adjacent building as well as machine gun and small arms fire from the steeple of a church two

blocks away that the Germans were using as an observation post and sniper nest. At great danger to himself, Private Johnson crossed the street, exposing himself to machine gun fire from the church steeple. He then scaled the wall of the courtyard of the building where the bazooka was located. Private Johnson climbed the drainpipe to the second story bazooka emplacement, tossed two grenades in the window, eliminating the enemy personnel. Private Johnson entered the building through the window and finding the German bazooka still operable, without assistance, loaded it and fired on the machine gun emplacement in the church steeple. On his third attempt he was able to destroy the emplacement and kill the German personnel in the steeple, thus removing all obstacles to K Company assuming control of the village.

This account is respectfully submitted to Command HQ as a recommendation for a bronze star as an appropriate decoration for unusual bravery on the part of Private E.W. Johnson.

Signed, Sgt. James T. Patterson, 2nd Platoon, K Company, 108th Infantry Division

Richard gave the document to Jamie who held it with both hands for some time, saying nothing.

"That's odd," Richard said as he looked at another document.

"What's odd?" Jamie asked.

He showed her the document. "Here's the roster of K company personnel. E.W. Johnson is not listed."

"But he must have been part of K company. My grandfather wrote the recommendation for his medal."

"You're right. This makes no sense." Richard pulled out several more documents and scanned them. "Here's the induction list. He's not on it. Neither is he on the personnel replacement list, and he's not on the paymaster list." He pulled out more documents and went through them while Jamie continued to look at her grandfather's medal recommendation. "And he's not on the discharge list," Richard said, "or the KIA or MIA list. That's Killed in Action and Missing in Action," he explained to Jamie. "He's on no list related to K Company."

Richard kept looking at the stack of papers on the table, his bewilderment evident on his face. "I've never come across this before, but I have an idea. However, it's nearly 4:30. I have to have these documents back in the basement by 4:45. Then everyone—that includes you—is dismissed at 5:00." He began re-organizing the stacks of documents.

"What is your idea?" Jamie asked.

"Before I tell you, let me ask you a question: Could you eat an early dinner?"

"Certainly. I never got to the cafeteria for lunch."

"An Italian place is within walking distance. We can go there for dinner and then come back here and do more research. Let me take this box back to the basement. You can wait for me in the lobby."

In the lobby, she saw Louise gathering items in her purse, getting ready to leave. Louise's face brightened when Jamie came near.

"I have a question," Jamie said. "This morning and again this afternoon I thought I heard someone refer to Richard as 'Clark'. Did I hear correctly?"

Louise had a mischievous smile on her face. "Just a little nickname Richard has around here."

"Clark?"

"Some of the girls refer to him as 'Clark Kent' … you know, wears glasses, very polite, sort of the mild-mannered type, but maybe underneath—"

"I get the idea," Jamie said.

TWENTY-FIVE

"IS YOUR SHOULDER bothering you, Henry?" the president asked.

"No sir … well, yes sir … a little."

The question caught Henry off guard. He and the president and the other members of the president's entourage were waiting in the wings of the White House Press Room. The press conference was scheduled to start soon, and Henry realized he must have been unconsciously rolling his left shoulder. It had been bothering him even more than usual the last couple of weeks—and the recurring skiing dream came almost every night. Every time it came, he sat up in bed just before he crashed into the tree.

"Old football injury?" the president asked.

"No sir, not a football injury, a skiing accident."

"Ah, well, you didn't impress me as the football type."

"No sir. I never played football."

The president held a folder—with the presidential seal on it—in both hands. In it were the notes for the press conference. Brent Arens, more agitated than usual, paced back and forth in the waiting area. Occasionally he peered out at the press members as they assembled in the adjacent room. He looked at

Henry scornfully, as if it were Henry's fault that the president was making small talk with him rather than studying the press conference notes. Arens had written those notes, and the bags under his eyes betrayed the fact that he had worked over them through the night. Arens believed—and he was probably correct—that this press conference was critical to the president's campaign for reelection. The president needed to counter all the exposure that Henninger was getting in the press and he needed to make a good personal showing to keep his poll numbers from slipping further.

"I know a good orthopedic guy," the president said. He flexed his knee. "He shot some cortisone in my knee and it really helped the pain. My secretary can give you his name. You may want to call him."

"Thank you, sir. If it gets any worse, I will do that."

Arens raised his hand—the signal for the president to get ready. The president stood and a moment later, the tape played "Hail to the Chief" and the president entered the room.

Henry had never attended a White House press conference before—and he really did not want to attend this one, but he had no choice. Hardly two hours earlier he had returned from meeting with Harrison Henninger, and he was scheduled to give the president a report on that meeting as soon as the press conference concluded. And if he did not look forward to the press conference, he really did not look forward to providing that report. Harrison Henninger believed—perhaps accurately—that he held all the cards in this contest with the president. Yes, it was true—Henninger held all the cards, and he was playing this at his own leisure.

Henry took a seat in the wings. He could see the president at the podium very clearly, but only the front row of the reporters. The president greeted the press and thanked them for their coming. He seemed relaxed, and the congenial smile—the Jimmy Stewart smile, some called it— seemed genuine. Wilson Cavanaugh was known for having a strong television image and a relaxed atmosphere with the press—even a hostile press. That image had been valuable in his campaign for president four years previously—and apparently, he still retained that calm image.

Mr. President, you need to tap into that charm for which you are noted. If you can pull this off today, you deserve to be reelected.

Brent Arens stood nearby with a folder identical to the one the president had open on the podium. He looked like a drama coach, holding a script, ready to prompt the lead actor if he should stumble on his lines.

The president's opening remarks were brief, citing the growing economy and some recent foreign policy achievements. Then he opened the floor for questions. The first question was about the current polls. The president looked at his notes. This was an easy question for Arens to anticipate. "Well," the president said, showing his famous smile, "we can't operate the executive branch of the federal government on the basis of polls. Our policy has always been to do what is right—and then let the polls take care of themselves."

Good enough. An insipid response really, but adequate for the purposes.

Henry couldn't hear much of the next question, but he did hear the name "Henninger". The president nodded thoughtfully as he looked down at his notes. Arens would have easily anticipated this question as well. "You will have to ask Mr. Henninger if he plans to run for president of the United States. That is none of my business. As for the second part of the question, whether he is qualified, that is a question for the American people to decide." He looked down at his notes again. "I don't think Mr. Henninger's lack of political experience should be held against him. We should not forget that Mr. Henninger has shown considerable leadership in the business world, having built one of the most significant companies in North America—and in the process, I might add, created thousands of jobs and helped make the U.S. competitive with other countries in a number of key industries—plus he has a remarkable record in the service of our country."

Henry saw Arens check his notes. He looked pleased. The president was following the script—if not word for word, very nearly.

Henninger is loving this ... and he's getting the signal. The White House is ready to cooperate.

A female reporter in the front row was recognized. "Mr. President, much has been written in the past few days about the advisory panel you have recommended to study the feasibility of a 'Pacific Rim Commission.' First, isn't this exactly what Harrison Henninger has asked for? And second, if so, wouldn't it be true what one of my colleagues wrote that you would be 'capitulating to Harrison Henninger' and 'that capitulation was the direct result of the threat he has posed to your reelection'?"

Henry saw some tension come into the president's posture. Arens squinted as he looked at the president.

This is the big one. This is the question that Arens was concerned about. This is the one the president has to get right.

The president flipped to a page in his notebook and paused for a moment. He put his hands on the side of the podium and leaned forward, dropping his voice slightly, looking directly at the cameras. It was a practiced pose—Henry knew that—but it was effective, just the same. "Just because a man does not have experience in the government, does not mean that the government should not listen to that man."

Good opening. Provide a little anti-government content.

"A government should always be willing to consider ideas that will benefit the citizens of that government. Any government that does not listen to its constituency is not a responsible government."

Of course we are open-minded; who could doubt it?

The president checked his notes again. "I think," he continued, "that we need to take a long-range approach to our trading agreements—in the Pacific Rim and also on the European side, particularly to those sectors of our private economy which are essential to the citizens of the United States. After all, the greatest responsibility of a government is to protect its citizens—not only from physical harm, but also from economic harm. We need to put policies in place that will ensure that our children and grandchildren have a guaranteed economic security. That is why I have asked this blue-ribbon panel to look into the feasibility of such a commission. I look forward to having that report on my desk. When it is there, I will consider it carefully."

Adequately imprecise—and it never hurts to mention the children and grandchildren. Henninger will love every word.

"Now," the president continued in his congenial manner, "if some members of the press want to characterize a studied response to global economic competition as 'capitulation', so be it, but I think my administration would be derelict in its duty to study this question to make a determination of its feasibility— and then bring it before the American people to see what they have to say about it."

Perfect—equal parts obfuscation and patriotism.

A thin smile—a smile of satisfaction—came on Bruce Arens' face. His man had gotten over the hump.

He's a genius. Arens is a genius. Not an honest genius or even a nice genius, but a genius just the same.

Henry unconsciously reached over and massaged his left shoulder.

TWENTY-SIX

MONDAY, MAY 14, 5:20 P.M.

"WHEN WE GET back," Richard explained to Jamie as they walked along the sidewalk, "I will run Private E.W. Johnson's dog tag number through the computer. Your grandfather referenced that number in his medal recommendation. That should clear up who he is—and why he does not show up on any of the K Company records."

The sidewalk was buckled in many places as the roots of the maples and oaks had pushed against them from below, requiring them, at times, to walk single file. A few of the houses beside them were neat and clean, but others were overgrown and had sagging porches and sagging roofs. They came to a small commercial area—a convenience store, a dry cleaners, a Chinese take-out and a few others, including Salvatores.

"It's not upscale," Richard said as they entered the restaurant, "but I can vouch for the food—and they use real cloth napkins."

Jamie looked around. The posters on the wall—Tuscany, Umbria, Abruzzo, Campania and others—had gone bluish as they aged. Fishnets hung in the corners and melted candlesticks sat in wine bottles.

"Don't apologize," Jamie said. "It's mostly cafeteria food or frozen dinners for me."

A young waiter with a beaming smile came to the table. "Hello Richard. You are early this evening."

"Hello Joseph. This is Jamie."

"Hello Jamie. You are welcome at Salvatore's." He bowed. "My name tag says 'Giuseppe,' for that is what my grandmother prefers, and she is the boss—and the cook—but my friends, which includes Richard, call me Joseph."

"Then I will call you Joseph also," Jamie said, "for I would like to be your friend."

"What can I bring you to drink? Some wine perhaps?"

"Iced tea for me," Jamie said.

"The same," Richard replied.

When Guiseppe/Joseph returned with the tea, he lit the candle on the table, even though it was not yet dark. He winked at Richard and stood behind Jamie as she looked at the menu. He gave Richard the look that says, *Very impressive, my friend. You have done well.*

House salad and spaghetti with tomato sauce please," Jamie said. "And extra noodles please. I'm on the track team," she explained to Richard. "I'm supposed to consume extra carbohydrates."

"House salad and veal parmesan," Richard said, turning in the menus to Joseph, who gave a bow as he left.

Richard looked at Jamie. "Duke ... track team ... Now it comes together. Sports Illustrated wrote an article about you—when? A month ago?"

"Close enough."

"Oops, I think I hit a nerve."

"Well, let's just say the article did not turn out exactly as it had been represented."

Joseph returned with the salads and breadsticks.

Jamie broke a breadstick in half. "Since you already know something about me, I think you should tell me something about yourself. How does one get to be Associate Research Assistant—if I recall your title correctly—at Moreland Center?"

Richard stirred his salad with his fork. "Desperation is the key requirement—along with the willingness to be underpaid and overworked during the day so that one can take classes in the evening."

"You're a grad student?"

"Georgetown—pursuing a doctorate in history."

"Military history?"

Richard sprinkled pepper on his salad. "Yes and no—it's related to military history—although my undergraduate degree is in psychology."

"Your thesis?"

He took a bite of his salad. "Let me write it down for you. It looks more impressive when written." He took a pad and a pen from his jacket. "An Associate Research Assistant must always keep a pen and pad handy."

Richard wrote on the pad and gave it to Jamie. She read the note aloud: "'Post-War Trauma in the United States: a study of the mental health of American soldiers after World War II.' Impressive—you were able to get a colon in the title."

"No self-respecting doctoral thesis could survive without a colon in the title."

"When do you defend it?"

"This summer. If it survives the scrutiny of the committee, it will be approved and it will take its place among the several tens of thousands of other doctoral theses on the shelf of a university library, never to be read again."

"Oh, who knows? It might become a best-seller."

"Not likely. Not much market for quasi-historical sociological academic stuff."

"I guess we're in the wrong market for mass appeal."

Richard smiled. "When you said 'we,' it reminded me how difficult it is for me to picture you as a historian."

"Not a historian, a history major—an *undergraduate* history major."

"But a pretty good undergraduate student, if one can believe Sports Illustrated."

"Don't tell me you actually read that article."

"I read it. 'The Fast Angel from Blue Devil Country.' The article, as I recall, said you were going to have to decide between the Olympics and a Rhodes scholarship—not too shabby".

"I don't want to talk about that. I want to know more about your thesis. Tell me how you got into the military history field."

"Son and grandson of Marines. Both bronze star recipients. Both purple heart recipients. Grandad was at Guadalcanal in World War II as a corporal; Dad is an Annapolis grad and did three deployments to VietNam, initially as a lieutenant, eventually as a colonel. He is pure Marine. He now has one star on his shoulder and hopes to get another before he retires.

"And you?" Jamie asked.

Joseph brought their spaghetti. Richard offered the parmesan cheese to Jamie but she declined. "I enrolled at Annapolis," he said, sprinkling the parmesan on his spaghetti. "I completed two years before I realized the military wasn't for me. It was hard on my father, but I think it was a relief for my grandfather—he's in his 60's now. Grandad laughed about it—he said there were enough purple hearts in the Roberts family already. My dad—well, I think he regrets that I was born into a world that had recently experienced the VietNam war, rather than World War II. In those days in which my father grew up—things, supposedly, were simpler. Everything that mattered—duty, patriotism, citizenship, honor—all seemed to be clearer then."

"Supposedly? I thought I heard a disclaimer."

Richard took a deep breath. "What I found in my research painted a different picture of the years immediately after World War II than the conventional picture. The pervasive public view—that the men who fought in World War II came back and seamlessly rebuilt their lives—just does not bear up to scrutiny. One significant statistic—which does not tell the whole story, but still is pertinent: divorce among veterans in the years immediately after the war was more than double the rate of that of civilians. PTSD, Post-Traumatic Stress Disorder, did not become an official diagnosis until after the war in VietNam, but it is apparent—or at least that is the position of my thesis—that the malady was just as prevalent, perhaps more so, after World War II."

"Why wasn't PTSD acknowledged?" Jamie asked.

"Well, you might have to read my paper to hear my argument, but the short version is that it just didn't fit the narrative of the time. Everyone wanted the war to be behind them. The cultural ethos of the time was to move on. But wars are not neat and tidy. The effects go on after the guns are no longer firing. I have a quote in my paper you may be familiar with: 'Must you have battle in your heart forever?—the bloody toil of combat?'"

"Homer, *The Odyssey,*" Jamie acknowledged.

"Yeah—I guess Homer was the first to diagnose PTSD."

"Very interesting," Jamie said.

"Enough about me for the moment. Back to you. According to the article, you may have to choose between the Olympics and the Rhodes scholarship."

"Well, neither offer is official, and I do not want to be presumptuous. I have not yet qualified for the

Olympic team and the Rhodes scholarship has not been offered. It's possible I will get neither offer, and it's possible I will get only one—which will make the decision-making process simple."

"If you were to get both offers, who will you consult for advice?"

"My dad, for sure. He will give wise counsel and I will talk with my pastor, and then I will also talk with Dr. Emerson—he's been my academic mentor. Fortunately the only one seriously affected by my decision is Aspasia."

"Aspasia?"

"My cat."

"Aspasia? Like Pericles' Aspasia?"

"I'm impressed—you know Greek history, it seems."

"Well, don't forget Pericles was a military man, but a cat—"

"Well, she's very pretty and very intelligent and her background is suspicious—she just showed up at my house one day—so Aspasia seemed like an appropriate name. But that's enough about me for the time being. You haven't told me about the funeral for Dr. Kincaid."

Richard shook his head from side to side. "So tragic. Dr. Kincaid was a pure academic. He loved information. He was the one who encouraged me to pursue this doctoral thesis. He told me that although it was true that there was a 'great dynamism' after the war, but there was also another side of the story as well;

that many who returned from the war were not only injured in their bodies but injured in their spirits and minds as well. Dr. Kincaid told me it was a woefully under-reported phenomenon and one that needed more attention." Richard paused for a moment. "What a tragedy. It still hasn't sunk in for me. It still does not seem real that I will not see Dr. Kincaid at Moreland again—run over just a block from his own home and the driver doesn't have the decency to stop."

They were both quiet for a moment. "Hey," Richard said, "let's get back to Moreland and see what additional information we can find about your grandfather. I'm anxious to run the dog tag number of Private Johnson through the computer."

"That's odd," Richard said as they approached Moreland Center.

"What's odd?" Jamie asked.

"Dotson's car is in his parking space. Spencer Dotson is the director at Moreland. I don't ever remember seeing his car here after closing hours."

Richard and Jamie went around the building. As they did, another vehicle—a black limousine—pulled into the parking lot and parked next to Dotson's Mercedes.

As soon as they returned to the conference room, Richard took a seat at the computer table in the corner. "Moreland's digitized records are minimal. Mostly they just tell us if there are paper records—and where to find them."

Richard made a series of keystrokes on the computer. The computer responded with a series of whirrs and blinks as Richard looked at the medal recommendation again. He shook his head in confusion. He punched some more keys and then drummed his fingers on the desk as the computer did its work. The screen flickered several times and Richard read the numbers aloud as he typed them in. He punched the enter key with a flourish. "Let's see what happens."

Jamie leaned over Richard's shoulder as the screen shimmered.

"Here it is—"

The screen read:

JOHNSON, E.W.   13125934   108th Infantry, 3rd Battalion, I Company

"I Company?" Jamie said. "How could he be in I Company if my grandfather wrote a recommendation for him in K Company."

"Don't ask me," Richard said, standing up. "I can't figure it out. But his records should be in the basement. I'll be back in a few minutes. Keep working through the other documents.

Jamie sat with her back to the window, sorting out the documents. If she had looked outside, she might have seen—in the dim light provided by a streetlight—a man, a large man, pacing around a black limousine. He looked up at the building. Two rooms had lights on.

One was in the conference room, where he might have seen—if he looked closely—the silhouette of a young woman sitting at a table. The other light was from the director's office on the top floor. He could not see into that office, but he knew who was in the room. The man walked around the car again. He walked with a nervous energy, impatiently. He stopped for a second and looked around to see if anyone was nearby. Apparently assured no one was near, he removed his jacket, folded it neatly and placed it on the hood of the car. He looked around one more time and then dropped down beside the limo and began doing pushups. After a great number of pushups, which he did with great energy and perfect form, the man stood up beside the car, brushed off his hands, put his jacket back on, looking around to see if anyone had noticed him. As he turned toward the nearest streetlamp the dim light hit his face. He was a man with a thick neck, thick shoulders and a bleached-blond crew-cut and a matching blonde goatee. He looked up at the conference room window and saw the silhouette of a man's figure enter the room.

"I have I Company's personnel records," Richard said as he came back into the room. He put a large box on the table.

"I thought all the records had to be returned to the basement before 5 p.m.—government regulations."

"Well, yeah, they do … but there is no specific government rule that says that they can't be taken out again *after* that time."

"Richard, why do I get the feeling that you break a lot of rules around here?"

Richard ignored her question as he thumbed through the files, "Hernandez ... Horowitz ... Ingram ... Johnson, Charles Andrew ... Johnson, Earl Wayne ... E.W. Johnson! Bingo! Here's our friend's records." He put the folder on the table and opened it.

"Johnson, Earl Wayne, volunteered a few months after his 18th birthday—that was 1942 ... from Jenkins Ridge, Virginia. I know that place. I've hiked in the mountains near there. It's right on the edge of the Shenandoah National Park." He looked back at the document. "Johnson was an original member of the 108th—not a replacement ... trained at Camp Swift and at Camp Henry. He shipped over with his outfit in 1944 ... they landed in Normandy about a month after the invasion ... the unit saw its first action east of Paris and ..." Richard paused for a moment. He had a perplexed look on his face.

"What is it?" Jamie asked.

"Some pages seem to be missing. There's nothing in the record after November, 1944 and then it shows the discharge date as December 1, *1946*— that's a very late discharge date for someone from the European Theater—that's a year and a half after the German surrender, and there's an unusual notation at the bottom—" He pulled another folder from the file.

"Ahh ... that's what I was afraid of," he said looking at a sheet from the file.

"What is it?" Jamie asked.

"A Section 8 dismissal. Private Johnson was a psychiatric case after the war."

"Oh, I suppose that explains the late date of his discharge," Jamie said.

"Yeah, probably in a hospital after the war," Richard answered, "but it doesn't explain the gap in the records—or why he was recommended for a medal in K company." Richard pulled a document for Jamie to see. "Hmm—Look at this. Private Johnson has an interesting record—two arrests by the military police during training. The first was for a fight with another soldier. For that he received only a reprimand and confinement to post. For the second infraction he served 15 days in military prison for assaulting an M.P. On another occasion he was brought before a court of inquiry on a charge of insubordination to an officer."

"Not exactly the ideal soldier, was he?"

Richard pulled another sheet from the file. "Here's another citation. While Johnson was in England, waiting to be shipped out—he was charged with striking an officer—a *major* at that! He actually was in military prison in Southampton awaiting trial when he was released to join his outfit when they crossed the channel for France."

"Mr. Johnson seems like an interesting person— do you think he might still be alive?" Jamie asked.

"Maybe we can find out."

"How?"

"I'll show you." Richard moved over to the computer and made some keystrokes. "I will cross-check his military I.D. with his social security number." In a few seconds the screen showed the name E.W. Johnson and his social security number. "Now I will run that number through the tax records. There will be an IRS record for him for every year until his death. Richard made several more keystrokes. The screen asked for a password and Richard made more keystrokes. Jamie could not read everything on the screen, but the words '**FEDERAL PENALTY**', and '**FOR AUTHORIZED INTERNAL REVENUE SERVICE PERSONNEL ONLY**' were in bold letters.

"Why is it that I have the feeling you are not supposed to have all these access codes?" Jamie asked.

"Well," Richard answered. "It makes the research process less complicated when you don't have to fill out all those government forms."

The screen flickered green and white for several seconds and then "**Johnson, E. W.**" came on the screen—and then after a moment "**No Tax Records**".

"No tax records!" Richard said, rocking back in his chair. "How can that be? That's not possible. *Every* American has a tax record! You can't live in this country without paying taxes!"

Richard sat back in the swivel chair and put his hands behind his head. "I can't figure it out. I'm stymied. 'Curiouser and curiouser' as Alice would say."

They were both quiet for a moment.

Jamie interrupted the silence. "Richard, I think it's time to call this off. This has become much more complicated than I expected. I'm grateful that I found out some valuable information about my grandfather. I can be satisfied with that. I've disrupted your schedule—"

"But," Richard interrupted, "*I* am not ready to give this up. My curiosity has been aroused. I need to figure this out. Look, before we give up, I need to take these files back to the basement. We can look there—"

"We? Am I allowed in the basement?"

"Well, we're going to make an exception in your case. While we're there we can look at Harrison Henninger's records. Maybe that will shed some light on our research."

At the mention of Henninger's name, Jamie had an involuntary reaction—a slight twitch, and despite her suggestion that they call off the research, she still was puzzled by her interaction with Mr. Henninger. Once again she fought the impulse to tell Richard about the strange response from Henninger a few days earlier. *Not now. This is already weird enough without Richard having to deal with female intuition.*

"Dotson must be leaving," Richard said as he and Jamie entered the elevator. He was looking at the indicator light on the elevator beside them. It indicated that someone was headed down from the third floor.

If Jamie and Richard had taken the elevator to the lobby, rather than the basement, they would have seen two men come out. One of the men was Spenser

Dotson, the director of Moreland Center. The other, despite the spring weather, wore an expensive full-length coat with the collar pulled up around his neck and ears. Had even a casual observer seen the two men walking down the hall, without hearing the conversation, he would have seen the tension between them. Dotson seemed to be making some sort of appeal, his hands open as he walked alongside the man in the long coat. But the man in the long coat walked quickly, with his shoulders and head down, making no response to Dotson. They walked to the back door, Dotson was still making his appeal, but the man in the coat put up his right arm—in rejection—and walked out the door. Dotson stood for some time watching the figure walk across the lighted parking lot toward a black limousine where a large man stood beside the vehicle's door.

"Impressive, don't you think?" The sarcasm in Richard's voice was heavy.

Jamie stepped out of the elevator into the Moreland basement. She stood for a moment at the door evaluating what she saw. What she saw—the giant underground warehouse—gave her an immediate sense of repulsion. The room was cavernous, more than the height of two regular stories, but, even so, the ceiling felt low because of the great expanse of the room. A broad corridor ran down the middle of the gigantic room—as wide as a one-lane road and on either side rows of heavy metal shelves, filled with cardboard boxes, rose up toward the ceiling. Several carts of various sizes lay around the room, apparently used for transporting the files. The room had no windows but there seemed to be hundreds of fluorescent lights, their low hum pervading the basement. Huge pipes ran across the ceiling. But the overwhelming sensation was the odor—it smelled like someone had burned their trash in a damp basement.

"Nice place, huh?" Richard said, smiling, looking over at Jamie's wrinkled-up nose.

"Yeah, I bet you bring all the girls here."

"I've got to wow them somehow. I wish I could tell you that you will get used to the odor, but I'm not sure you will. Some of these files are fire damaged and then water-soaked, so the aroma lingers."

"Where are those files?" Jamie asked. "Let's get this over with."

"Follow me."

Jamie's shoes squeaked on the concrete slab floor and echoed back to her as they walked down the corridor. On both sides the metal frames rose up nearly twenty feet. Thousands of boxes of documents filled the shelves.

"You really like this place, don't you?" Richard teased.

"It's like a set for a horror movie. I keep expecting a mad scientist—or a mad researcher—to jump out of one of these aisles."

"When you've been here as long as I have, you come to love it."

At the end of the corridor was an office area with a small window beside a metal door. Richard used his key to open the door and he turned on the light inside. A bank of four computers, identical to the one in the conference room, sat on four tables.

"Let me run a quick search. Henninger served in battalion headquarters for the 108th. We should be able to find some records. "Harrison Henninger, 108th Infantry," he said as he made keystrokes. He leaned back and waited. After a moment a message on the screen said: **Special Records Vault. Director's Approval Required.** "Hmm … Henninger's documents are in the Special Records Vault."

"And what is a 'special records vault' if I may ask?"

"It's where the government keeps some particularly fragile documents—some from the Revolutionary War, the War of 1812 and the Civil War and some things that have never been declassified— and apparently some stuff that *really* must be secret— because no one has told me what it is."

"And where is this vault? Is it here in the basement?" Jamie asked.

Richard flipped on a light that illuminated a concrete-block hallway that ran about ten feet away from them. Steel bars framed the end of the hallway, and just beyond them, a heavy metal door. "Down the hallway, just beyond those steel bars, you will find your government's 'Special Records Vault'.

Jamie looked down the hallway—her expression betraying her disgust. "Have you been in there?"

"Once—with Dotson. He's the only one with a key. Standard operating procedures require him to personally escort researchers in and out of the vault. I was doing some research about the Battle of New Orleans on behalf of a congressman from Louisiana and I needed some records from the vault. Dotson accompanied me. He acted as if it was an awful imposition on him to spend a few moments in the basement—but that is my only experience in that vault."

"Why would Harrison Henninger's records be in the Special Records Vault?" Jamie asked.

"That's the question I'm asking myself. Maybe because he has become a national figure, his records have been moved."

"Will you ask Dotson to see the records?"

"Sure—oh, look at this," Richard pointed at the screen. It said: **Inquiry Log** and below it was the name: **Milton Kincaid**. "Dr. Kincaid was the last one to inquire about this record."

"Oh, how sad," Jamie said.

"Yes, just four days ago, he was alive and working on research—"

"Working on *my* research," Jamie interrupted. "Oh Richard, this whole effort has become too heavy for me. I need to give this up and get back to campus. I have track practice tomorrow afternoon. Tomorrow's Tuesday. The conference championships are on Saturday. I need to give that my focus."

"Don't let the ambience of this basement get to you. Before you give up, I have one more thing I would like to explore. It would take only an hour—maybe two—in the morning. You could be on the road by eleven. Can you do that?"

"Well, I guess so, but what is the idea you want to explore?"

"The Internal Revenue Service. It's extremely odd that the IRS does not have a tax record for Mr. E.W. Johnson. The IRS has the best records in the U.S. government—better records than the Secret Service. I don't understand why Johnson's tax records don't show up. Maybe Neal can help. Neal is my friend at IRS—like me, a part-time student at Georgetown. Let me shoot him an email."

Jamie watched as Richard typed on the screen: "Neal: Flummoxed at Moreland. Dog tag #1312594-34 shows no tax record. Apparently, Johnson, E.W. is not paying taxes. Please explain. (And will it work for me?) Richard

"Neal should be able to help us. He's gone home for the day, but he's generally responsive to emails. Let's wait for his reply."

They didn't wait long. The reply came almost immediately: Hmmm … not paying taxes? We can't let that happen, can we? Can you meet me in the morning? Our doors open at 8:30.—Neal

"Okay, we're set," Richard said. "We can meet Neal at the IRS office—"

"I don't know." Jamie interrupted. "This has gotten much more complicated than I expected. Maybe I should head back to campus first thing in the morning. That would—"

"Jamie," Richard interrupted, "do what you need to do, but I can't leave this alone. I plan to meet Neal in the morning."

Jamie said nothing for a moment as she considered her options. "Okay, 8:30 at the IRS office."

Jamie had trouble falling asleep, and it had nothing to do with the fact that she was in a strange bed. Her mind was whirling … the handshake from Henninger … the conference track championship … the Rhodes application … this trip to Washington … the anomalies of the military records—and she also found herself thinking about Richard.

No Jamie. Don't go down that road. Your life has enough complications already.

TWENTY-SEVEN

TUESDAY, MAY 15, 7:30 A.M.

JAMIE THREW HER travel bag in the trunk of the Civic. She had checked out of the motel. Now, after the appointment at the IRS, she would be able to make a quick get-away back to campus—in time for track practice.

She started toward the train station and rehearsed the day's schedule in her mind. She would take the train into town and meet Richard at the IRS office at 8:30 a.m. to talk with Richard's friend Neal. Then by 10 or 10:30 at the latest, she would take the train back to the hotel and then drive back to campus. Unless traffic was a problem, she should make it back in time for practice.

This is a big building! How many columns are there? Thirty?

Jamie stood near the flagpole by the sign that said **Internal Revenue Service-1111 Constitution Avenue.** The Constitution Avenue entrance—which was not the longest facade—ran from 10th St. NW to 12th St. NW. She looked up at the seven-storey building. The brown limestone gave the edifice an imposing presence.

The better to intimidate dishonest taxpayers, I suppose.

She walked up the steps. Richard was at the entrance waiting for her.

"Good morning," he said.

Jamie had the impulse to give Richard a hug, but thought it might not be appropriate, so she extended her hand instead. "Richard, I feel like I have disrupted your life. I'm sorry—"

"Don't be sorry. This mystery about E.W. Johnson and his missing records and his failure to pay his taxes has me intrigued. And I'm—" Richard was about to say he was glad he had gotten to meet her, but before he could say that, the guard opened the door and several people brushed by them to enter the building.

Richard and Jamie joined those entering the building and as they did, Richard heard a voice, "No, it will not work for you."

Jamie looked at the young man with unruly blonde hair wearing a plaid shirt.

"Neal!" Richard said, giving a strong handshake.

"Neal, this is Jamie Patterson." Jamie extended her hand.

"Welcome to the Internal Revenue Service, Jamie, where our motto is 'Doing all we can to brighten your day.' Well that's not actually our motto. I wish it could be—but I'm afraid we would fail miserably if it were. And actually we receive almost no correspondence thanking us for brightening someone's day and—"

"Neal," Richard interrupted, "I don't want to break up this enthralling story about the IRS, but Jamie has only an hour or so before she has to head out of town."

"Enough said. Follow me."

Five minutes later, after winding their way past an endless number of office bays, Neal led them to a small glassed-in conference room. Richard looked around. "You have better computers than we do at Moreland," he said, pointing to the workstation.

"Yeah, that's true." Neal smiled mischievously. "The U.S. government apparently gives priority to those of us who are actually *generating* income." He pulled two chairs near the swivel chair in front of the computer. "Sit here, Jamie."

He typed in some keystrokes with passwords and "**Entry Allowed**" popped up on the screen. "Okay Richard, tell me what I'm looking for."

"Johnson, Earl Wayne—U.S. Army dog tag number 13125934."

Neal typed in the name and number. "**No Tax Records**" came on the screen.

"That's what I saw yesterday afternoon," Richard said. "How can that be?"

"Hmm …" Neal mumbled. "Let me do a little work-around." He typed in "TRUANT RECORDS and the dog tag number.

Richard looked at the screen "Truant Records? What is that? You never told me about 'Truant Records'."

Before Neal could answer, the screen on the computer filled: **Johnson, E.W. Serial Number 13125934 Jenkins Ridge, Virginia November 26, 1924-. Truant Records Division.**

"So Johnson does have some records," Richard said.

Neal nodded. "Apparently so. Wait here," Neal said. "I will be right back."

"With Johnson's records, I hope." Richard said.

"I hope so, too," Neal said as he hurried out.

Jamie and Richard had a moment of awkward silence when they were left alone in the room. "I've never heard of 'truant records'," Richard said, in an effort to break the silence. Jamie nodded, but said nothing.

Another moment of awkward silence followed before Jamie spoke: "Richard, there is something I should tell you—it's about Harrison Henninger. You know he spoke at the awards ceremony at Duke last week."

"Yes, you told me—and I saw the news reports."

"Well, it was that event that triggered my interest in finding my grandfather's history in the war."

"That's understandable. Did you speak with Henninger? Were you able to mention to him that your grandfather was one of those killed at St. Lautern?"

"Well, sort of, but—"

At that moment Neal returned with a plastic tub filled with file folders.

"You even have better *boxes* here than we do at Moreland," Richard said. "Ours are cardboard."

"Once again, the benefits of working for a revenue-generating sector of the government." Neal put the tub on the table. Neatly stenciled on the side was **Internal Revenue Service—Truant Records—Jod-Joh.** "I ask again," Richard said. "What is this 'Truant Records Division'?"

"Ah, let me explain," Richard responded. "Unlike the Canadian Mounted Police, we at the IRS don't *always* get our man. Now, if you reveal this to the general public, it might cause the breakdown of civilization as we know it—or at least the civilization of U.S. taxpayers, but the naked truth is this: there are a few—it's a very small number—but a few, American citizens, who do not pay any taxes. I realize this is a radical revelation, and one which the general populace should not be made aware of—lest they seek to join this elect club, so please swear—"

"Neal—"

Neal raised his hand. "I know. You want me to get to the point. Here. Look at the title of this file: **Determination of Infeasibility of Pursuit of Further Collections.** If you translate that from 'bureaucratese', it simply means 'We at the IRS are not going to try any longer to collect your taxes'."

"But why—"

"Let me explain. It appears that in the early sixties, Mr. Johnson's name showed up on a list of non-filers, and that a certain IRS agent, Lyle Goodwater, from the Richmond regional office, was assigned the case. This was 1963, twenty-one years ago." Neal pulled out a stack of documents. "It appears that Agent Goodwater exhibited considerable diligence in his effort to communicate with Mr. Johnson. We have copies of more than a dozen letters sent to Mr. Johnson, as well as documentation of an equal number of attempts via the telephone. Failing in all those attempts, Agent Goodwater requested—and received—permission to make a personal visit. That visit took place on October 18, 1963. One week later, on October 28, 1963, Agent Goodwater, in his report, requested permission to 'discontinue efforts of tax collection'. He says future efforts would be 'impractical and unfeasible'."

"Is that unusual?" Jamie asked.

"Very." Neal said. An amused look came on his face. "And the circumstances that led to that recommendation are unusual as well. Look at this photograph." The picture showed an early 60's black Ford sedan with a pock-marked fender."

"What?—" Richard started a question.

"Buckshot. Agent Goodwater, in his report, does not specifically allege that Mr. Johnson fired his shotgun *at* him, but the buckshot that splattered the fender of his government-issued Ford sedan—and so, in the mind of Agent Goodwater—created the possibility that the other barrel of Mr. Johnson's double-barreled shotgun might possibly be redirected toward him."

Richard and Jamie looked at the photo more closely. The pock-marks on the black fender were obvious.

"Has it ever occurred to you," Neal asked, "how few IRS agents are afforded hero status? Are there any references that you can recall, in our school's history books, of IRS agents laying down their lives in an effort to collect taxes? Is there a statue anywhere in this country, on a horse or otherwise—"

"Neal—" Richard interrupted.

"Yes, yes. I digressed again. Let's go back to the record. Agent Goodwater, it appears, stayed in Jenkins Ridge for another couple of days, interviewing local townspeople, and based on those reports, Agent Goodwater cited 'correlative reports of mental imbalance' and 'corroborative evaluations of instability.' Upon his return to Washington, D.C., Agent Goodwater was able to obtain Mr. Johnson's military records, including the information about his Section 8 dismissal. Anyhow, Goodwater attached the entire file to the record and cites 'remoteness of subject location' and 'minimal income projections' as further mitigating factors in his request to cease efforts to collect Mr. Johnson's taxes."

A mischievous smile came to Neal's face.

"What is so amusing?" Richard asked.

"The appeal that Agent Goodwater wrote—if you read between the lines—seems to be screaming 'Please don't make me go back there again!'"

"Did he go back there again?" Jamie asked.

"He did not. Here's the letter from the regional director—dated January 17, 1964. It authorizes Agent Goodwater to transfer the record to the Truant Records file."

They were all quiet for a moment before Richard spoke: "You mentioned Johnson's military file—which is missing from the records at Moreland."

Neal pulled a thick file from the plastic box. "Here it is." He plopped it on the table. "Take a look. However, I need to go to my desk for a moment. How long do you think you will need this folder?"

"Thirty minutes," Richard answered.

"Okay," Neal said as he left. "Just remember—this is secret stuff. You can't make this information public. We can't have our citizens shooting at IRS agents in the hope of not paying their taxes, can we?"

Richard and Jamie looked at each other as Neal closed the door behind him. "Well," Richard said, "let's take a look at our friend Mr. Johnson's medical records." He opened the folder and began scanning the documents.

"That's odd," Richard said.

"What's odd," Jamie asked.

"The date. The first entry is September, 1945. Johnson's first medical records begin in late September 1945." Richard turned over a page in the folder. "Hitler had been dead for six months. Germany had surrendered. The war in Europe was over in May. Why so long? Where was he during those months? And here is more odd information, the first entries in his medical records are not medical at all, they are background materials—the reasons he was referred to the psychiatrists."

"What do they say?" Jamie asked.

"A lot. Listen to this: 'Patient was initially referred while in military prison in Frankfurt."

"Military prison?" Jamie asked.

"AWOL—Absent without leave. He had been missing since December, 1944, about nine months."

"AWOL since December, 1944? But my grandfather wrote a medal recommendation for him in March 1945."

"Yeah, I know. That's extremely confusing. Add that to the list of things that don't make sense."

Richard returned to the records. He ran his fingers over the page as he read: "Johnson was due to be tried for desertion, but he was saved from that by an army doctor who referred him for psychiatric evaluation. He was sent to the V.A. hospital in Rome, Georgia and that is where the psychiatric records begin." Richard scanned through the documents. "There's a great deal of psychiatric language in these records 'neurasthenia … traumatic war neurosis … combat exhaustion …' all of which we would now call Post Traumatic Stress Syndrome—which, as I said, was a name that was not coined until about 20 years after World War II. But in the common vernacular of the time, it was just called 'shell shock.'"

"What else do you see?"

"Still wading through the general diagnosis—'co-morbidity … psychic numbing … anxiety reactions … antisocial personality disorder … hallucinations …'. All of these traits, unfortunately, are fairly standard for PTSD patients."

"That is sad," Jamie said. "I had no idea."

"Okay, we're coming to more specific information. This is interesting."

"What is interesting?"

Richard read the report aloud: 'Prevalent hallucinatory behavior has been noted. Night terrors are regular. Patient has difficulty sleeping—often wakes up screaming in the night and must be restrained. Sodium pentathol injections achieve only temporary relief. Other medications are minimally effective. Recurring narrative is that of betrayal by an officer. Patient consistently maintains that one of his fellow soldiers was murdered by an officer. Other examples of paranoia have been cited. Counseling sessions have provided no evidence of improvement. Patient demonstrates exceptional nervousness. Patient requires a bed in the corner of the ward and will not go near windows. Patient often requires restraint. Patient often becomes combative when other patients approach.'"

Richard looked up from the documents. "These observations are classic PTSD. Our Mr. Johnson fits the profile. His symptoms, unfortunately, are not unusual. These descriptions are similar to what I consistently saw in my research."

Jamie was quiet for a moment as if she were working something over in her mind. "Richard," she said firmly, "I'm going to Jenkins Ridge. I want to talk to Mr. Johnson."

TWENTY-EIGHT

THE POLITICAL PUNDITS were energized. They had a new story and new questions; Harrison Henninger had canceled his planned speech in Tampa and the media were asking, "What does this mean?"

In the Oval Office, Brent Arens was asking the same question. He stood looking out the window over the White House lawn, hands folded behind his back, the president and James Olmstead nearby. "Something has happened," Arens said. "Something has upset Mr. Henninger's plan. I sense it—but what is it? And how do we find out what it is?"

James Olmstead and the president looked at each other. They were certain that Arens' instincts were right—they always were.

"What about Pursley? Does he have any information?" the president asked.

"I talked with him less than an hour ago," Olmstead replied. "He has left messages at Henninger's office, but there has been no reply."

Arens continued to look out the window, "What is it, Mr. Henninger," he mumbled, "that has upset your little apple cart?"

TWENTY-NINE

RICHARD LOST THE argument.

Jamie and Richard were now forty miles outside Washington headed due west on I-66 in Jamie's Civic. "This is not a good idea!" he had said repeatedly, but Jamie was determined. Her mind was made up. She was going to Jenkins Ridge. She was going to talk with Mr. E.W. Johnson, and nothing Richard could say could deter her from that ambition. "I will miss this afternoon's practice, but I can work out on my own tonight," Jamie said, talking more to herself than to Richard.

"You can't go alone, " Richard had said. "If I can't talk you out of going, I will go with you."

"How will you get back to Washington?"

"You can drop me off in Middleton. It's nearby. There's regular bus service from there. I took that bus last year when I hiked in the Shenandoah." He looked at her firmly. "I can't let you go by yourself."

Richard drove. He kept the speedometer in the mid-60s as they drove through the Virginia hills where yellow and white flowers peppered the roadside. Above them, two hawks drew circles against white clouds fixed against the rich blue sky. The drive afforded the opportunity for the two of them to talk—and to get to know each other better. Richard had a sister who was two years younger and who had finished a clinical psychology degree and got married right after graduation. Jamie was an only child. Richard asked about the Olympics, but Jamie's response was perfunctory, and Richard realized that was not a topic she wanted to talk about.

"Tell me," Jamie said, "about the Naval Academy."

"The academy? I spent two years there. It is a wonderful—and necessary—institution. It just wasn't the place I needed to be."

"And why not?"

Richard laughed. "Probably lack of ambition. When I thought about my dad's career—going from Lieutenant to Captain to Major to Colonel and now to Brigadier General—I realized I just didn't have the energy to follow that path. May God bless those who do. We desperately need those men—but I knew—after two years at the academy, I was not one of them."

"What about your father? How did he accept that decision?"

"It was hard on him. He wanted me to follow in his footsteps—to be a career officer in the Marines. That was his dream for his son, but I realized it wasn't my dream. And I would say that though our relationship was damaged, it was never severed. We're still on good terms."

They were quiet for a while. Outside the hills in the distance became steeper as they neared the Shenandoah mountains. The sky above the hills held inert white clouds that seemed fixed against the blue sky, holding their place as if they would never move again.

"Once again," Jamie said, "I appreciate your going with me today, Richard. It wasn't necessary and I feel like I'm taking you away from your work."

"It's good for me to get out of Washington. If you stay there too long, you begin to think it's the real world."

The fields on either side of them became steeper as they approached the Shenandoah Mountains. Cows grazed in lush meadows. Red barns, nearly pink due to decades of sun and rain, were set against gray-green hills that rose up in the distance.

"Richard, I would like to know more about your thesis."

Richard took a deep breath, strumming his fingers on the steering wheel. "I wish I could tell you I enjoyed every part of the research, but the truth is … much of it was painful. And it was revelatory. I was unaware of the level of personal suffering that World War II veterans endured when the war concluded. Our country has done a great disservice to those veterans. Those of us who were born after the war, when we see any film or photographs of the era, or when we read books or articles about it—the story is invariably rendered in two stages; first, the horror and tragedy of the war and then, the euphoria after the war. That neat outline does not do justice to the truth. That narrative assumes all the struggles of the war—for those who fought in it—were suddenly over with the signing of the peace treaty. But the evidence—and it's painful evidence—is that that jaunty and uncomplicated narrative does not hold up under scrutiny. It just wasn't that simple. The truth is that many veterans—a great many—continued to fight a war even after the war concluded—a war at home.

Richard paused. He looked at Jamie as if he were unsure he should go on.

"I think," Jamie said, "this topic has become more than just a thesis program for you."

Richard nodded. "That's true. The more I read and the more I researched—and some of the research included personal interviews—the more I realized how much suffering these men endured when the war was over. The images in their brains—of men dead and dying, often dying grotesquely—were not immediately erased with the announcement that a peace treaty was signed. Likewise the decisions men made in the field have haunted them the rest of their lives. One Pacific theater veteran, a Marine sergeant, told me, "I killed those men. I killed them as surely as if I had shot them myself." He was at Tarawa. He had sent a squad, nine men, to an outcropping below a hill where there was a Japanese emplacement. They had been there only moments when a mortar round fell on them, killing all nine instantly. That old Marine's wife told me her husband, 40 years later, still wakes up screaming in the night."

Richard paused. "I'm sure, based on my research, that there are untold thousands of veterans who have misgivings about their decisions—decisions which caused other men to lose their lives. The point I am trying to make is that World War II was not clean and neat—with a clear demarcation between the war and the post-war. The aftermath of the war, contrary to the nostalgic adulation of the historical media, was not as rosy as we have been led to believe."

He looked at Jamie. "I have a quote from the thesis. I've been over it so many times it is now memorized. Here it is: 'The view foisted on us of returning World War II veterans by the historical authorities has been sanitized and sentimentalized and it does not accurately describe the complex stories of alienation and mental suffering of those veterans. When we see videos or photographs of that era—what do we see? Ticker-tape parades, jubilant crowds and public euphoria, but those images do not tell the complete story. We have been given a reassuring assessment, an uncomplicated portrait of the years immediately after the war. That view was pervasive—and still is—but it is not accurate. The war had an aftermath—a painful aftermath. The men who returned from combat were different than when they left. Not all the wounds our World War II veterans sustained were in their bodies. Many were damaged in their brains …

and in their souls. That sad fact is something our nation needs to acknowledge."

Richard paused again.

Jamie moved her head from side to side. "Thank you, Richard. I certainly have had no appreciation for the trauma of those veterans—and I hear your passion. And I genuinely hope your thesis gets a wide reading."

Richard nodded. "Part of the thesis—the psychological part, I suppose—is that human beings are not mentally equipped, in their psyches, for the brutality and bestiality of war. Killing other men is not a natural thing for the human brain to witness. Watching other men blow apart, or seeing innocent women and children killed, has an effect on a man. He can never be the same again. And I make no effort to quantify this theory, but I came to believe that the level of psychological trauma a returning veteran experienced, was proportional to the amount of battle horror he endured—which, honestly, gives me great concern about our proposed meeting with Mr. E.W. Johnson. While I feel sorry for him for what he has endured, I also know, based on my research, that those who endured the most trauma are often the most volatile."

He looked at Jamie. "We need to be cautious with your Mr. Johnson."

Both of them went quiet, each pondering what lay before them in the effort to meet Mr. E.W. Johnson.

THIRTY

BRENT ARENS STOOD at the window of his office overlooking the South Lawn. Tourists were walking on the sidewalks at the edge of the lawn—many posing for pictures, but he did not notice them. He was deep in thought. He had told his secretary that no one should interrupt him—unless it was the president—for the next two hours. He was writing a speech—a speech for the president, an important speech, but he himself was having trouble concentrating. He was thinking about Harrison Henninger.

Something has disrupted your tidy little world, Mr. Henninger. I sense it. My instincts tell me so—and my instincts are rarely wrong. What is it, Mr. Henninger, that is bothering you? What is it that has caused you to get out of character? Is someone prodding you like you are prodding us? If so, I hope they take that prod and shove it—

He did not finish the thought. He returned to writing the president's speech.

THIRTY-ONE

A BILLBOARD WELCOMED them to Jenkins Ridge. It noted the meeting times of the Lions Club, the Rotary Club, the Kiwanis Club, and the Jaycees. An attachment at the bottom honored the Lady Hawks, who had won the 2A girls' state basketball championship three years earlier.

Richard pulled into a gas station at the edge of town. A newly painted sign said "**Carruthers Convenience**", but the new sign could not conceal that it was an old service station trying to adjust to new times. Richard started the gas pump and he and Jamie went inside.

"Greetings, folks." A man wearing overalls which swelled out over an ample stomach was behind the counter and he spoke to them as they entered. "I hope you are having a good day. Thanks for stopping in." He drummed his fingers on the counter. His face was broad and engaging. A woman, whom Jamie assumed was his wife, was filling the refrigerated cabinet with soft drinks. She smiled and nodded toward the bathroom before Jamie could ask.

"Great weather we're having these days, isn't it?" the man at the counter asked and Richard nodded in agreement. "But there's rain in the forecast for the

234

weekend, I heard." Richard nodded again and excused himself to go outside and finish pumping the gas. When he returned, Jamie had chosen a fruit juice. Richard gave the man a twenty dollar bill. "Perhaps you can help us," Richard said. "We're looking for a gentleman named E.W. Johnson. Do you know how we can contact him? Perhaps you have directions to his house." The man's countenance changed. Both Jamie and Richard noticed it.

"You want to go to Earl Wayne's house?" The way he asked the question seemed to indicate "*Are you sure you want to go to Earl Wayne Johnson's house?*"

"Yes," Jamie answered. "Can you tell us how to get there?"

"Well … yes, it's not difficult to get to his house, but—"

"Is there something wrong?" Jamie asked.

"No—but Earl Wayne don't get many visitors."

"Let me explain," Jamie said. "Mr. Johnson and my grandfather were in the war together. I would like to talk to him about that."

The man nodded. "Yes, ma'am. I understand. Earl Wayne was in the war, for sure, but as far as I know, in the last forty years, he has never said one word about the war. The truth is—Earl Wayne don't talk about much at all."

Richard looked at Jamie, his face forming a plea that she would call this search off.

Jamie looked at the man in the overalls. "It's important to me that I meet Mr. Johnson. Can you tell us how to get to his house?"

"Directions to Earl Wayne's house—" the man said to himself. He shook his head slightly. "Here's what you do: Go on into town—to the main intersection—turn right on Highway 22. You'll go nearly three miles and you will see the sign for Porter's Mill Road on the left. It's a gravel road. Follow that about a mile and a half and you will see Earl Wayne's house sitting up on the left. It's the only house on the road—and the road turns into a logging road just a few hundred yards beyond the house. If you come to the logging road, you've gone too far."

"Richard, do you think we should call before we go?" Jamie asked.

"Earl Wayne don't answer his phone," the man said. "Not since Margaret died—Margaret was his wife. When was that, Roberta?" he called to the lady putting the drinks in the cabinet. "Was that last summer or the summer before?"

"It will be three years this summer," she answered.

The man shook his head, "Time gets away—well, anyhow, good luck with getting Earl Wayne to talk to you. As I said, he has never talked about the war—of course, some people in town say he's got good reasons for not talking about the war, but some of those people talk too much."

"What reasons?" Richard asked.

The man took a deep breath, leaned forward, and lowered his voice. "Oh, you know, they talk about that hospital he was in—right after the war. But I don't put any stock in that. Earl Wayne was always a little odd, even before the war—and prone to get into a fight every now and then. I can't deny that, but I never thought he was—well, you know what I mean."

"Carl," the lady called. Her voice was a reprimand.

The man smiled. "My wife thinks *I'm* one of the ones who talks too much."

Richard looked at Jamie. "I'm not sure this is a good idea. Mr. Johnson sounds like he is unpredictable."

"Well, there have been a couple of incidents," the man said.

"Incidents? What incidents?" Richard asked.

Carl lowered his voice again and leaned toward Richard and Jamie. "Well, it's probably been a little more than three years ago—before Margaret died. Earl Wayne ran the only sawmill around here. Right after the war, he went to work for Old Man Porter at that sawmill and just a year or two later, he married Margaret, Old Man Porter's daughter. He worked there nearly twenty years before Mr. Porter died and then he ran the mill himself for another twenty. He finally shut it down a couple of years ago—"

"But what was the incident?" Richard prompted.

"Oh yeah. Three young men were here in town for a couple of weeks working on a construction job—that warehouse for Dent's Plumbing, as I recall." He scratched his chin. "Now that I say that, I'm not sure. It could have been that addition at the back of the dry cleaners, I can't—"

"But what happened?" Richard asked, some exasperation in his voice.

"Well, these three young bucks went out to the sawmill to pick up some lumber. I heard this from one of those boys himself, so I know it's true. Well, one of these young bucks, probably twenty years old, was kinda full of himself—and he had heard the stories in town about Earl Wayne and the hospitals he was in after the war. Anyhow, this boy, when Earl Wayne isn't watching—or at least he doesn't think he's watching—started making faces, walking funny—Earl Wayne has a limp, you know—and acting like he's crazy. If Earl Wayne saw it, he ignored it. He put on his safety glasses to cut another board for these boys. Now, again, I want you to know I heard this directly from one of those boys. This is not second-hand. Well, Earl Wayne cranked up his saw and stood over it, feeding a log into it. Well, this boy, the one that's full of himself, starts snickering and picks up a short two-by-four and sneaks up behind Earl Wayne, giggling all the time. Well, he took that two-by-four and shoved it up under Earl Wayne—goosing him, you know what I mean?"

Richard nodded.

The man quit talking and began to shake his head back and forth.

"What happened?" Richard said impatiently.

238

The man continued to shake his head back and forth. "Now, you just don't do that. You don't touch a man when he's at a mill-saw. That's just not done. It's dangerous."

The man paused and began shaking his head from side to side. Richard thought he was going to have to prompt him again, but he picked up his story, "Well, I saw that boy myself right after that. They came by here with that boy laid out in the back of their pickup. When I first saw that boy, I thought he had got caught in the saw himself. I've never seen such a sight. His face was a bloody mess. Both eyes were completely closed and it looked like he had teeth missing. They asked me for directions to the doctor, but I told them to take that boy to the county hospital. He needed more attention that Doc Smith, here in town, could give him. I don't know how many stitches that boy needed or how many bones was broken, but it was a considerable number, for sure. Those other two boys said it was all they could do to keep Earl Wayne from killing that boy. He knocked that boy down, jumped on top of him and beat him unmercifully. They said it didn't last thirty seconds but if it had lasted much longer that boy would have been dead."

An overweight woman came in and paid for gas and bought two packs of cigarettes.

The man thanked her for her business and went on with the story. "Now there was some talk that there could have been charges brought against Earl Wayne, but I think that boy was so embarrassed that he had taken such a whupping from a sixty-year-old man—he just let it drop."

Richard looked at Jamie again, his face showing his concern.

"Yeah, that was really something," the man said, replaying it over in his mind, rocking his head back and forth. "And I got it from one of those other boys."

Jamie noticed that the man's wife had moved to the front of the store. She stood with one hand on her hip, looking directly at her husband.

"Well," the man said, "you folks have a good day. You've got the directions?"

"Yes, thank you," Jamie answered.

"This is definitely not a good idea," Richard said when they got back in the car. "Believe me, I know enough about these cases—similar cases—to know that our friend Mr. Johnson is unpredictable, and we have heard of two cases of violence. Jamie. Don't forget that our Mr. Johnson fired his shotgun at an IRS agent. I will be honest with you, Jamie. Despite all my curiosity about this man, I had hoped that when we arrived here, we would find that Mr. E.W. Johnson was dead and that would have been the end of this—"

"Wild goose chase?" Jamie interrupted. "Richard, you're probably right and I'm sorry I have gotten you entangled in this wild goose chase, but I'm so close I don't want to give up now. I need to talk with Mr. Johnson."

They were quiet for a moment. "This is definitely not a good idea," Richard repeated, "but I'm not going to let you go by yourself. If you're determined to go, I will go with you."

Following the directions out of town, they passed clusters of white frame houses with neat geometric gardens laid beside. Emerging crops—lettuces, onions, radishes—created rich green lines against the brown earth. The yellow blossoms of forsythia bushes swelled up in round clusters in the front yards. Pink azaleas grew next to the porches. In one yard a ceramic deer posed in full alert. A tractor with a disc slowed their progress for half a mile or so, but as they crested a hill, the farmer pulled over to the shoulder and waved them around. The road carried them along the edge of the hills which flanked the left side of the highway. A line of telephone poles, some slightly askew, like soldiers out of step, traced the line of the highway. Swaths of cultivated crops in shades of various greens marked the contours of the land.

Richard checked the odometer and slowed the car. A sign came into view, the lettering barely visible: **Porter's Mill Road**. Richard looked at Jamie as if to ask one final time if she wanted to reconsider. She did not look back at him. He flipped the turn signal and made the turn. After a few yards the road turned to gravel and the crunching noise underneath them seemed especially loud. The trees on each side of the road came closer as they moved along. The road curved slightly, rising up, taking the contours of the land and then fell away for a few hundred yards. A slow-moving stream joined them on the descent, going down to a stone trestle of an abandoned railroad line. The vine-covered pillars looked like miniature versions of the Mayan ruins in South America. They passed under the trestle and over a low bridge with no rails. Dozens of frogs, startled by the car, jumped into the languid green water under the low bridge. The road rose up on the other side and the thick undergrowth thinned out as they came into open fields edged by hardwoods. Dozens of rusty signs were nailed to the trees: "NO TRESPASSING", "POSTED", "NO HUNTING", "PRIVATE PROPERTY".

Richard and Jamie kept their eyes straight ahead. Neither of them spoke.

The sawmill, a long shed open on three sides, came into view on their left. A timber saw and a diesel engine lay idle, both gone to the brown-rust color of neglect. An assortment of other pieces of machinery were stacked in piles on the concrete floor of the mill. Dozens of young saplings, taking advantage of the site's abandonment, rose up along the edge of the concrete floor, some reaching up to the edge of the roofline.

"Can't be much further," Richard said, breaking the silence.

A clearing came into view sooner than Richard expected. A small house—with small windows—seemed oddly out of place on a treeless hill. Not a single shrub, tree, or bush grew on the rising slope in front of the house. Richard estimated there must have been four or more acres that were cleared. A long gravel driveway over a culvert ran more than fifty yards straight up the hill to a one-level ranch-style house with three windows that seemed too small for the house.

Richard slowed the car and stopped at the edge of the driveway. The ditch that ran alongside the road was overgrown with weeds. The same weeds grew in clumps in the yard. The small shutterless windows on the house, and the lack of trees or bushes gave the site a strange severity. In front of the culvert, a rusted mailbox was set on a heavy square post. A profusion of cattails grew in a swampy area by the concrete culvert. A thin stream managed to make its way sluggishly through the garish-green muck that thrived there. A drooping power line ran up alongside the gravel driveway to the house.

Richard put the car in park. "Let's keep your car out of buckshot range." He looked up the slope toward the house. "Mmm ... I don't think Mr. Johnson is going to win this month's garden club award,"

"Richard, there's no reason for you to go. Just wait here."

"Well, that is not going to happen. I'm going with you."

As they closed the car doors, Richard saw a curtain in one of the small windows flutter.

He stood by the mailbox and surveyed the area. "He's cleared the perimeter."

"What do you mean?"

"He has cleared the perimeter. He's made the place into an outpost—a fort. Look. No trees within a hundred yards—no visual impediments around the house—nothing to block his view. That's not unusual. It's a classic PTSD symptom. PTSD patients often require a view of everything around them. They won't sit with their back to a window, for example." He opened the mailbox. It was stuffed with old, and soggy, catalogs. "Looks like Mr. Johnson doesn't check his mail very often."

Jamie said nothing. She paused for a moment looking up at the long straight driveway. She took a deep breath and started up the driveway. Richard followed, only a step behind. The gravel crunched under their feet. Richard looked over at Jamie, but she kept her eyes straight ahead. Looking back at the house, he thought he saw the curtain flutter again. The sound of the gravel underneath their feet seemed oddly loud. Richard unconsciously moved in front of Jamie as they neared the house. The driveway had no sidewalk leading to the porch, a small square porch with no rails. Richard thought that made sense—if you don't have any visitors, you don't need a sidewalk. They walked across the yard and up the two concrete steps to the porch. He raised his hand to knock on the door, paused a moment, blew out a breath, and knocked.

No answer.

Richard knocked again. Still no answer. Jamie stepped in front of Richard and knocked insistently. "Mr. Johnson, we would like to talk with you." Still no answer. Jamie knocked again even more insistently. "I know he's there," she said to Richard. "I know he is."

Jamie knocked again and then stood waiting, but there was no response.

"Mr. Johnson!" she shouted.

"Jamie, it's time to give up. I don't feel good about this. If he won't answer the door, there's nothing you can do."

Jamie stood on the porch, taking deep breaths. Richard put out his hand. Jamie looked at the door and started to knock again but then thought better of the idea and took Richard's hand. They stepped down the porch. Richard led her through the coarse clumps of grass in the yard. Her lips and chin were clenched. Her face was full of frustration and exasperation. They took a few steps down the gravel driveway—

"I'm going back," Jamie said, dropping Richard's hand.

"Jamie—"

"Richard, he is not going to shoot a girl. You stay here." She stepped quickly back up the driveway, through the yard and onto the porch. She hammered on the door with both fists. "Mr. Johnson!" she screamed. "I know you are in there. My name is Jamie Patterson. My grandfather was Sergeant James Patterson. You fought with him in the war. I want to talk with you!"

The window shade fluttered, and Richard thought he saw a face in the window.

"Mr. Johnson! I know you can hear me! You were in the 3rd Army. 108th regiment. You fought across France into Germany alongside my grandfather! He wrote a recommendation for a medal for you. I want to talk with you! I want to know about my grandfather! I will not leave until you answer the door!"

Jamie stood and waited. She looked back at Richard. No sound came from inside the house. She was about to pound on the door again, but … a sound, the sound of a deadbolt sliding open … and then the sound of a door-latch being thrown … and then another door-latch …

The door cracked open slightly. When it did, Jamie saw a man with a bewildered face. The man spoke. "You're Sergeant Patterson's granddaughter?"

THIRTY-TWO

TUESDAY, MAY 15, 12:55 P.M.

ABRAHAM LINCOLN WAS looking directly at Henry Pursley. Or at least his statue was looking directly at Henry Pursley. Or, more likely, it just *seemed* to Henry as if Abraham Lincoln's statue was looking directly at him.

The Lincoln Memorial had become a regular place for Henry to visit the last few weeks. At the Commerce Department, where he was supposed to be working, and where he had an office, he now had no responsibilities. He, effectively, was on loan to the White House and his only job there, serving as a liaison to Harrison Henninger—difficult as it was—did not consume a workday.

As a result, Henry regularly spent much of each day wandering around the Washington Mall area. The Smithsonian had been his favorite place. The treasures there, at one time, seemed endless, but after more than a dozen trips, he decided he had seen almost everything on exhibit. Recently he found himself regularly drawn to the Lincoln Memorial—where he now stood, looking up at the solemn eyes of "The Great Emancipator".

During his first visits to the memorial, it seemed to Henry that Lincoln's pensive gaze was directed toward him—and the observation made Henry feel guilty. But now, Henry had decided his first impression was self-centered, that Abraham Lincoln was not looking at Henry Pursley—rather those contemplative eyes were looking beyond Henry seeking answers to the difficult issues that pressed on him and the nation.

Henry tried to find consolation in the fact that *his* worries were for himself only; Lincoln, however, had the worries of the nation on his mind.

Lincoln, when this memorial was dedicated, was cited for "the virtues of tolerance, honesty and constancy in the human spirit." The word "honesty," each time Henry read it, stuck in his craw.

What advice would you give me, Honest Abe? I am not honest—and I am becoming more dishonest each day.

THIRTY-THREE

THE INTERIOR OF Johnson's house was less severe than the outside, showing evidence of a woman's presence at one time. Crocheted items abounded—a coverlet on the brown vinyl couch where Jamie sat, arm covers on the matching brown vinyl chair where Mr. Johnson sat. Richard sat farther away in a green upholstered chair. A large piece of cream-colored crocheted piece draped over the dining table in the adjacent room. Doilies of the same color decorated the coffee table and end tables. Bronze candlesticks—without candles—sat on the fireplace mantle, along with a few small black-and-white photos in frames.

Richard looked at the man in the chair. "Sergeant Patterson's granddaughter," he said, "Sergeant Patterson's granddaughter. I can't believe it." E.W. Johnson wore denim overalls, a green and red plaid shirt and work boots—as if he were going to the sawmill. He was not a big man, but lean and wiry. Richard thought he looked like he would be capable— if he needed to- of putting in a full day's work.

"Mr. Johnson," Jamie said, "I'm sorry I shouted at you."

"That's okay. I don't mind. When you hollered, you put me in mind of Sergeant Patterson. I heard him holler only once—and he had reason to." His eyes took a far away look as if he were recalling deeply embedded memories—events hidden in a private, inner place.

"You favor him," Johnson said, coming out of his reverie, looking at Jamie. "I see the resemblance."

"We saw the medal recommendation my grandfather wrote for you," Jamie said. "You must have been a very brave man. You exposed yourself to machine gun fire. You climbed a drainpipe to capture a bazooka emplacement—and then you destroyed the sniper nest in the church steeple."

Johnson rubbed his chin. His eyes took a far away look again. "Never felt good about shooting that steeple. Didn't seem right, tearing up a house of God. No, never felt good about that. Missed it the first two times I shot."

"What can you tell me about my grandfather?" Jamie asked.

Johnson squinted his eyes. "When you hollered at me on the porch, you put me in the mind of your grandfather. The last time I saw Sergeant Patterson—before the Germans overwhelmed us—he was shouting—shouting into the radio, 'Where is our support?!' he hollered into the radio. "Where is our support?! We need backup! I need answers!' You sounded just like him—just like Sergeant Patterson."

The elderly man's expression went vacant, as if he were seeing that image of forty years ago in his mind's eye. "Sergeant Patterson was your grandfather," he said again, as if confirming it to himself. "It just doesn't seem possible. But he used to carry a picture of his little boy with him. He showed it to me just a couple days before—" he caught himself. "That was your daddy, I guess."

Jamie nodded. The man's eyes again took a faraway look, and no one spoke for a moment, until Mr. Johnson squinted his eyes and looked across the room at Richard. "Young man, I don't like the way you're looking at me. You're looking at me the same way those doctors did in the hospital."

"I'm sorry," Richard answered, putting up his hands, "but before you tell Jamie about her grandfather, can you explain to me why the records show you as part of I Company, but your medal recommendation and the AAR indicate you were with K Company at St. Lautern?"

"Confusion," he replied. "A lot of confusion. I was I Company. I trained with I Company stateside and I fought with them up to the battle at Metz. Our unit got really torn up at Metz. I got separated from the rest of my platoon. It was really disorganized. My company commander and my platoon sergeant were both dead. The company was in confusion. We had units all over the town and the Germans did too. They were holed up in buildings and just as disorganized as us. It took us two days to flush out all the Germans—most of them surrendered. Those last two days I fought alongside K Company and Sergeant Patterson's platoon. His platoon's lieutenant had been wounded and sent to the rear. We heard that they were going to give Sergeant Patterson a battle-field commission—make him a second lieutenant, but before—" his voice broke off. "But when we had control of the city and things quieted down for a while, Sergeant Patterson asked me if I wanted to go back to battalion headquarters and rejoin I Company or if I wanted to stay with him in K Company. I decided to stay with him."

"Why?" Jamie asked.

"I don't know. I guess I thought I would be a coward if I went back to battalion headquarters—but part of it was Sergeant Patterson. My previous sergeant had been a real jerk—but let me tell you this, in combat a man learns about another man and what he is made of much quicker than you can in any other way. Sergeant Patterson took care of his men. He was a god-fearing man—used to read his Bible at night. He was a little older than the rest of us—twenty-three or twenty-four as I recall. That seemed awfully old to a boy only nineteen."

"Twenty-three or twenty-four," Jamie thought, *"only a year or two older than I am now."*

"What happened at St. Lautern?" Jamie asked. "What happened on the day my grandfather was killed?"

Mr. Johnson looked at Jamie, then at Richard and then back at Jamie. He had the look of a man reluctant to say what he needed to say. His lips trembled slightly.

"We were betrayed."

"Betrayed?" Richard asked. "Who betrayed you?"

The man looked at each of them before he spoke: "Henninger. Henninger betrayed us."

THIRTY-FOUR

TUESDAY, MAY 15, 1:30 P.M.

PRESIDENT WILSON CAVANAUGH sat at his desk in the Oval Office reading a sheaf of papers. James Olmstead sat nearby reading an identical document. The president put the papers on his desk. "James, what do you think about Brent's speech?"

James Olmstead, during his years in Washington, had learned never to answer any question quickly—even from the president of the United States, who also happened to be his best friend. "Still reading," he said.

A smile came to the president's face. "James, do you remember when we ran for student body president?"

"You ran for student body president, not I."

"Well, yeah, but you were the one who talked me into running. We were just a couple of fraternity boys in those days—too full of ourselves, to be sure. Do you remember our platform? What were we running on?"

"Lowering the drinking age to eighteen," Olmstead responded.

"And how in the heck did we think we were going to convince the state of Virginia to lower the drinking age?"

"We didn't think," Olmstead replied.

"But we had a good campaign. The fraternity brothers put up signs all over campus and I made one speech. You wrote it. Fewer than thirty students, I suppose, heard it—there in front of the student union, and I don't remember being very eloquent, but somehow, I got elected. I've made a lot of speeches since then, and you've been with me all the way—lieutenant governor, governor, vice-president and now president—and I have to keep making speeches. The crowds are bigger now—and tougher, but we have to keep making the speeches, don't we?" He paused for a moment. "Brent says this is an important one."

Olmstead nodded. "He says every one is an important one, doesn't he?"

The president agreed. "He does—and I guess he's right. And, as usual, he's given me a list of questions to anticipate from the press." A wry smile came to his face.

"What is it?" James Olmstead asked.

"The only question lacking," the president said, "is: Do you still hope to lower the drinking age in Virginia to eighteen years?"

THIRTY-FIVE

As E.W. JOHNSON told his story there were several times Richard was glad the man had left his shotgun propped at the front door. He remembered that he had fired that shotgun at an IRS agent and the man's expression when he looked in Richard's direction was *I would just as soon shoot you as look at you.*

Earl Wayne Johnson, it was obvious, was not a man accustomed to talking. The words came slowly at first and after a while it seemed he was not telling the story to Jamie and Richard—he was recounting the story to himself, a subdued story, a story withheld for forty years.

"Our first training was in West Texas—in the desert, so we figured they were planning to send us to North Africa. Then we trained down in the Louisiana swamps, so we figured we were going to the Pacific. After that they sent us up in the mountains of West Virginia for a couple of months. Most of us, at first, thought we were going to Italy, but then we heard about Normandy and we were fairly certain that was where they would send us."

The little whirling clock on the mantle made a continuous, rhythmic tick as Johnson squinted his eyes, bringing back memories of forty years before. Neither

Jamie nor Richard said anything. Both realized they needed to let the man talk. After a moment he looked at them and shook his head. "I don't usually talk this much. Anyhow we sailed to Europe. We were worried about getting torpedoed by one of those German subs, but we got to England okay. We were there for a few weeks before they sent us across to France."

"Your record," Richard said, "indicated you almost didn't make the trip."

Johnson looked at Richard squarely. Richard was forty years younger and forty pounds heavier than the man who looked at him, but there was fearlessness in the face he saw.

"A lot of those things you might have seen in my record are true—but I ain't crazy." He gave Richard a hard look to make his point.

"I had a bunch of scrapes in the Army, and I did some stupid things—things maybe I wish I hadn't done—but I wasn't crazy then and I ain't crazy now, no matter what your record says."

If a man's eyes could hurt another man—Richard would have been dead.

No one spoke for a moment.

"Hitting that major got me in trouble," Johnson said.

"Tell us about that," Richard said.

Johnson nodded. "Yeah, I hit that major—but he needed hitting. He kicked our dog. We were bivouacked in tents in England—thousands and thousands of tents in the fields, full of American soldiers, just waiting—waiting for the word to go across the channel. The beaches at Normandy had been secured. We knew we would be going across soon, so we were just waiting for that word. Well, this little scrawny dog showed up. I gave it some of my dinner, and so did some of the other guys. We all took to that dog. We called it 'Tommy'—that was our nickname for British soldiers. He took to sleeping right outside our tent door. Well, one night I had just gone to sleep, and I hear Tommy yelping, and I hear some guy cussing Tommy and kicking him. I jump up and run outside—it's pitch dark and I'm in my underwear—and I knock the crap out of this guy. He tries to get up and I knock the crap out of him again. By then, my buddies are all outside, and they are holding me back, because I'm about to beat the—" Johnson caught himself.

"Someone brings a flashlight and we see this guy in a major's uniform laying on the ground moaning, blood pouring out of his mouth. As it turns out he was some West Pointer who was going around checking to see if the trenches around our tents were up to specifications. But how in the hell was I to know he was a major in the dark?"

"So you were sent to prison," Richard said.

"About ten days. They were waiting for the major's jaw to heal so that he could testify—but then our unit got orders to ship out, and I guess they thought the worst punishment I could get was to send me across the channel."

Johnson took a deep breath. He seemed to be forming some pictures in his mind. "You have to excuse me. I haven't talked about this in a long time."

"Take all the time you need," Jamie said.

"We got to Normandy in early August—went ashore at Omaha Beach. It had been two months since the invasion. Those guys—the ones who came on the beach in June—did the hard work. We could only imagine what it would have been like then. Our group got a lot more sober when we arrived there—a lot less horsing around. We knew we were going to be thrown against the Germans ourselves really soon. They told us they were going to put us in Patton's 3rd Army." A wry smile came to his face. "Sunbitch didn't wait for us." He looked at Jamie. "Sorry for my language."

"It's okay," she assured him.

"Patton had pushed the Germans halfway back across France, so the Army had to figure out how to get us to the line. They ended up putting us on boxcars—they were called '40 and 8's". On the side it was written in French '40 men or 8 mules'. The men laughed about that, but it was nervous laughter. I think men have a tendency to laugh when they're afraid—and we were all afraid, no matter how hard we tried to act like we weren't."

He looked at Jamie as if to ask if he should continue.

She nodded. "Go on."

"We got to the line the middle of September. No need to tell you everything except for the next two months we were continually fighting the Germans. Most of the fighting was in the villages but some of it was out in the field. The Germans would put up a fight and then fall back. We hated it when they fell back because that was when the shelling started. We hated that. A man with a gun can fight another man with a gun, but a man can't fight against those shells. It's an awful thing to lay in a muddy foxhole and hear those shells coming in. The trees would just explode around us. A lot of guys went over the edge during those days—they just couldn't stand the noise. Some took off running. Most of them got sent back to HQ for a few days and then they were sent back to the line—but they were never the same."

Johnson gave Richard a hard look. "I never ran."

Richard nodded, acknowledging the statement.

"The worst night was the night our division relieved an armored unit. When the Germans heard the sound of the motors of our tanks moving out and no sound of truck motors coming in, they figured it out. They weren't stupid. They laid in their artillery all night. It was an awful night. We could hear those shells above us and you never knew if the next one was going to drop on top of you. My company, I Company, was hit hard. We lost a lot of men that night. Some of them were just blown up in their foxholes. The Germans tried a counter-attack in the morning, but we were able to hold our position, but we took a lot of casualties— and there was a lot of confusion. I ended up fighting alongside K Company the next few days and when the

Germans had fallen back, Sergeant Patterson asked me if I needed help getting back to my company, but I told him, if it was okay with him, I would just like to stay with his platoon."

Richard interrupted. "So you were never officially a member of K Company?"

Johnson shook his head. "Nobody, during those days, when we were along the edge of the Siegfried Line, was really concerned with paperwork. We were just trying to stay alive."

His eyes took on a faraway look. "As far as the Army was concerned, I was always a member of I Company—and that is probably why I'm still alive today."

"Why do you say that Mr. Johnson?" Jamie asked.

He looked at Jamie and then at Richard and then back at Jamie. "Because there was somebody, who, if he knew there was a survivor from 2nd platoon of K Company, he would have killed me."

The look that Johnson gave Richard reminded Richard of the story he had heard a couple of hours earlier—how Johnson had almost killed a man forty years younger. *This is a man who would like to hurt me and he might be able to do so.*

"My throat's dry. All this talking has made my throat go dry. I'll get us some tea," Johnson said.

As Johnson turned away Richard looked at Jamie and shook his head, his expression demonstrating his skepticism.

"I'll go with you," Jamie said as she followed Mr. Johnson into the kitchen. She noticed his limp as he walked across the kitchen. He extracted ice cubes from a metal tray and dumped them in a plastic bowl. She looked out the window to the back porch. Several clay pots—none with flowers—were arrayed on the porch. She imagined that Mrs. Johnson had once kept those pots full of flowers. Only one tree disturbed the openness of the backyard—an apple tree in full blossom. Otherwise, the area around the house was open in a hundred yards in every direction. The field behind the house had been recently mowed and the yellow cuttings lay at angles across the clumpy green grass. A small garden plot with onions, lettuces and tomato vines made a neat rectangle behind the house. Near the apple tree was a root cellar with a shingle roof dug into the gently sloping hill. Concrete blocks formed the entrance with earth bermed up around it. Jamie looked around the kitchen while Mr. Johnson poured the tea. A crocheted tablecloth covered a table with aluminum legs. She brought Richard a glass of tea and the three of them took their seats.

"You mentioned St. Lautern, Mr. Johnson," Jamie said. "That's where my grandfather died. What happened there?"

He held his tea in both hands as he squinted his eyes. "Caught the Germans by surprise at St. Lautern. They had wired the bridge to the village with four 500 pound bombs. Their orders, we learned later, was to blow the bridge if we tried to go across. We fooled them though. During the night, we sent a small group across the river in rafts, about a quarter mile downstream. They killed the guards at the bridge and the rest of our company rushed across."

Johnson took a sip of his tea. "Some awful fighting that night. The Germans and us were packed in close. No battle lines, just house to house fighting. Our platoon was assigned the north end of the village. We caught some Germans trying to retreat up the main road that led out of town. We caught them in a little village—only a few dozen buildings—less than a mile out of St. Lautern. They were pretty disorganized and our bazooka guy threw some shells in their direction but they were not disposed to fight. They just ran. Some of us wanted to chase them down, but Sergeant Patterson knew better. He did not want us to get separated from the rest of the company. We stayed in place until the sun came up and I heard some commotion from some of our guys in the street. I went to see what they were talking about and I saw them milling around this truck. 'Hey, come look at this,' one of my buddies hollered. The truck had taken one of the bazooka charges on the passenger side and inside was a dead Nazi. 'Look at that collar,' my budd said. 'He's SS.' I looked and sure enough, he was wearing the gray uniform with the skull insignia stitched on it. None of us had seen an SS guy before. 'Wonder what an SS guy was doing here?' my buddy asked. 'Well, whatever the reason,' another guy said, 'it turned out to be a bad idea on his part.'

The truck was different from any German truck we had seen before. The top was not canvas. It was solid and the loading doors were padlocked. One of the guys had found a file and he was filing away on the lock.

Meanwhile Sergeant Patterson is on the radio. He's worried about our platoon being separated from the rest of the company. Like I said, we were less than a mile from St. Lautern, but it might as well have been a hundred miles if the Germans decided to counterattack. Our back is against the river. Sergeant Patterson is on the walkie-talkie, talking to some communications officer at HQ and he gives him the situation and he tells him about the SS officer and the truck. The communications officer tells him that we should sit tight and that he will come out right away. About that time our guys had cut through the padlock and they pulled the doors open."

"What did they find?" Jamie asked.

"Crates."

"Crates? What kind of crates?" Richard asked.

"Wooden crates—heavy, four of 'em with stencils on the side."

"What did the stencils say?" Richard asked.

"Reichsbank."

"The German national bank?" Jamie asked.

"We were ready to pop 'em open, but Sergeant Patterson stopped us."

Johnson looked first at Jamie and then at Richard—as if he were uncertain if he would continue with his story. He took a drink of his tea. A thin smile came to his face.

"One of our guys had found a salted ham in the basement of one of the houses—and some sauerkraut. We built a fire, made some coffee and had a little feast. Gosh, that ham was good. We hadn't had anything but C-rations for several days. Well, we ate that pork and that sauerkraut and then we fell asleep in the grass. Maybe an hour and a half later we hear this jeep roaring into the village. Had this lieutenant from HQ in it, driving it himself. He parks the jeep and hops out. His uniform is all clean and neat and starched and he's wearing this 38 caliber on his hip. 'Has Patton come to see us?' one of our guys snickered.

Anyhow this lieutenant looks at us and he's got his nose wrinkled up—and I have to admit we probably looked pretty bad. None of us had had a bath in a week. We're laying there in the grass and he looked at us like we had some kind of disease. Then he says, 'Don't any of you men know how to salute an officer?' Hell, we hadn't saluted anyone in a month. The officers on the line didn't want to be saluted. That was the best way to draw a sniper's bullet."

Johnson looked at Jamie. "You have to realize, all that military crap didn't mean anything when you were in combat. You fought and you obeyed orders because there were men depending on you—not because of military protocol.

Anyhow, this twerp stood there like he expected us to get up and give him a salute. So I stand up and give him what we called an 'up-yours' salute. I take my middle finger and bring it to my forehead and bring it toward him real slowly. The other guys get a big kick out of this and they are rolling around in the grass laughing. But this lieutenant—his face gets red and he looks like he is going to have a stroke.

Sergeant Patterson shows up, and being a better soldier than the rest of us, gives the lieutenant a proper salute. The two of them walk over to the truck and open the loading doors of that truck and this lieutenant goes inside. After a minute or two he comes out and he and Sergeant Patterson talk—but it's not a friendly conversation. I can't hear what they are saying but Sergeant Patterson is not happy. He's arguing with this spit-shined squirrel from HQ and that argument goes on for several minutes. In the end the lieutenant salutes Sergeant Patterson as if he is dismissing him. Sergeant Patterson pauses for a second, but then he returns the salute."

Johnson went quiet for a moment. Jamie looked at him as his mind went back to the memories forty years earlier. She tried to imagine him as a nineteen-year old young soldier lying in the grass with other young men like him—all caught in a horrible war.

"What's the word, sarge?" one of my buddies asked.

"We're staying put. We're to watch the German truck carefully. The lieutenant has left to get a truck to carry the cargo back to HQ."

"About two hours later, the spit-shined lieutenant returns. He has commandeered a two-ton cargo truck and he comes wheeling in and he backs it up behind the Nazi truck. Me and a few other guys come over to help move those crates. They were heavy. The crates had rope handles on each corner and it took four of us to move those crates."

Johnson paused again. He looked at both Jamie and Richard. He seemed reluctant to go on.

"One of those crates was damaged. We could see inside one corner. We all saw it. All four of us saw it."

"What was it, Mr. Johnson?" Jamie asked.

"Gold," he said, his eyes squinting. "Bricks of gold."

Jamie looked at Richard. She saw the skepticism in his face.

"What happened then?" Jamie asked.

"The sergeant and this lieutenant had another argument, but it didn't last long. The lieutenant took off in the two-ton. 'What are our orders, Sarge?' someone asked. We could tell the sergeant wasn't happy about the orders. 'Our orders are to hold this village until further notice.' Some of the guys groaned. We knew there were still some Germans in the area and we knew we didn't have enough men to hold them back. Those are the orders," Sergeant Patterson said. "Set up two-hour patrols along both roads coming into the village. I'm going to get on the radio to see if I can get us some support."

"Yes, sarge," we answered, but all of us were grumbling.

"'Let's take care of each other,' Sergeant Patterson said. And then he said it again. 'Let's take care of each other.'"

Johnson's eyes took a faraway look. He did not speak for several moments.

"Those were the last words I heard Sergeant Patterson say."

"What happened?" Jamie asked.

"A road ran through that little village from the north. Me and this guy Langston had guard duty on that side. Everybody called Langston 'Iowa'. All he could talk about was going back to Iowa after the war. We kidded him a lot about that. To hear him talk, Iowa was heaven. All he talked about was getting back to his farm in Iowa. He said he wanted everybody in the platoon to come visit him. Anyhow, me and him had patrol duty on the edge of the village. We found a spot in some bushes alongside a ditch that ran beside the road. We had been there about an hour when I thought I heard something. I stood up. Big mistake. I saw the muzzle blast and felt my leg fall out under me. A round caught me just below the left knee—just shattered the bone. It still bothers me. Iowa was hit too, twice—once in the leg and once across the edge of his shoulder, but neither round hit any bone. We returned fire in the direction of the muzzle blasts and the rest of the platoon showed and began to put up a fight. As long as the Germans fired at us, we kept shooting back. After a few minutes, there was a lull in the fighting and Sergeant Patterson bandaged my leg and Iowa's wounds as best he could. We didn't have a medic in our unit. I had lost a lot of blood and so had Iowa. Sergeant Patterson had some guys carry us to a house and put us in the basement.

Johnson looked at Jamie. "I said that the last thing I heard Sergeant Johnson say was 'Let's take care of each other.' I guess that's not entirely true. Just as they put Iowa and me in the basement, I heard him on the radio trying to contact HQ. '2nd platoon needs support! 2nd platoon needs support!' I heard him say. Then all hell broke loose. What I figured out later was that a full company of Germans who had abandoned St. Laurent had hid in the woods outside town. They didn't want to fight. They were trying to retreat, but they had to go through this little village to get to the road to the east. Like I said, they didn't want a fight, but our platoon was in the way of their retreat. It took them a while to figure out how few of us there were, but when they did, they came at us strong. Me and Iowa were both in the basement of that house. There wasn't anything we could do to help. The shooting couldn't have lasted thirty or forty minutes. German guns, American guns, but mostly German guns. Our guys were outnumbered. The shooting tapered off and finally stopped. Then we heard the German trucks coming through the village, headed east. We could hear the Germans talking as they went through the village. After a while it became quiet—absolutely, totally quiet. I hope I never hear such quiet again—not a bird, not a dog, not a machine. It's hard to describe how quiet it was. It seemed like all the sound had gone out of the world. Me and Iowa sat there for a long time—not saying anything. The sun went down and I heard Iowa whimpering. He knew what had happened. I knew what had happened. We knew everyone in the platoon had been killed. I knew Iowa wasn't crying about himself—but about the platoon."

Johnson paused again. His eyes were focused on something that Jamie and Richard could not see. The hum of the refrigerator in the next room and the 'tic-toc' of the clock on the mantle were the only sounds in the house.

"Your grandfather was a good man, Miss Patterson. He was a brave man. You should be proud of him. I'm grateful I knew him and I'm sorry you didn't."

Jamie nodded. "I know this must be painful for you, Mr. Johnson. Thank you for telling me. But what happened to you—and your friend?"

Johnson's eyes tightened. Jamie had the impression that he was no longer telling his story to her and Richard, but that he was reliving the story for himself. His voice was flat and emotionless when he spoke: "About daybreak we hear this motor. 'Sounds like one of ours—' Iowa says,'a jeep.' He hobbles up the ladder. My leg is so bad I can't climb the ladder. Iowa hollers back to me, 'Yeah, it's one of ours!'

Then I hear him holler 'Hey! Over here!' and I hear the jeep drive up and the motor cuts off. There's a little bit of conversation which I can't make out and then I hear a second pair of boots on the floor above. There's a little more conversation. I'm listening but I still can't hear what was said and then I hear two quick shots—a handgun—and a thump, the sound of a man falling to the floor.

It startles me. I don't know what is going on. I'm confused. Iowa didn't have a handgun. It must have been a German in the jeep, I tell myself. He must have shot Iowa. But I know I need to hide. I look around. There's a coal closet in the basement. I drag myself over there and pull the door closed behind me. I'm doing this as slow as I can, trying not to make any noise. Just as I close the door to the closet I hear footsteps near the basement ladder—and then the sound of the door to the basement opening, and then the sound of a boot on the top rung. Whoever it is— he's going slowly, testing the step. Then he takes another step, then another—all very slowly—and then onto the dirt floor. It's quiet and I know this guy is letting his eyes adjust to the dark. I'm laying flat on that dirt floor and I feel like my heart is banging against my ribcage. He walks in the direction of the closet. I try to control my breathing. There's a gap—maybe a couple of inches—at the bottom of the door and I see the boots coming toward me. They stop right in front of me. They are GI-issued. Those are not German boots. They're spit-shined! I recognize those boots. I saw them the day before. They are the same boots of that lieutenant! I'm sure of it, but I'm confused and I'm scared.

I'm afraid he is going to hear me breathing, or smell me sweating. Then I hear a shell off in the distance—and then another shell. This guy must have gotten worried about those shells, because he moved away from the closet—and then I heard him going up those steps, and a moment later I hear the jeep crank up and pull away.

It became quiet again. I waited a long time—or at least it seemed like a long time, and I crawled out of that closet and hollered for Iowa, but there was no answer. I drug myself over to those wooden steps and tried to pull myself up—but I couldn't do it. My legs started bleeding again. And then I just broke down and cried—I just bawled like a baby. Me, Mr. tough guy, just laying in that basement, my face in the dirt at the bottom of those steps, just heaving and crying with no shame. I guess I cried myself to sleep. When I woke up my face was caked in mud and there was a puddle of blood around my legs. And I suddenly realized how thirsty I was, but my canteen was less than half full. I drank a little of it, and I realized I had no way to get any more water. I tried again to get up those steps, but I realized I had lost a lot of blood and I'm really weak.

Anyhow I laid there all day just listening—but I didn't hear anything. That night I woke up when the mice were nibbling at my legs. I swatted at them all night, trying to keep them away. It was an awful night. The next morning I drank the rest of my water and tried again to get up the steps—but I couldn't do it. I sat there at the bottom of those wooden steps for a while— assessing the situation. I find a glass jar in the corner of the basement, and I break it into pieces and put a big piece in my pocket. I figure if I can't get up the steps by the end of the day, I will cut my wrists. Better to bleed to death than get eaten by rodents.

It was probably the middle of the day when I heard voices. They weren't American voices—they're German voices, but at that point I don't care. The worst thing they could do was to shoot me, I think, but maybe they will take me prisoner. I start hollering as loud as I can and in a few minutes I hear steps above and then the hatch opens. It's a German—but not a soldier. He's a local—a farmer. I put my hands up like I'm surrendering. He starts jabbering in German and then I see some other faces looking down at me—it's his wife and two daughters, teenagers. In a few minutes they have a piece of canvas they bring down into the basement and the four of them hauled me up out of the basement.

That family had a donkey and a cart, and they laid in some straw and we headed out of town, the wife and the daughters making all sorts of commotion about my injuries. Their farm was a couple of miles out of the village, and it appeared it had not been affected by the war. The farmer's wife cleaned up my wound, the girls watching, making faces. The farmer made a splint for my leg. 'Kein artz' he said. 'No doktor'.

And they fed me. Gosh, how they fed me. Eggs and potatoes and cheese and bread and turnips—and I ate it all. I was pretty woozy for a few days—I guess because I had lost so much blood, but my head began to clear and that splint worked pretty well. In a couple of weeks I was able to hobble about and help with the farm chores. Those two girls—they were 14 and 15— treated me like a big brother. They taught me some German and I helped them with some English."

Richard interrupted. "That was in March. The war was over in May, but according to what I read in the records, you did not rejoin the U.S. Army until September."

"And you want to know," Johnson answered, a bitter expression on his face, "why I didn't rejoin the army earlier? You're just like those Army idiots in Frankfurt. They asked me that question a thousand times. After I answered it a few dozen times, and they didn't believe me I told them to kiss my sorry—excuse me." he said, looking at Jamie. "The truth is I never rejoined. The Army found me. I didn't find them. I didn't want to find them. And I certainly didn't want them to find me. I would have stayed with that German family at their farm forever. I was safe there. They took care of me. They tried to keep me out of sight, but I'm sure some German farmer saw me, who told somebody, who told somebody else and eventually that information made its way to the Army."

He squinted his eyes again as the memory came back to him. "Anyhow, one morning—I was picking onions and the two girls were in the field with me when I look up and see a jeep headed our way, throwing dust as it came nearer. Right across the front, under the windshield, in big letters, it says 'MILITARY POLICE'. Even before those two big MP's get out of the jeep, I know it's over. I dropped my bag of onions and walked toward the jeep. There was no use prolonging anything. As I got near the jeep one of the MP's put handcuffs on me and the girls suddenly realized what was happening. They started screaming and wailing, but I didn't look up. I didn't want to make it worse than it was. I never got to say good-bye. That family saved my life. If it hadn't been for them, my sorry carcass would have been eaten by rodents in the basement of that village. You'll never hear me call the Germans 'Krauts'. That's what we all called them during the war, but you will never hear me say that again. That family saved my life."

"You mentioned Frankfurt," Richard said. "What happened there?"

"Put me in the stockade. Accused me of desertion. I told them what happened at St. Laurent—about the gold in the truck—and about Henninger. A couple of days later this Colonel shows up, but he's different from the lawyers. He talks in a very calm voice, asking a lot of questions about my time in combat. I'm not stupid. With that voice—like he's talking to a two-year-old—I realize he's one of the doctors from the psycho ward. I'm not stupid, and I'm not crazy either. But apparently somebody thought so, somebody decided I was crazy—at least crazy enough that they sent me to that psycho hospital. I was there for more than a year."

The man shook his head. "Some bad cases in that hospital—really bad cases, men so badly ruined they could never get well. It was awful to see those men, but—" He interrupted his thought. Anyhow, I guess the doctors got tired of me. I was certainly tired of them. They finally discharged me—a dishonorable discharge, but I didn't care. I was ready to come home."

"What about Henninger?" Richard asked. "You accused him of betraying the platoon and of killing Private Langston. Why didn't you bring charges against him?"

"The only way I was going to get out of that nut-house was to quit talking about Henninger. Any time I mentioned the gold or about Henninger killing Iowa, I could see their faces. They didn't believe me—so I quit talking about it. But I was not mistaken. It was Henninger. I recognized the spit-shined boots—and there's one other thing—"

Johnson got up and walked down the hall to a bedroom. Jamie and Richard looked at each other. They heard a drawer open and close. When Johnson came back he had a cardboard tube in his hand—the kind used for packaging hand grenades. He pulled the tube open and brought it over to Richard and poured the contents into his hand."

Richard looked at the two items in his hand. "Shell casings—38's?"

Johnson nodded. "When that German family carried me out of the basement of the house, I saw Iowa laying there, dead, two rounds in his chest. On the floor I found these—two shell casings, 38's. I picked them up off the floor. I've had them ever since. It don't prove anything—leastways to anyone but me, but I know Henninger betrayed our platoon and I know he killed Iowa."

"Mr. Johnson," Jamie said. "If you were able to do something to bring Harrison Henninger to justice, would you do it?"

Johnson rubbed his face with his hand as he considered Jamie's question. "I'm not the one. I wish I were, but no one believed me forty years ago and no one will believe me now. I owe your grandfather a debt, but I don't know how to pay it. You've seen my record—insubordination, striking an officer, desertion, Section 8 and a dishonorable discharge. Who would listen to me? Once I got to that hospital in the states, I quit talking about Henninger. I haven't mentioned his name to anyone in forty years—not until today."

The refrigerator motor clunked as it finished its cycle and went silent.

Richard and Jamie looked at each other, but Johnson was looking at the floor.

Jamie stood up. "Mr. Johnson. Thank you for your time. I'm sorry if we have intruded and I'm sorry if we have brought back painful memories."

"I wish I could help you, but I'm not the one. No one would believe me."

Richard was about to extend his hand to Johnson, until he saw the look on the man's face. He and Jamie let themselves out the door and down the steps. Jamie turned and waved at Mr. Johnson as they walked away.

"Bizarre story, huh?" Richard said as he put the car in gear.

Jamie didn't answer. She was slumped in her seat, her head straight ahead, deep in thought.

"It's not hard to see why he was a Section 8," Richard went on. "He fits a lot of the profiles of those suffering from PTSD. I'm not blaming him. I've read about dozens of cases like his. Men who endured the horrors of combat often cracked. A key part of my thesis statement is that *every soldier* who endured combat suffered some degree of what we now call PTSD. Some, of course, had it worse than others—but all had *some* symptoms." Richard shook his head. "But our friend Mr. Johnson seems to have a severe case— but then, what he endured was severe."

Richard looked over at Jamie who still had not spoken. She looked straight ahead, the expression on her face serious and fixed.

"Richard, I am going to tell you something. When I do, you may want to have me put in one of those 'Section 8' hospitals you mention." She took a deep breath. "I think Mr. Johnson is telling the truth."

Richard looked over at Jamie.

"I have hesitated to tell you about this but—" She explained her interaction with Henninger at the award ceremony. "When he heard my name, his whole countenance changed. It was odd how completely he changed. But that's not the only reason I have concerns about Henninger. When I began my research into his military records I found out that the writer in San Francisco who was doing a series on Henninger died tragically—they found his boat capsized in the bay. Then, your friend Dr. Kincaid, shortly after he started the research on Henninger, was killed in a hit-and-run. All of this sounds weird, and it all may be coincidence, but I don't think so—and it makes me worried about you Richard. I know it sounds crazy, but I am convinced that there was something wrong when I shook hands with Harrison Henninger, and he heard my grandfather's name. So there. Call the psychiatrist. Throw me in the loony bin, the nut-house, the wacko ward—whatever you want to call it. I fit your profile. Give me a Section 8, just like Mr. Johnson."

Richard did not respond.

"Richard?"

Richard took a deep breath and blew it out. "Listen Jamie. I think Henninger is bad news. He's bad for the country and he's bad for the world—and I appreciate your concern for me—"

"But do you believe me?"

"It doesn't matter what I believe. Think about it—what if we took these concerns to the authorities—the FBI, the CIA, the U.S. Army, whoever. What would you tell them? —that Harrison Henninger gave you a weak handshake? That a 60-something-year-old army deserter with a criminal history, certified as insane by a board of psychiatrists, who thinks his army buddy was killed by an army officer because he saw some boots he thought was the officer's—and all this happened because this mental patient saw a crate full of gold bullion."

Jamie sat tight-lipped, staring ahead. "We need more proof," she said. "I've changed my mind. I'm not going back to Duke tonight. I want to return to Washington. I want to look at those records more closely."

Richard turned his head to look at her.

"Are you looking at me," she asked, "for evidence of some psychosis?"

"No, and I'm glad to have you return to Washington, and I'm glad to help you with further research—but I'm not certain we will find any additional information."

"Perhaps not, but I want to look."

They rode several miles—neither of them speaking. The highway rose and fell in gentle waves through the countryside. Soybeans grew in tight straight rows near the road. Young corn, not yet waist-high, made green ribbons on the low rolling hills.

Jamie broke the silence. "What about records from the German side? Do the Germans maintain records from World War II?"

"Well, yes—"

"Can we check their records?"

"Sure. We'll just hop on a Concorde and zip over to Bonn—"

"No, smart aleck. Do you know someone in Germany who can help us? Surely in your research you have had a contact in Germany. Am I right?"

"Well, yes. I have a friend, Detlef—"

"Then, let's contact him and ask him to look into their records."

"To look into what records? What would the request be? What would I ask him to research?"

"The Reichsbank truck. Maybe there would be a record of a missing Reichsbank truck near St. Laurent around the dates of the capture of the bridge. If there were such a record, wouldn't that lend credibility to Johnson's story?"

Richard looked at his watch. "It's almost closing time in Bonn. I can send him an email tonight. Maybe we will get an answer in the morning."

"Why not call him right now?'

"Call him right now? But—"

"Don't you have an account at Moreland? Something that allows you to make international calls?"

"Well, yes I do. I've rarely used it—"

"Will it work over a pay phone?"

"I guess so. I've never used it on a pay phone, but it should work."

"Then, let's look for a pay phone."

Richard stood in a phone booth outside a truck stop and punched in numbers. "No answer," he told Jamie. "I'll leave him a message." He spoke slowly into the phone: "Greetings Detlef. This is Richard Roberts. Thank you again for your past help in the research for my doctoral thesis. I hope you are doing well. To the point: I need a favor. This is a somewhat urgent request for some information about a Reichsbank shipment in the proximity of St. Laurent, in the spring of 1945. The U.S. 108th was opposed by the German 18th Division at the capture of the St. Laurent bridge. I need information about a missing truck, possibly from a convoy carrying a Reichsbank shipment. I apologize for the urgency of this request. Thank you. I appreciate your help. It may be difficult to reach me by phone. Please send an email."

After Richard hung up, Jamie called the Holiday Inn and made her reservation for the night. Then she called one of her teammates and asked her to tell Coach Barton that she would not be back in time for today's practice, but that she would maintain the regimen that had been laid out.

As they got back in the car, Jamie reached over and touched Richard's arm. "I'm sorry. I can be bull-headed at times—"

"You know what I think would be a scary sight?" Richard answered. "I think it would be unnerving for some member of a women's track team to look over her shoulder in the final turn of a race and see Jamie Patterson closing the gap. That would be a scary sight."

Jamie smiled as she squeezed Richard's arm. "Thank you, Richard. Thank you for helping me."

"Let's do this," Richard said. "I will drop you off at the Library of Congress with a list of some books about stolen booty during World War II. Those resources will give you some background on the topic. I will run by Moreland for a moment and then pick you up back at the library."

THIRTY-SIX

TUESDAY, MAY 15, 3:30 P.M.

HENRY SAT IN the lobby of the Westin at Dulles International Airport. He was thirty minutes early for his four o'clock appointment with Henninger. Henninger's secretary had confirmed the appointment just the day before—and she had threatened him that he should not reveal that Mr. Henninger was in Washington.

A message at the desk was waiting for Henry when he arrived. It instructed him to wait in the lobby until he was summoned.

Summoned! I'm waiting to be summoned. That is my relationship to Henninger. I spend my time waiting for Henninger to summon me.

Henry thought it odd that Henninger was not staying downtown at one of the luxury hotels, but as Brent Arens had noted, Henninger's recent behavior had been unpredictable.

I guess he wants to stay near his airplane.

So Henry sat in the lobby—waiting for his summons.

He used the time to think about his future. He had quit trying to project how long he would be in prison— two years? ... three years? ... five years? Surely no longer than that. Whatever the duration, he needed a plan for life after prison. He couldn't go back to Sacramento. That wouldn't work. There would just be too much stigma for Myra and the girls. The house at the beach had possibilities, but what would he do for income?

He came out of his reverie long enough to look at his watch: 4:02. He went back to his thoughts.

At 4:20 the bellboy came over to Henry. "Are you Mr. Pursley?" Henry nodded. "Mr. Smith," he said, "the gentleman in the presidential suite, has asked you to come upstairs."

Henninger's secretary answered the door to the suite. She maintained the same expression of disdain she held at Henninger's headquarters. Henninger sat at the desk in the work area of the suite.

"Don't sit down," Henninger said, hardly looking up. "Take your sorry butt back outside and wait. I have something I want to send to that pathetic boss of yours. When I get that list typed up, you can take it to him."

Henry stood in the hallway for twenty minutes. The receptionist came out and handed him a 9x11 white envelope with the **HHI** logo on it. Henry took it, went to the elevator and downstairs where he found a taxi outside. Inside the taxi he opened the envelope. Only one sheet was in it. He read the text.

"Oh, my goodness," he said out loud.

THIRTY-SEVEN

TUESDAY MAY 15, 3:55 P.M.

JAMIE RAN UP the steps at the Library of Congress between the aqua-colored lamp posts at each side. *Control yourself. Save your speed for the race this weekend.* As she approached the great bronze doors, she was held up for a few seconds by a tour group receiving their initial orientation. She slid around the group and went through the doors to the Great Hall. She looked around. White marble walls, rising up several stories, defined the spacious interior. She was certainly not unfamiliar with libraries—but there was no library like the Library of Congress—more cathedral than library. She would have liked to wander around, walk through the corridors, let the aura of the place soak into her soul and give the building the appreciation it deserved, but she knew this was not the time. She stepped quickly through the center of the hall toward the Main Reading Room. Her eyes were caught by the allegorical paintings under the vaulted ceiling. She saw *Government* and *Good Administration* and *Peace and Prosperity*, but also *Corrupt Legislation* and *Anarchy*.

In the reading room, under the great rotunda, she found a vacant seat on the edge of one of the curved rows. Several dozen people, many of them with laptop computers, were at work in the room. The brass plate at her station read 170. She placed her legal pad on the desk and took the list of books she needed to the desk in the middle of the room. It was the list that Richard had compiled—related to World War II booty in Europe. She wished she could browse the stacks herself, but after all this was the Library of Congress, the biggest library in the world. She gave her list to the library attendant at the central desk and went back to her desk to wait. When she did, all her doubts came back. *What are you doing here, Jamie? Sitting in the Library of Congress researching a truckload of gold that went missing forty years ago? Why aren't you back at Duke getting ready for the conference championships?*

The attendant brought three books. Jamie flipped on the brass reading lamp and placed her pen on the legal pad.

Over the next hour Jamie was amazed to read the stories of stolen art, stolen jewels and stolen bullion that occurred during the war and shortly after. The Nazis were the worst culprits, appropriating billions of dollars worth of artwork, mostly from Jewish collections. Hundreds of caves were used by the Nazis to store the stolen loot—the most famous of which was the Merkers Salt Mine in Hungary where more than a billion dollars of gold, jewelry and art was discovered by personnel in the U.S. 3rd Army—only hours before the Russians arrived at the site. But many American soldiers were also offenders—on a smaller scale. They often appropriated "war loot" and simply mailed the items back to the states. A few Americans were more intentional; Norman Byne, appointed by the U.S. government to preserve European artwork, sold hundreds of works to private American collectors, enriching himself in the process. Kathleen Nash, a Captain in the Women's Army Corps, stole the Hesse crown jewels from Kronberg Castle and mailed them to various family members in the U.S.

At 4:05 Richard ran up the steps of Moreland Center, entered and waved to Louise as he headed to his cubicle—but she motioned for him to come to her desk.

"Give me a progress report," she said.

"A progress report?" Richard asked. "Are you making reference to any particular research project?"

"Listen, you big doofus. You know what I'm talking about."

"Aaah, you could be referring to research project 19840504A. Yes, that must be the inquiry you are alluding to. Was that a Miss Patterson who initiated that inquiry? Do I have the correct name?"

"Listen, you—" Louise started, but Richard put his hands on her shoulders. "Let me say this: a less professional research consultant might say that Miss Patterson is the most delightful, most attractive, most intelligent young woman that has ever inquired about services at Moreland Center. She is certainly the most delightful, most attractive and most intelligent young woman that an associate researcher could ever expect to encounter in his efforts to serve the American public. However—my being a purely professional researcher, I have noticed none of that. To me, she is simply case number 19840504A."

"Well, you big lug," Louise answered, "just in case you happen to notice any of those things, you might want to remember who it was who introduced you to case number 19-whatever."

Richard put his hand to his chin as if thinking. "Let me see if I can remember who that was. Now who was that?" He leaned over and kissed her on the cheek. "Thank you, Louise."

"Oh, by the way," she called to Richard as he hustled away. "The boss-man wants to see you."

"Sims, my supervisor? Is he back?"

"No, the big boss-man—Dotson."

"Dotson is here? This time of the day? And he wants to see me?"

"That's what his secretary said. There's a note on your desk."

As Louise had said, the note was on his desk. It was hand-written on Dotson's personal stationery and signed by his secretary:

Mr. Roberts,

Please call Mr. Dotson's office as soon as you return. He would like to speak with you as soon as you are available.

Doris Weatherly,
Personal Secretary to Director Dotson

Ugh—Mrs. Marjorie Adams Prescott must have filed a fresh complaint.

Richard made the call and the secretary asked him to come upstairs as soon as "his schedule would allow".

Ten minutes later Richard was seated in the director's outer office. He declined the secretary's offer of a cup of coffee. "Mr. Dotson will see you soon," she said. He began to formulate a defense for whatever accusation Mrs. Marjorie Adams Prescott had filed with the director. In the end, he decided that no defense was the best defense. He would just acquiesce to whatever the director recommended. *You have only a few more months at Moreland. Just keep Mrs. Prescott mollified until you can turn over her file to your unfortunate replacement.*

He looked around at the office. It looked more like an upscale Washington lawyer's office than a U.S. government office. It would have been out of place in almost every government building in Washington, but it was particularly out of place in Moreland Center, noted for being drab. Only on two other occasions had Richard been to the director's office—both times with a group. The first event was a reception for a retired four-star general and the other a retirement party for the associate director. He was struck again by the contrast between the meager furnishings on the floors below and the surroundings of this office. He sat in what he knew was an expensive wing-back leather chair which sat on what he assumed was a more expensive Persian rug. Chinese prints, and several large oriental vases completed the effect. The only incongruity in the decor was a series of photographs of Dotson with recent presidents. They seemed out of place—but in Washington such photographs were badges of prestige.

Richard thumbed through a copy of Architectural Digest while he waited. He chuckled to himself as he looked at the pictures and thought about his own apartment. *The Gainsborough portrait might look a little out of place alongside my Rolling Stones poster.*

After a few minutes the phone on the secretary's desk rang and she said, "Mr. Dotson will see you now."

As Richard entered, Spencer Dotson was writing on a pad. Richard had the impression that the man was trying to appear busy. He had been in the company of the man only a few times, but Dotson always seemed nervous. Many of the employees in the building made jokes about his absenteeism and his nervousness. "He's more comfortable around ceramics than he is around people," one of the research assistants had said. No one seemed able to explain how an assistant curator at the National Gallery of Art came to be the director of the Moreland Center.

"Ah, Roberts," Dotson said, rising from his chair. "Please come in." He pointed to a chair in front of his desk. "Please. Have a seat." He did not offer a handshake and Richard took a seat. The inner office was spacious and decorated in the same oriental motif as the outer office. The walls were rosewood. More oriental prints—larger than those in the outer office—hung in the panels. oriental vases, the height of a small person, were situated around the room, some of them exhibiting palms with flowing fronds. Jade and ivory pieces filled the spaces on the bookshelf behind the large desk. A large window looked out over the parking area to the surrounding trees and the row-house neighborhood.

"Roberts," Dotson said, looking at the pad on his desk. "Thank you for coming in on such short notice."

"It is not a problem, sir."

Dotson picked up a file folder on his desk and he took on a serious expression. "Roberts, I've been remiss in my failure to commend you on your work here at Moreland. I have your file here and it demonstrates exemplary effort on your part."

Somehow, I don't think you invited me here to pat me on the back.

"Sims' evaluation of your efforts is at the top of the chart. Here's what he says, 'Richard Roberts' expertise has been invaluable in the installation and maintenance of the new software system—' He goes on at some length commending you in that regard."

"Did he," Richard asked, "note my recommendation that the office needs upgraded hardware?"

Dotson nodded. "Yes, I think he did—but of course, we, like all the government agencies, suffer from the constrictions of budget constraints." He shrugged his shoulders. "I couldn't agree with you more. We certainly could benefit from having better computers, but until Congress approves an increased budget—"

Maybe you could sell a couple of vases. I'll bet one of these hogs would buy a few dozen new computers.

"Yes," Dotson went on, "we will certainly keep your recommendation in mind, but there is another issue I would like to discuss with you as well."

Aha. Now we are getting to the point. What is it that Mrs. Marjorie Adams Prescott, the purported descendant of John Quincy Adams, has complained about?

"Yes sir," Richard answered.

"It concerns your request for the Harrison Henninger file."

Oops. I had it wrong. It's not Mrs. Prescott.

"One of the things we have to be concerned about here at Moreland," Dotson continued, "is the potential abuse of personal files of prominent persons. You understand that, don't you?"

"I'm not sure I do."

Dotson seemed surprised by Richard's answer. He walked over to the picture window. He ran his hand along the lip of a large vase decorated by a red, entwined dragon. "We have a responsibility to those who have served their country and have subsequently entrusted their military records to their government— to Moreland Center for Military Records—to make sure that those records are not used in a manner harmful to the veteran. While that is true for every veteran, it is particularly true in the case of a prominent veteran, particularly a prominent veteran in the political arena. In those cases there is a greater possibility of distortion and—"

Why is this man so nervous? Richard asked himself.

Dotson continued running his hand over the lip of the vase as he looked out the window. "—it's our responsibility at Moreland to remain aloof from the political arena, to always maintain neutrality when approached by those with political motives. You understand that, don't you Roberts?"

"I suppose so, but I don't think there should be any concern about political motives in this request. The one who made the request is an undergraduate student at Duke, whose grandfather fought in the same unit as Harrison Henninger."

"Yes, I'm sure you are right. This young lady who made the request, did she do so in person?"

Richard suddenly felt uncomfortable. *How did Dotson know this was a young lady, not a young man? And why would he want to know if the inquiry had been made in person?*

"Initially by letter, then in person," Richard answered.

"I see," Dotson replied. "I'm sure what you say is true, and I'm sure this young lady has only the noblest intentions, but you understand why it's necessary for the center to take all appropriate precautions."

Why doesn't this man look at me when he's talking?

"However, with your assurance that this inquiry has no political implications, I'm sure I can arrange to have the file unlocked. I will attend to it personally—"

At that moment Dotson's secretary opened the door. "I'm sorry, Mr. Dotson, but that phone call you have been expecting has just come in."

Dotson's face had a pained expression. He looked at Richard, "I'm sorry—"

"It's not a problem," Richard interrupted. "I can wait outside."

Richard again declined the secretary's offer of coffee and began thumbing through more copies of Architectural Digest. The phone on the secretary's desk rang and she had a short conversation before she said to Richard. "Mr. Dotson apologizes for this interruption. He asks if you could come back this evening at eight to pick up the documents you need?"

"Eight? This evening?" Richard asked, not sure if he heard correctly.

"Yes. That's when Mr. Dotson said he would have your documents ready."

"Okay. Eight p.m it is. I will be back then."

Richard went by his cubicle and booted up his computer. He made a series of clicks with the mouse and waited for the internet connection to process. In a few seconds he heard the computer voice say, "You've got mail." He scrolled to the one he was looking for:

'Deadly@germgov.mail.bonn', his friend Detlef's email handle. Richard double-clicked the message and it came on the screen:

Richard,

I send you greetings from Bonn. I trust your doctoral program is going well. When you finish, you must make a visit to us here in Germany.

Concerning your request (there is no need for apology). However, I found no record of a Reichsbank shipment in the vicinity of St. Laurent in the spring of 1945 (or any other time). I will be glad to investigate further, but I am not hopeful that it would serve any purpose. Because of the various international tribunals' investigations into war reparations, the records concerning war booty are extensively researched and the records of bank assets are perhaps the best-cataloged of all the files. Also, this note: a bank shipment in that area so late in the war would have been unlikely. Reichsbank assets were moved away from the French/German border several months earlier.

This may not have been the information you were looking for, but I hope it was helpful.

Your friend,

Detlef

Richard double-clicked on the PRINT command and waited as the printer began printing the message. He felt oddly disappointed. He was sure that Johnson's story was preposterous and was the product of a mind distorted by the cruelty of combat—yet, unconsciously he had held some hope, perhaps for Jamie's sake, that the story had some credibility. But it didn't. That was obvious.

The printer read PRINTING COMPLETE. He stared at the message. *Yes, the printing is complete, and the inquiry is over. Is there some finality in this message? Is this a conclusion? Will Jamie Patterson go back to Duke and I will never see her again?*

It was 4:40 when Richard tapped Jamie on the shoulder. "Almost quitting time."

"Yeah, your little local library closes quite early," she said.

"Well, we can't have people in Washington reading books after 5pm," Richard said. "It would interfere with the cocktail parties."

"Richard, I had no idea about the looting at the end of the war!"

"It was probably much worse than is reported. The books report on only those who got caught. More than likely, a greater number got away with it. Europe was in a state of chaos at the end of the war. There is no telling how much gold and jewelry and artwork was stolen at that time. And there are still thousands of pieces of artwork that have never been returned to the families of the rightful owners."

"What's in your hand?" Jamie asked.

"Let's go outside," Richard replied.

Richard led them out the entrance and down the stairs to a spot near the fountain in front of the library.

"What is it Richard? You look serious."

He gave her the printed copy of the email and she began reading, mumbling some of it aloud: "… no record of any Reichsbank shipment … records are extensively researched … Reichsbank assets moved away …"

Jamie took a deep breath and blew it out slowly. "Well, I guess that is the end of that. I guess you were right about Mr. Johnson."

"I'm sorry," Richard replied.

"You shouldn't be—and I shouldn't be either. I suppose it means that Harrison Henninger is not a traitor and a murderer. For that we should be grateful. Richard, I'm sorry for the trouble I have caused—"

"No apology is necessary."

"You know what is odd, Richard? Do you know what is the most distressing thing about this wild goose chase? It all started with Harrison Henninger's handshake—and now I can't even remember the handshake. I've replayed it so many times in my mind that now I can't separate the event from the recollections. I can't remember the actual event. And then we have Mr. E.W. Johnson—the former resident of the Army's psycho ward—"

"Jamie—"

"No, let me finish. We have a diagnosed mental case who tells us a preposterous story about gold bullion and betrayal—and I believed it. I believed it because I wanted to believe it."

"We can't blame Johnson," Richard said. "A great number of American soldiers went over the edge during combat."

"No, I don't blame him. But I realize now how much I wanted his story to be true. It made my grandfather a hero and it seemed to explain everything—how he was in the wrong unit … the platoon was wiped out … why Henninger reacted to my name … and how he became a millionaire after the war. Richard, now I realize how foolish I was to—"

"Don't beat yourself up Jamie. And your grandfather is still a hero. That part of the story remains true."

Jamie nodded. "Thank you, Richard. I know you are trying to make me feel better, but now it's time for me to recollect myself. I need to get back to campus and get back to my life."

They were quiet for a moment. Along the sidewalk pedestrians passed quickly—some were tourists with maps in their hands, men in suits carrying leather briefcases, young women in walking shoes, carrying the high heels they had worn in their offices all day. A breeze blew some mist from the fountain behind them onto Jamie's arm. She chuckled as she wiped the mist from her arm.

"What's funny?" Richard asked.

"Oh, I was just thinking about you sometime in the future when you are a college professor and you're at some cocktail party and you are asked about your experiences at Moreland Center and you say, 'Well, there was this one incident—this college girl accused Harrison Henninger, the billionaire, of treason, and said he stole a truckload of gold from the Nazis, and her witness was this psycho who lived in the boondocks—"

"No stories," Richard interrupted.

"But it would be a good one."

"No stories."

They were quiet again for a moment before Richard spoke again. "Jamie," he said in a deliberate voice. "I'm not very good at this—" he paused. "Why do I feel like I'm in junior high asking for a date for the dance?"

Jamie smiled.

"What I'm trying to say, I suppose, is that I would like to see you again. That's the best I can do. If that isn't enough to sweep a girl off her feet, I don't know what will."

Jamie smiled again. She reached over and took his hand. "Richard, you have been delightful."

"Uh-oh, I'm in the past tense."

"You *are* delightful." She squeezed his hand. "And you have been patient and considerate—"

"Why is it," Richard asked, "that I feel like I'm not going to get that date to the dance?"

"Richard, I like you. I really do, but right now I am emotionally exhausted. In a few days I have a track meet. Soon after that I have to make a decision about my immediate future. I need to run my race; I need to go through graduation; I need to talk to my father; I need to curl up on my couch with my cat; I need to—"

"At least give me your address," Richard interrupted.

"Deal," she said, squeezing his hand again.

A little boy, perhaps seven years old, holding his mother's hand stopped near them, pointed and giggled.

At first Jamie thought the little boy was pointing at her and Richard, but then she realized he was pointing at the statue. She turned and realized how gloriously naked was Neptune and his sea nymphs, the water streaming over their stone bodies as the sea-horses pulled them through the small ocean. The mother pulled the boy along, but Jame felt strangely uncomfortable holding Richard's hands.

"Let's walk," she said.

He led her down the sidewalk in front of the Supreme Court building. "Richard, I'm ready to pick up my car. I need to get to the track for a work-out and then head back to Duke first thing in the morning. Can we walk to your place?"

"Sure, but what should I tell Dotson?" Richard asked. "He's holding Henninger's files for me. I'm supposed to pick them up at his office tonight."

"Do whatever you need to do. I have no need to see the files. I'm through with Harrison Henninger. If you want to look them over, that's up to you."

They took a route through a neighborhood similar to the one two days earlier. The row-houses, with shutters of blue, green and yellow, were trimmed by small flower-laden front yards, some tidy, some disheveled. They walked slowly along the uneven sidewalk, maple branches hanging over them. The conversation went away from Harrison Henninger and E.W. Johnson. They talked about many topics, including Richard's prospects for the teaching position at Colorado State.

"I just hope I don't get saddled with Friday afternoon classes, because I will have my backpack and camping supplies in my car, and I will be leaving for the mountains as soon as the bell rings in my last class."

"Maybe," Jamie laughed, "you could teach your last class in your hiking shorts and boots."

"Well, the department head might have something to say about that. I'll wait until I have tenure before I make any demands for class schedules."

Jamie realized she felt more relaxed than she had been in the last week, as if some burden had been lifted. *I'm glad to have this behind me.*

They came to an intersection and Jamie looked across and saw the parking lot of the Moreland Center.

"That's Dotson's car," Richard said, surprise in his voice. A late model cream-colored Mercedes was parked in the space closest to the back door. Richard looked at his watch. "Huh. It's 7:05. Maybe that file is ready now. If I could pick it up now, I wouldn't have to come back at 8:00. Do you mind if I run in and get the file before we go to the train station? We could stop by my apartment and take a quick look at the records."

"I don't mind," Jamie replied.

Richard went in the back entrance and Jamie strolled around the building. When she came to the front of the building, she laughed at herself. *When you came here less than 48 hours ago, you were determined to see Harrison Henninger's records. Now that you are about to get them, you don't even care.*

As she walked, her thoughts took her to her plans—*get back to campus ... run in the conference championships ... the NCAA is next ... then think about the Olympics ... and the Rhodes scholarship. One thing at a time Jamie. Don't presume on the future, Jamie. That's your father's advice.*

Richard found her on the steps when he came out. He had a pocket folder in his hand. "Is that the file?" Jamie asked.

"It is—but I wasn't sure Dotson was going to give it to me after all."

"Why not?"

"I don't know. He's always an odd bird, but he seemed even odder than usual. When I knocked on his door, he seemed startled. 'I thought you were coming at 8:00,' he said. I explained that I was walking by and saw his car and thought perhaps the file was ready. He seemed distraught—as if my coming forty-five

303

minutes early had upset his whole life. I saw the file on his desk. I asked if I could take it. He mumbled something that I took as assent, so I picked up the file, thanked him, and left him at his desk, distraught—like I had chipped his best Ming vase."

They walked across the parking lot and went down one block. When they reached the corner, Richard said as he took her arm. "Let's cross here,"

As they began to cross, Jamie looked down the street and suddenly stopped. "What's wrong?" Richard asked as he stepped back on the curb.

Jamie blew out a deep breath. "Nothing—except perhaps a recurring case of paranoia."

"What—?"

"It's nothing. I saw a black limo down the block, turning toward Moreland. I guess I can't see a black limo without thinking about Henninger and his blonde-headed goon. This city is full of black limos. I know that and I thought I was over this, but it may take a while."

Jamie looked over the photographs in Richard's apartment—situated over the detached garage of a large white frame house. Richard broke ice out of a tray and put the cubes in two glasses. "I rent this place for less than a third of what it's worth. The lady who owns it is gone more than half of the year—mostly on cruise ships. She says her husband would never take her anywhere when he was alive, so now she's making up for it. And she gives me a break on the rent so I can keep an eye on the place while she's gone."

"Your grandfather?" Jamie asked, pointing to a World War II portrait of a young man in a Marine uniform.

"Yes, that's him—and that's my dad beside him."

Jamie moved closer to see the photo of the VietNam era photo. "I see the resemblance." Next to that photo was a family photo of Richard in a high school graduation gown, his father in uniform, his mother and his younger sister. "Tell me about your sister."

"Kelly got married two years ago," Richard said as he handed Jamie the glass of water. "She married one of my Annapolis classmates—a Marine. At the wedding I told him to try to get shot as soon as possible so the family could carry on the purple heart tradition."

"Richard!"

"Yeah, I felt bad when he was deployed to Lebanon, but he survived—and didn't get shot. Hey, I know you need to go, but I want to take a quick look at Henninger's file."

Richard started reading. "Pretty dull stuff," he said. "Volunteered in 1942 … went to Officer Candidate School … received his commission … spent a year and a half at a desk job … then assigned to Colonel Cable's staff as a communication officer. That unit was sent to Europe in mid-summer 1944. Here are his test scores—all well above average. His physical performance was okay, but not exceptional. Colonel

Cable's evaluations of Lt. Henninger were all exemplary. Here's an AAR by Captain Marshall Adams: 'The securing of the St. Laurent bridge and the subsequent rout of the Germans on the other side was one of finest actions by the battalion during the push toward the Siegfried Line. Special commendation should go to Lt. Harrison Henninger, who, although assigned to HQ, came to the aid of his fellow soldiers in the field, fighting alongside the members of 2nd Platoon, K Company at the battle at the bridge, suffering what was considered a debilitating injury, but continued to engage the enemy troops, although fighting against overwhelming odds. As soon as positions are fortified I will recommend Lt. Henninger for the Silver Star.' There's a note," Richard said, "that Captain Adams was killed by sniper fire two days later."

"I think I've heard enough," Jamie interrupted.

Richard stared at the document, mumbling as he re-read a section.

"Is something wrong?" Jamie asked.

"I don't know. I've read dozens of these AARs, but this one is different. The language is odd. It's too smooth. This sounds like it was written by a public relations agent—not a field officer. And a silver star? Those are not easily earned."

"Oh, Richard. Have you caught a case of paranoia? I didn't realize it was contagious. Please, close that file and let's hope I never hear the name Harrison Henninger again."

"Well, I will close the file, but you may want to get used to hearing Henninger's name. There are some people who think he might get elected president."

"If that bleached-blonde gorilla who tried to look up my dress becomes Secretary of State, I will move to Costa Rica or somewhere else. I wish I could laugh about this—and maybe I will someday, but not now. I need to recollect myself. I feel like a complete idiot. This is all so out of character for me. I've always been little miss do-it-by-the-book. I never colored outside the lines. I always won perfect attendance awards in elementary school. I made straight A's and I always called home when I was going to be late. I've never done anything impulsive in my whole life and then two days ago—"

"I'm glad you had that one impulsive moment," Richard interrupted. "I'm glad I got to meet you."

"And I'm glad I have met you, Richard. I really am, but I need to go. Will you walk me to the train station?"

"Not until I get that address you promised."

"Pen and paper please."

Richard pulled a pad and pen from a drawer. "You know," Jamie said, "I will be at this address only a couple of more weeks."

"You'll have a letter before then. Count on it."

At the train station, Jamie bought her ticket from the machine and then began laughing.

"What's funny?" Richard asked.

"Remember, you promised—no stories. No stories about that goofy girl who—"

"No stories," Richard interrupted. "Scout's honor."

They were both quiet for a moment.

"Richard," Jamie broke the silence. She looked directly at him. "I am going to do two things: First I am going to thank you—as effusively as possible for your help—and then I am going to kiss you on the cheek. The thanks comes first. I am truly grateful—"

"I'll settle for the kiss."

Jamie smiled and then kissed Richard's cheek. She squeezed his hand and walked down the steps to the train.

Theo's face brightened when Jamie came to the front desk. "You're back."

"Yes, a change of plans. I called to make the reservation for another night."

"It was not a problem," Theo replied. "I put you in the same room as last night. If you need anything, just call."

"Thank you, Theo. I will drop off my bag and then I'm headed to the track for a workout."

A fine mist was falling when she reached the track. She pulled her cap down on her brow for protection. Except for one older man wearing a hooded raincoat, no one else was there. *It's Tuesday. Four days until the conference championships. I have to push myself today.* Coach Barton's pattern, which was the pattern the ancient Olympians developed, was to exert oneself four days prior to an event, and then, on succeeding days, conduct lighter workouts—letting the body recover.

She jogged two laps to get her muscles warm. The falling mist became a little heavier. She did her stretches and then ran one more lap just to be sure she was warm. She walked a lap and then set her watch for a 200 meter run. Her intent was to find the pace she needed for the 800 meters. She had run less than half the 200 meters when her internal clock told her she was running slow. She looked at her watch when she came across the 200 yard marker—a full second and a half below her needed time. *What is wrong with me?*

She walked a lap to catch her breath and then ran another 200. This time she made her goal, but she realized she had to push herself to make it.

The older man was still walking, impervious to the rain and to Jamie. He was considerate enough to walk on the outside lanes so as not to impede others. She walked two laps to get her heart rate down to normal. It was time to run a full 800 meters and she knew that Tuesdays and Wednesdays were the best predictors for Saturday's time. *Put everything else out of your mind. Concentrate on your running—nothing else—right now.*

She punched the button on her watch and started. She tried to find the pace she had established earlier. Her strategy had always been to establish a consistent pace for two laps. Others might have better sprint speed at the end, but Jamie's strategy—first taught by her father—was to establish an adequate lead so that no competitor could catch her on the final straightaway. *Consistency, Jamie. You've been known for your consistency. Where is your consistency now?*

Despite her cap, the rain covered her face. Her inner clock told her she was not on pace. She fought the impulse to speed up. She tried to keep relaxed, to stay with her pace. She finished the first lap. *Maintain your pace.* Water on the track spattered with each stride. She rounded the last curve for the straightaway. She pumped her arms higher. That was her plan for the final one hundred yards—to force her legs to keep pace with her arms. As she crossed the line, she punched the button on her watch and looked at it. 2:10.6 *Awful!* She groaned aloud. She bent over and heaved to catch her breath. Yes, the track was wet and yes that would cost a couple of seconds, but even so, she knew this performance was slow. She supported her shoulders with her hands on her hips, her chest heaving and her face in pain. The rain had become steadier and the older man had left the track. She was alone. She watched the raindrops create thousands of concentric circles on the red pebbled surface of the track. She suddenly felt discouraged. *What are you doing here, Jamie? Go*

home and go on with your life. Tomorrow you will be
back at Duke and everything will return to normal.

THIRTY-EIGHT

TUESDAY, MAY 15, 5:50 P.M.

BRENT ARENS, AS he sat in his office in the West Wing, looked over the article in the *Washington Post*. The headline said: "Henninger Cancels Again." The article went on to say that the organizers of the rally in Cincinnati had no information as to why the event was canceled. Some speculated that Mr. Henninger was ill, but his whereabouts, according to the writers, was unknown, although his private jet was not in its hangar. Brent Arens carefully refolded the newspaper and put it on his desk. He squinted his eyes as he considered what he had read. His political instincts were seldom wrong, and those instincts told him that Harrison Henninger had a problem.

What is it, or who is it, Mr. Henninger, that has jolted you off your course? Something has distorted your plans, Mr Henninger. You may be ill, Mr. Henninger, but I don't think it's a common virus. It's something else—and I really wish I knew what it was. Whoever is causing you this pain, I wish them well.

THIRTY-NINE

WEDNESDAY, MAY 16, 8:30 A.M.

THINK, JAMIE, THINK.

She surveyed the hotel room.

Do I have everything?

Her sleep had been fitful and she found herself unable to think clearly as she was getting ready to depart. She wore her running suit, thinking she would just go directly to the track when she arrived on campus. However, her mind would not turn loose of all the turmoil of the last few days. She zipped up her duffel bag, threw it over her shoulder, grabbed her car keys and opened the door to leave—but the hotel phone rang. She dropped the duffel bag and picked up the phone.

"Hello."

"Jamie."

"Richard, I—"

"Jamie, don't say anything. Just listen to me very carefully. I need help. I need to meet you as soon as possible.

"Richard, what is it?"

"Listen carefully, Jamie. I don't have much time. Dotson is dead. They found his body in his office this morning. I can tell you more later, but I need your help."

"But what—?"

"Jamie, Dotson is dead, and they think I killed him."

This traffic is horrendous, Jamie said to herself. *How do these people endure this every morning?*

She reviewed what Richard had told her: Park in the City Center deck; walk to the Library of Congress; meet him under Hawthorne. *Meet him under Hawthorne? What did that mean? I wish I had asked.*

She found a parking spot on the top floor of the deck, ran down the stairs and then walked briskly toward the Library of Congress. *Under Hawthorne? What does that mean? Maybe it's a street. If it's a tree, it better have a label on it.*

The normalcy of the activity around her—politicians, business people, tourists, —all going about their efforts, made her thoughts even more bizarre. *Richard—accused of murder!?*

The mystery about Hawthorne was solved as she approached the library. Above the portico she saw the busts of Demosthenes, then Emerson, then Irving. *Aha. Hawthorne that's what—*

"Ah!" The hand on her arm startled her. "Richard! You scared me." He had been standing inside an alcove on the lower level of the front entrance. He wore an oversized jacket that said "Ron's Janitorial Services" and a baseball cap—pulled low on his brow. His laptop bag was on his shoulder.

"Richard, what is going on?"

He took her arm. "Let's walk."

They walked quickly at first, but then Richard put out his arm. "We're walking too fast. We need to slow down. We don't need to draw attention to ourselves."

"Richard—"

"It's Henninger. I'm convinced of it. You were right with your first impression. I understand it all now. It's Henninger. He's behind all this."

"Why? —"

"There's no time to explain about Henninger. Let me tell you about the current situation."

"Please do."

"When I arrived at Moreland this morning, there were half a dozen policemen in the lobby. They were checking ID's and wouldn't let anyone on the elevators. I asked one of the girls in the lobby what was going on and she said, 'Mr. Dotson is dead. They say someone killed him. His head was crushed. It's awful.' All of Moreland's employees were in the lobby. The police were checking ID's, asking questions and herding everyone to the auditorium on the main floor. I looked across the lobby and I saw Mrs. Weatherly, Dotson's secretary, talking to a policeman. She looked in my direction and the policeman did too, and he took a step in my direction. Then it hit me—I was in Dotson's office last night—and his secretary knew that!"

"How—?"

"I slid along the wall and headed toward the hallway that leads to the back door. The policeman hollered at me to stop. He started pushing his way through the crowd. I ran by the elevator and pushed the button for the top floor, hoping to distract the policeman, but I went into the custodian's closet. I left my coat and tie there and took this jacket and cap. It was the best I could do for a disguise."

"Where are we going?" Jamie asked.

"I will show you, but listen, I've had time to think about this and it all makes sense now. It's Henninger who killed Dotson—more likely his bodyguard did the dirty work. And he had the others killed also—the reporter from San Francisco, Dr. Kincaid, and now Dotson. Everyone who has gotten close to his records from World War II—has been killed. No doubt I was on the list also. Henninger planned to kill me and Dotson together last night. He was the one who told Dotson to have me come to his office at 8:00. When I showed up early, Dotson was perturbed—but he didn't know Henninger's purpose for the meeting."

They went by the Library of Congress and turned onto the sidewalk of Pennsylvania Avenue.

"Richard, where are we going? Shouldn't we go to the police?"

"Not to the police. I need to get online. I need to check the records. I need to find a phone jack I can use."

None of this made sense to Jamie, but she didn't know what questions to ask.

"Walking too fast again," Richard said as he checked himself.

Jamie saw the White House directly in front of them. "Let's turn here," Richard said as they came to 15th Street. The White House was on their left when they turned. "It's only a few more blocks to the Carlton."

"The Carlton?" Jamie asked.

"The Carlton Hotel. I can find a phone jack there."

FORTY

IF JAMIE AND Richard had been able to hear what was being said in the Oval Office as they passed by—they would have heard a tense exchange between the four men in that office.

"Blackmail! This is blackmail!" President Cavanaugh had the reputation of a calm demeanor, but his voice, at this instance, was harsh. He crumbled the sheet of paper in his hand and threw it on his desk. It bounced off and fell to the floor of the Oval Office.

Don't shoot the messenger, Henry Pursley thought. *The messenger just brings the message. The messenger doesn't write the message.*

The atmosphere in the Oval Office—with every visit Henry made—seemed to deteriorate. James Olmstead sat in his customary seat studying his copy of the document, while Brent Arens stood at the window examining a copy of the same document.

The president looked at Henry and asked for verification: "Does he actually think I will sign this document—this guarantee that the Pacific Rim Commission cannot change its bylaws? He wants my signature?" He picked up the document from the floor and began opening it.

"Yes," Henry replied, trying to remain matter of fact. "That is my understanding. The specific wording calls for the guarantee that—" Henry began reading from the document, '... you will never use the powers of the presidency, including the powers of executive orders or any other similar presidential powers, to alter, change, revise, adjust or countermand the provisions, stipulations or agreements of the said original charter of the Pacific Rim Commission—"

"Look!" the president said. "The arrogant you-know-what has already put my name at the bottom!"

"And dated it with today's date," Olmstead added.

"How did he know, Brent?" the president asked. "How did he know what we planned?"

"I can answer that question," Olmstead replied, "He knows what we planned because he is an unprincipled and devious S.O.B. and that is how such people think."

Henry saw a flush of red come up in Brent Arens' neck, just above his white starched collar. He turned to Olmstead as if he were going to say something, but restrained himself.

"Is that all, Henry?" The president's voice seemed fatigued.

"Actually, no. There is another document." Henry pulled a folder from his valise. He gave copies to all three men.

The president stood by his desk as he read the document. A perplexed look came on his face. "James, what do you make of this?"

Olmstead shook his head. "Odd-he wants an executive pardon, in advance 'if implicated for any real or imagined accusation of previous illegal activity.' There's a lot of legalese here, but essentially he's asking for *carte blanche* to be pardoned for anything in his past history."

"Brent?" the president asked. Arens was still standing at the window, studying the document. "What do you make of this?"

Brent Arens continued to look out the window. "I'm not sure—but it seems our Mr. Henninger is worried about something?"

The president sat down at his desk, shaking his head, the two documents in front of him. "I don't know. I just don't know. I don't see how I can sign these documents. I just—"

"Do you want to be president?" Brent Arens said without turning from the window.

"Excuse me?" the president responded.

"Do you want to be president?" Arens repeated, as he turned toward the president.

"Of course I do, but—"

"Then sign the papers," Arens said firmly. "If you want to be president, sign the papers."

"But—" the president started.

"It's very simple," Arens interrupted. "If you want to sit in that chair next year at this time, you need to sign the papers. Otherwise, Henninger will throw his support to your opponent. He will win the election and *he* will be the one sitting in that chair next year."

The president looked at James Olmstead who had nothing to say. He turned to Henry. "Is that all, Henry?" the president asked.

"One more thing—Mr. Henninger wants a purple heart."

"A purple heart? Henninger wants a purple heart?" the president responded, incredulity in his voice.

"He claims," Henry said, "that he should have received a purple heart during the war. He wants one now—by tomorrow night when he gives his speech." Henry decided he would not report Henninger's actual words: "Tell that spineless excuse for a politician that he should be grateful I don't ask him to personally pin it on my chest." Some things, Henry knew, are better left unsaid.

The president looked at James Olmstead in such a way as to ask if such a thing could be accomplished— that a purple heart could be arranged on such short notice. Olmstead nodded.

"So—" the president said, "—if I sign these two documents … and if I get him a purple heart—"

"Then," Brent Arens interrupted, "Henninger will endorse you for president and you will win the election by a wide margin." He walked over to the president's desk, pulled out a drawer, took a pen from it and handed it to the president.

Wilson Cavanaugh, the president of the United States, took a deep breath, looked around the room, making eye contact with both James Olmstead and Henry Pursley. Henry heard the president mutter

Henninger's name and some obscenities as he signed the two documents. When he finished, he pushed the two documents across his desk toward Henry. When Henry reached for the two pieces of paper, a jolt went through his shoulder. He put the two documents in a folder and put the folder in his valise.

We're all going to prison. All of us. I know we are.

FORTY-ONE

BELLMEN IN SILVER vests and black bowties looked at them oddly as they came to the entrance of the Carlton Hotel. "Act like you belong here," Richard said, "Let's go in."

"I thought you were looking for a private place. This is private?"

"It's the best I can do right now."

The Carlton Hotel is a Washington landmark, one of a few key sites around the city where the powerful—and those hoping to become powerful—gather for lunch or drinks. Lobbyists, out-of-town businessmen and foreign dignitaries often choose the Carlton in Washington and a great many decisions affecting millions of people have been made among the leafy palms surrounding the numerous alcoves of its lobby.

"Richard, I'm wearing a running suit. How can I look like I belong here?"

"Well, I'm wearing a janitor's uniform, but we won't be here long."

Strains of Mozart filled the lobby. A few Asian men in western business suits sat together at a table; two African women in bright print dresses stood at the reception desk. A tall Arab in a white thobe and red keffiyeh talked with some Westerners. Several other discreet conversations were taking place alongside the marble columns and potted plants, for this was the place where a great deal of international policy—at least in its preliminary phases—was shaped. Here and in a couple of other hotels in the city, these private sessions between middle-level leaders would become the groundwork for broader sessions among higher-ups in the chain of authority, which would lead to official appointments among "decision-makers" which would lead to legislation and agreements and contracts, and as a result politics and business would continue and there would be more meetings in the lobbies of Washington's hotels—and the world would go on.

Richard led Jamie to an unoccupied alcove. A potted ficus tree sat next to a marble topped table along the wall. An old-style telephone sat on the table. An array of chairs and a couch fitted snugly into the space insulated by ferns and small palms.

As they sat down a bellman came by and gave them a condescending look, and Jamie offered a weak smile. As he walked away Jamie said, "I think someone is concerned about the riff-raff in the lobby," but Richard did not answer—he was unzipping the bag with his laptop.

"What are you doing?" Jamie asked as Richard unplugged the phone jack from the phone and plugged it into his laptop computer. Richard ignored the question as he began punching the keys on the laptop. After a moment Jamie saw Richard's face as he read something on the computer screen, the green screen reflecting off his glasses.

Richard blew out a long breath. "Look at this," he said, turning the laptop toward Jamie. "It's from Detlef."

Hello Richard:

Greetings again from Bonn. After I sent the previous message I had another thought. Your request was for a record of a German gold shipment in the St. Lautern area, which of course is along the French/German border. It occurred to me that I should run a search for a French gold shipment—which is a separate category as far as the records are concerned. When I made that search, I found that indeed there was a missing shipment of gold. However, the gold was from a French bank, not a German bank. A convoy of five German trucks, ordered to relocate the gold, left Talange, France on March 1, 1945 as the U.S. 3rd Army approached. That convoy arrived at the storage center in Merkers on December 8; however, one of the five trucks in the convoy failed to arrive. There is an extensive file on this subject, which I will be glad to send you. The gold from the other four trucks was eventually returned to the French government in 1946, but the issue of the one missing truck was never resolved.

Have you by chance found the missing truck? If so, perhaps you will send your friend in Bonn a gold bar or two. Ha Ha. Just a little joke.

Detlef

Richard took the laptop from Jamie. "I need to check the Moreland files."

"Do you have to do it here?" Jamie asked. "I feel out of place."

"It won't take long," Richard answered as he began typing.

As Richard typed, the bellman returned and paused long enough to look through the palm fronds in their direction.

Jamie took the phone receiver from its cradle and began talking loudly enough for the bellhop to hear: "But Daddy, *must* we go to the Riviera again this summer?" she whined. "You know how I dislike the servants at the villa. Their English is so poor. It does seem like someone would send them to a *proper* school. And why did you send me to Washington with Brother? He is *such* a bore. He insists on visiting all the dreary historical things and writes about them in his computer."

She peeked at the bellman through the corner of her eye. He was looking at the phone in her lap with a puzzled look on his face. And then she realized what the bellman was looking at— the phone line was not attached to the phone. Her charade was exposed. She looked up. The bellman was gone.

"Uh, Richard, we need to leave."

"Look at this," he answered.

"Look at what?"

"Look at the screen. Henninger's file is no longer there." Jamie looked at the screen: **NO RECORDS MATCH THIS REQUEST.**

"Can we talk about this somewhere else?" Jamie asked. "I think the management is about to evict us. She pointed toward the lobby where the bellman was talking to a security guard and they were both looking in Jamie and Richard's direction.

Richard zipped the laptop into its case. "Follow me. There's another way out." He led her out the back through a courtyard and out the wrought-iron gates. Richard looked back. No one was following.

"How did Henninger's file disappear?" Jamie asked.

"Henninger must have had Dotson remove the file. It now makes sense. Henninger had Dotson remove the file. He arranged the 8pm appointment last night with the intent of killing both Dotson and me. And the email from Detlef confirms what Mr. Johnson said—"

"Mr. Johnson!" they said in unison. They looked at each other, realizing that he also was now certainly on Henninger's list of those to kill.

Despite Richard driving 80 most of the way, it took them two and a half agonizing hours to get to Jenkins Ridge. They passed through town, past Caruthers Convenience Store, then out of town on Highway 22.

They came near the turnoff, Jamie shouted, "Richard, look!" A plume of smoke rose up into the open sky.

Richard put on his signal to turn left on Porters Mill Road. As he did, a gray sedan pulled out and turned right onto the highway.

"Richard, that was Blondie!" Jamie screamed.

Richard drove as fast as he could on the narrow gravel road. Both he and Jamie were jostled around as the car's wheels bounced through the ruts in the road. They went by the abandoned sawmill and then to the clearing.

The house was on fire.

Richard turned up the driveway. The wheels threw gravel behind them as he accelerated. He threw the Civic into park and ran up to the house. He tried to open the door, but the door handle was too hot to touch. He ran around to the back and Jamie followed. "Mr. Johnson! Mr. Johnson!" she called. Richard found a rock and smashed the sliding glass door. He put his head in and shouted, but drew back choking on the smoke. The fire gained in intensity and began to pour through the roof. They backed away from the heat. Jamie began crying and Richard put his arm around her. The fire hissed and popped as they stood watching the orange flames gather in intensity as gray-black smoke curled up into the air. Jamie shuddered. "It's my fault! It's my fault!"

Richard put both arms around her. "I should have left him alone," she cried. The roof collapsed and fell with a crash throwing millions of sparks into the sky.

Jamie buried her face into Richard's shoulder, crying again. "I should have left him alone," she repeated.

Both of them jumped when they heard a loud metallic sound behind them. They turned to see the open door of the root cellar and Mr. Johnson, shotgun in hand, emerging. "Sunbitch burned me out," he said.

FORTY-TWO

HENRY LEFT THE White House, but he did not return to his office. There was nothing for him to do there, so why go? He came to Constitution Avenue and turned left—away from the Lincoln Memorial. *Am I afraid to have you look at me again, Abe? Am I afraid that you will ask me all the questions I do not want to answer?*

Dozens of government officials hurried by him, hustling to get to their lunch appointments, but Henry had no appointment, and he wasn't hungry. He rubbed his shoulder. The dream last night had been more intense than usual—careening down the icy slope, faster and faster, the enormous tree in front of him coming closer and closer—. He awoke to Myra's hands on his arm as he sat upright in bed. "It's okay, Henry," she said. "It's just a bad dream."

I wish that were true. I wish it were just a bad dream—but it's not. It's more than that.

The plans were made. Brent Arens would keep the documents the president had signed until Friday. On Friday afternoon Henry would take those documents to RFK Stadium and meet Harrison Henninger just before he made his culminating speech in his "War on Washington." If all went well, Henninger would accept the documents … *Why wouldn't he?* … and announce in his speech that he was now endorsing Wilson Cavanaugh for president—who would subsequently be re-elected. Henry did not look forward to that meeting with Henninger, but he hoped it would be the last one.

What then? What happens after Henninger gets his agreement?

FORTY-THREE

RICHARD, JAMIE, AND Mr. Johnson were driving toward Washington on the interstate. Mr. Johnson sat in the back seat, his hands in his lap as they drove. "I heard a car go by," he explained, "but I didn't think much of it, but then a few minutes later I see a guy coming up the driveway with a gasoline can in his hand and a rifle slung on his shoulder."

"What did he look like?" Jamie asked.

"Big guy. Really big—with a blonde crew-cut."

Jamie and Richard looked at each other in acknowledgement. "I grabbed my shotgun and came on the porch and hollered at the guy. He took his rifle off his shoulder and fired. That bullet whistled by my ear and tore a hole as big as my fist in the front door. Well, I realize my 12 gauge wouldn't hurt him at that distance, so I jump inside the house. I go from window to window trying to get a shot at this guy, but the next thing I know is I smell smoke. The house is on fire. I know I'm in real trouble. I went out the back. I didn't see the big guy so I got in the root cellar. I sat there for a while with my shotgun pointed at the door just waiting for that guy to open it, but he never did. I waited a long time. Then I heard the two of you."

He went quiet for a moment. "Sunbitch burned me out."

"Mr. Johnson," Jamie said, "This is all my fault."

"No ma'am. It is not your fault. It's Henninger's fault. He's the one."

"Mr. Johnson," Richard interrupted. "I need to apologize—for not believing you previously. Yes, Henninger is behind all this. I realize that now."

Johnson did not seem to hear the apology. "I'm burned out. Everything I had is gone."

They drove in silence for a few moments until Richard spoke: "We need to find a place to stop. We need to gather our thoughts."

"This will have to do," Richard said. They were an hour outside Washington. He was parked under a sign with a giant green cloverleaf that said, "Cloverleaf Motel" and underneath it the "VACANCY" light was visible. It was a one-level facility, probably built right after World War II. Aluminum chairs, painted dark green to match the color of the cloverleaf, sat beside each door of the same color.

"Not exactly the Carlton, is it?" Jamie said.

Richard stayed in the car while Jamie checked them in. She got two rooms, one for her and one for Richard and Mr. Johnson.

Mr. Johnson had not spoken for the last thirty minutes of the drive, and he had a faraway expression when Richard led him to the room and suggested he lie down and rest. Richard and Jamie went into her room next door and Richard plugged in his laptop. "I've had another thought," he said.

Richard pointed to the screen and started to say something, but the proximity of Jamie's face so close to his made him lose his train of thought momentarily. "Here," he said, getting up from the chair. "Sit here and you can see better."

Across the top of the screen, she saw "**The Moreland Center—Director's Private Files**". "How did you get access?" she asked.

"When I helped install the new software a few months ago, I had to dump all the passwords for the various systems at Moreland into a file. No one ever asked me to delete that file, but I had forgotten about it until just now—so I was able to get into Dotson's private files."

"And—?"

"I'm not sure what to make of this. Look at this page. It's a list—maybe two dozen files—each with an odd name: 'Water Warrior', 'Drag Queen', 'Limp Wrist'—"

"What—?"

"I think," Richard interrupted, "these are files for individuals—with code names—files that only Dotson accessed."

"But why—?"

"Why would Dotson keep such files? To cover his back. This is Washington. Suppose a reporter or a congressman requested the records of one of these men. Dotson could provide the public file, but he would always have the private file available—"

"Blackmail," Jamie said.

"Exactly," Richard responded.

"What do the files say?" Jamie asked.

"That's the problem," Richard replied. "Look at what happens when I request those files." **ON SITE ACCESS ONLY** popped up on the screen. "Dotson was smart—smart enough to make sure these files could not be accessed remotely. I can't get to the data remotely. The information we need is resident on Dotson's personal computer.

Jamie turned around slowly. "Richard, surely you are not thinking about—"

"It's the only way. It's the only way we can get to Henninger's records and it's the only way I can prove that I did not kill Dotson. I have to get into Dotson's office."

"Oh, Richard. Are you sure? Surely—"

"There's no other way. I need to get into Dotson's computer."

"But how? How will you get into his office?"

Richard reached in his pocket and pulled out a key. "I have Dotson's key. I've had it since I installed that software a few months ago."

"I just don't know about this, Richard. I just don't know. I'm overwhelmed right now. Last week I was more or less an average college senior about to receive a diploma. Now I'm at a low-end motel with two men—one of them a former psychiatric patient and the other a murder suspect. And we are discussing the possibility of breaking into a government building—"

Richard interrupted. "Likewise last week I was a faceless government employee whose greatest worry was mollifying Mrs. Marjorie Adams Prescott of Stone Mountain, Georgia. Also, last week Mr. Johnson was living in his own house and minding his own business. And last week Dr. Kincaid was alive, as was Dotson—but all of that has changed, Jamie. All of that has changed."

Jamie was quiet for a moment and then nodded her head. "You're right. All of that has changed—and Harrison Henninger is at large and is a threat to this country. Count me in—but in the meantime I need something to eat. I saw a diner just down the street. I will bring sandwiches for all of us."

When Jamie returned, Richard had the Gideon's Bible in his lap. "I know we need inspiration," she said, "but—"

"I just thought of an ancient parallel to Henninger's actions at St. Laurent. Do you remember David and Bathsheba?"

"Of course. In fact, my pastor preached on that passage recently."

"Here's the key part. David, in his effort to cover up his sin with Bathsheba, decides he must kill her husband, Uriah the Hittite—but not directly. He sent a letter to Joab, the commander of the army. Let me read it: 'Place Uriah in the front line of the fiercest battle and withdraw from him, so that he may be struck down and die.'" Richard closed the Bible. "Do you see the parallel? Henninger exposed the 2nd platoon to the enemy. He left them vulnerable to the enemy. He did that—like David—to cover his own sin. The difference is that David's sin was lust; Henninger's sin was greed."

Jamie nodded. "We need to check on Mr. Johnson and give him this sandwich."

They found Mr. Johnson sitting on the side of the bed, eyes squinted, deep in thought. "Mr. Johnson," Jamie said. "I've brought you a sandwich."

He did not respond at first, still in thought. "I can't remember those two names," he said, without looking up.

"Whose names, Mr. Johnson?" Jamie asked.

"That PFC from New Mexico and the corporal from Michigan. I promised myself I would never forget any of those men from 2nd platoon, but I can't remember those two names."

Less than thirty minutes later the three of them got into Jamie's car to drive to the city. Mr. Johnson remained quiet in the back seat the entire time. Several times Jamie turned around in her seat to check on him, but he seemed deep in thought.

"The cleaning crew will finish by 9:00," Richard told Jamie, as they approached the area near the Moreland Center. "You and Mr. Johnson can watch from the car—"

"Mr. Johnson can watch from the car. I'm going with you. You will need me inside to watch out for you while you look for the files."

"Okay," Richard answered. "It probably will not do any good for me to argue with you."

At 8:45 Richard parked the car across the street from the Moreland parking lot at the back of the building. They rolled down the car's windows. The air outside was still. A few crickets chirred under the big oaks. "There's no cleaning crew tonight. That makes sense. The cops have probably sealed the doors. Still, let's wait a few minutes before we go in."

Jamie tried not to admit how nervous she was. *You are about to break into a government building—with a murder suspect!*

"Mr. Johnson, are you okay?" Jamie asked.

"I still can't come up with that name," he answered. "I promised myself I would never forget those names."

Richard and Jamie looked at each other, their concern for Mr. Johnson evident in their faces.

"Mr. Johnson," Richard said, "I need you to move up front to the driver's seat. If you see anyone pull into the parking lot—or enter the building—I need you to flash the headlights. Can you do that?"

He seemed to have trouble processing the request, but he said, "I can do that."

Although they tried to stay out of sight by skirting along the shrubs surrounding the parking lot, the lights seemed like searchlights. She had felt courageous when she told Richard she would watch the doors for him, but now her courage had failed. They came to the back door. Jamie looked around the parking lot and back at her car where Mr. Johnson sat in the driver's seat. She felt totally exposed as Richard put the key in the lock. The sound of the bolt turning seemed like the sound of a sledgehammer. Richard opened the door, stepped in, and motioned for Jamie to come inside. They walked slowly to the stairs and started up. At each landing Richard paused to listen.

When they reached the top floor, Jamie realized she was out of breath. *Must be the tension.* The sound of her breathing seemed to echo down the staircase. The only other noise was the low hum of the exit lights. They made their way down the hall and came to the door of Dotson's outer office. Yellow police tape was strung across the heavy door. Even in the dim light she could make out what it said: DO NOT CROSS. Jamie inhaled. *A man was murdered here last night!* That realization hit her anew and she also realized she was about to violate the tape's message. She was going to cross. Richard opened the door and slipped under the tape, then reached back to take Jamie's hand to help her under.

They walked by the secretary's desk to the door to Dotson's office. More yellow tape. DO NOT CROSS. Richard opened that door, and they slid under the tape.

"Check the window," Richard whispered. "See if you can see Johnson." Jamie nodded and went to the window. Below she could see the well-lit parking lot and across the street she saw her car. The headlights were not flashing. She gave a thumbs-up sign to Richard. As she turned back to the office, Richard took a seat at Dotson's desk. Even in the dim light she could see the chalk outline the police had drawn around Dotson's body and the bloodstains around the outline. *A man was murdered here last night!*

Richard booted up Dotson's computer. His face turned green with the glow of the monitor. The computer seemed unusually loud as it whirred to life. Richard started typing. Jamie looked outside again. No flashing lights on her car. *I hope Mr. Johnson is alert— and I hope this doesn't take long.*

"Ah!—" she gasped as the printer in the outer office came on.

"Sorry," Richard said. "I'm printing a file. I think I found something."

He turned off the computer and went to the printer in the outer office, motioning Jamie to follow him. "Look," he said, taking a page from the printer tray. He pulled a penlight from his pocket and pointed to the page "It's a list of coded names in a special file."

Jamie looked at the list. At the top it said: **Special Records**. A column listed about a dozen entries with strange names: Drag Queen, Water Warrior, Limp Wrist, Pistol Packer ....

"I think," Richard said, "that Dotson had some code names for these special files—"

"Pistol Packer?" Jamie read. "Henninger? Do you think? —"

"Could be," Richard interrupted. "I think Henninger had Dotson killed—probably by your friend Steroid-Boy. As I said, I think he intended to kill me also—and make it look like murder-suicide, but when I came early, it upset the plans."

"But where is the file you are looking for?"

"In the basement."

"The basement? Uhh ... not *the* basement."

"Yes, *the* basement. We need to get down there and find the file."

"And how—?"

"How will I get in?" Richard held up a post-it note. "Dotson's combination was in the records."

Richard took Jamie by the arm, and they started out the door under the yellow tape—but as they left, they failed to look out the window. If they had—they would have seen the headlights on her Civic blinking furiously.

Jamie held Richard's hand firmly as they descended the back stairs—too firmly, she realized as she loosened her grip. When they came to the landing on the main floor, Richard paused for a moment and listened—as if he had heard something. "Just my imagination," he whispered, and he led Jamie down the stairs.

When they came to the bottom floor, Richard punched a sequence of numbers into the keypad. Richard pushed the huge door. Jamie cringed as the hinges groaned in protest. The heavy odor of the room poured out of the room into Jamie's nostrils. The day before, when Jamie had been in this huge room it had been well-lit and still it seemed like a great burial vault. Now in the darkness—the only light in the room was the exit light above them—it was even more ominous, even more foreboding. Richard left the door ajar and pulled out his penlight, which seemed puny in the great cavernous underground auditorium.

Richard took her hand and led her through the main corridor as the shadows of the high steel shelves played against the walls like macabre monsters. It was a full one hundred paces across the cavernous auditorium. With each step the sound of their shoes on the concrete floor came back to them in a dozen echoes. Jamie felt herself shudder.

"The vault is inside the inner office," Richard whispered.

They made their way into the inner office, down the narrow hallway and came to the vault. Richard gave the penlight to Jamie and she held it on the post-it note. Jamie realized—when she saw the light flickering—that she was trembling. Richard put his hand on her shoulder to calm her. She took a deep breath and concentrated on keeping the light still as Richard punched in the code to the vault. When he finished, he put the note in his shirt pocket and reached for the wheel on the vault door.

It wouldn't budge.

Richard tried again. The wheel would not turn.

"Why? —" Richard said in exasperation. He pulled out the note from his shirt pocket and looked at it carefully. "I know I entered it correctly. Why doesn't it—"

"Oh!" Jamie was jolted by a low whirring sound coming from inside the vault.

"Aha," Richard said. "The dehumidifier. The vault has a delay mechanism to allow the dehumidifier to kick in." A metallic "click" came from the vault door. Richard tried the wheel. The door opened.

He pointed the penlight inside the vault. A heavy file cabinet sat in the corner—the only item in the vault. With the penlight on his shoulder, he opened the drawer and pulled out a file box. Inside were several pocket folders, each tied with string. None of the folders had names, only a file number. Richard opened one and began reading.

"Well, how about that!" he said.

"What?" Jamie asked.

"Guess which retired admiral and former Under-Secretary of the Navy fathered two children in the Philippines when he was stationed at Subic Bay as a Lieutenant?"

"Richard," Jamie whispered. I don't care about admirals. I care about Henninger. Find his file."

"Hmm … here's the file of a ranking member of the House Ways and Means Committee. It seems he has a cross-dressing habit. The file has photos—uggh." He closed the file and pulled out another one. "It's just as we thought. Dotson had a little cottage industry—protecting prominent Washingtonians with military records. He would simply remove all the incriminating information from the public record—for a fee, no doubt—but he was smart enough to keep copies of the original records for his own protection. That explains how he was able to live the country club life and collect all that porcelain."

"Just find Henninger's records and let's get out of here."

"I'm looking.

"Shh—" Jamie whispered. "Did you hear something?"

"Probably the dehumidifier," Richard answered, opening another file. "Another congressman—I wish I had time to see his records, but—"

"Richard—"

"Aha! I think this is it. Yes, this is it—Henninger's file, the thickest one." He began thumbing through the papers. "The first section is from 1942—letters to his draft board. Henninger is protesting his draft status. His first objections are medical. There are a series of letters from a local doctor describing 'heart palpitations'—but in 1942 the army didn't care if a man's heart 'palpitated' as long as it was beating. Then he turned to the 'essential nature of his business to the war effort' excuse. After that appeal failed, he began exploring the requirements for conscientious objector status."

"But he was drafted anyway?" Jamie asked.

"Technically he volunteered. However—if I can read between the lines, it appears he—or his father or his congressman—struck a deal with the army that Henninger would remain stateside. However, apparently that agreement got lost in the Army paperwork. The next records are a series of letters to members of congress from 1943, protesting his impending overseas assignment—some from Henninger and some from his father. And once overseas, it appears he did not get along swimmingly with his superior officers. There are some notes about 'attitudinal problems,' among other things."

"Richard, can we read these records later?"

"Ah! Here is what we need—Colonel Cable's file. Let me take a quick look. Yes, here is a letter dated June 1, 1945, and it's addressed to General Bernwald at Division Headquarters. Listen to this—"

"Couldn't I listen somewhere else?" Jamie asked.

"This won't take but a second. Look at this: **Re: Request for reenlistment for Lt. Harrison Henninger. Dear General Bernwald, Lt. Harrison Henninger, a communications officer in my HQ command, has requested an extension of duty subject to an assignment with a Military Postal Service. With an awareness of the desperate need for personnel for occupation duty, I am forwarding Lt. Henninger's request for reenlistment. Why the griping SOB, who has talked of nothing else but getting out of the Army, suddenly wants to stay in, or** why he wants to hand out mail at the post office, I don't know. But if you can use him, you can have him. And honestly, I will be glad to be rid of him. Sincerely, Colonel D.C. Cable."

"Jamie, do you see? Henninger requested the postal service assignment so he could control the shipment of the gold back to the U.S."

"No doubt he melted down the gold and—

Jamie screamed as a light hit her face.

Blondie!

The giant stood in the doorway with a flashlight in one hand and a metal bar in the other. "Well, aren't we so clever?" he said. "I'm sure Mr. Henninger will be grateful that you have found his papers for him." He looked at Jamie. "Well, well—if it isn't 'little miss blue dress'. We meet again."

Richard stood up and moved Jamie behind him.

The big man tested the weight of the iron bar in his hand. He took a step toward Richard and Jamie. "Just hand me that pack of papers and everything will go so much better."

Jamie felt Richard push the folder into her stomach. "Run Jamie!" he said as he lunged toward the big man. He threw up his arm as the giant brought the bar down on him. Jamie heard an awful "crunch" as the bar caught Richard on his arm and his head. Then she heard an 'ummph' as Richard's head caught the big man under his rib cage. "Run Jamie!" Richard said again—more insistently—as the behemoth fell to the floor.

Jamie tucked the folder under her arm and made for the door. The big man cursed as he struggled to his feet. He tried to grab her ankles, but she slipped away—out of the vault into the darkness of the cavernous basement. The exit light, two hundred feet away, was the only light in the great room, but it gave her orientation. *Richard's hurt! Must go back! Can't go back! Must take care of this pouch.* When she looked back she saw the silhouette of the big man coming from the vault., his flashlight in his hand. "You little bitch!" he hollered. "*Bitch ... bitch ... bitch ...*" bounced off the walls, reverberating through the basement.

"Oof," Jamie heard herself say. She had run into one of the file carts and the pouch flew out of her hands. She fell to the floor. *Where is the pouch?* She was frantic. She couldn't find the pouch. She could see nothing. She knelt down on all fours and scrambled around, feeling for the pouch on the concrete floor. She could hear the steps of the big man coming in her direction. Her hand found the pouch. She picked it up, held it close to her chest and crawled down one of the aisles. The flashlight came nearer, exploring the aisles, but she was behind one of the shelves, out of sight— for the moment.

"Where are you, little miss blue dress?" The behemoth struck one of the steel cabinets with his iron bar, sending great metallic echoes through the basement. He continued to bang on the shelves turning the huge room into a jarring cacophony. Jamie huddled against a steel cabinet, flinching with each successive echo.

"You and I need to get better acquainted, little miss blue dress." He rapped on successive shelves as he moved down the corridor, using his flashlight to explore each aisle. "Mr. Henninger won't mind waiting a short time while we get better acquainted. You are going to need another boyfriend, you know. Your other one got his head cracked. As soon as I get those papers you are holding, I will need to go back and finish the job on him."

Oh, Richard! Please be okay! Please be alive!

Jamie checked her breath, trying to be as quiet as possible. Blondie was walking slowly now, casting the beam of the flashlight from side to side, exploring the aisles. He was only two aisles away. Jamie found a section of the shelves where the files had been removed. She curled her body into that slot, tucking the folder into her stomach, as the flashlight beam came closer. Blondie banged the pipe on the shelves as he came to the aisle where Jamie was hidden. "Where are you, little miss blue dress? I will find you eventually," he taunted.

The flashlight beam illuminated the aisle where Jamie was hidden. She tried to control her breathing, fearing she would be heard. The beam lingered for some seconds on the aisle where she hid.

Bang! Bang! Bang! The big man hit the shelves with the iron bar. "I'm getting a little impatient!" he said, but the flashlight beam was now pointed the other direction.

Got to lead him away from Richard. Oh, Richard. Please be okay.

Blondie banged on the shelves in the next aisle. Jamie used the echoes to cover the sound of her slipping onto the floor.

"Alright blue dress!" His voice was angry now. "It's time for you to come out of hiding."

Jamie walked quietly to the main corridor. The behemoth had his back to her now, his big silhouette framed by the flashlight in his hand. Farther down the corridor she could see the exit sign above the doors she and Richard had entered earlier.

Jamie, you are about to run the most important race of your life. Richard's life may depend on this race. You must run the best race of your life. Unconsciously she began to shake her legs to loosen her leg muscles, just as she always did before a race. She tightened her shoestrings, just as she did at every race.

Blondie banged on the shelves again. Jamie used the echoes to cover the sound of her stepping into the corridor. The big man was thirty feet in front of her, walking slowly toward the exit sign, moving the beam of the flashlight from side to side. When he banged the shelf again, Jamie tucked the pouch under her arm and took off in a sprint—directly toward the giant.

"Wha—!" he said as she went by him at full speed, close enough that she could have touched him.

She sprinted toward the doors as she heard Blondie starting to run. "Come back here, you little bitch!" She pushed the door open and went toward the stairs. She took the steps three at a time. She heard Blondie explode through the doors below. She made as much noise as possible on the stairs to make sure he followed her. She came to the main floor and ran to the door that led outside—but she waited to make sure Blondie saw her. "I'll catch you now!" he hollered as he came to the main floor. Jamie stepped outside. The headlights on her car were flashing.

Mr. Johnson. I forgot about Mr. Johnson. Can't run in that direction.

She headed across the lawn away from the car—and away from Moreland Center. The big thug emerged from the building. He held the iron pipe in his hand. He saw her and started in her direction. He was thirty yards behind her, screaming at her, running as fast as he could. Jamie ran only fast enough to keep the big man at the same distance. His stride was that of a weight-lifter, not a runner. She ran to the street corner stopping under a streetlight allowing him to close the gap between them. She adjusted her pace. She went to a sprint. When she did, the big man was unable to keep up. He lost ground—at first only a few yards, then twenty yards, then thirty. Now a full block behind her, he stopped, leaned against the post of a street sign, hunched over, hands on his knees, trying to catch his breath.

When she was certain she was out of sight of the big man, Jamie turned left for a block, then turned left again to make her way back toward Moreland Center. *Must check on Mr. Johnson. Must get some help for Richard.*

She began walking. *Compose yourself Jamie. Walk slowly. Don't bring attention to yourself.* She walked a block, watching carefully to see if the blond goon appeared. A cat ran across the sidewalk in front of her and startled her. A man in a tee shirt leaned on the post of his porch, smoking a cigarette, the glow illuminating his unshaven face. The air seemed unusually still. She laboriously walked another block. The Moreland Center came into view.

Richard is inside. He's hurt, or—She wouldn't let herself finish the thought. She saw her car about fifty yards in front of her. The headlights were no longer flashing. She crouched down behind the line of cars making her way to her car—and Mr. Johnson, she hoped. *Be careful. Blondie will be coming back here.* She moved along slowly, raising up regularly to see if she saw the big man. She had made her way along a dozen cars or more when she squatted beside the back wheel of a car to take a look in the direction of the center. She moved forward a step so she could see through the windows of the car.

She screamed.

Henninger! Harrison Henninger's face was six inches from her own! And he was just as startled as she was!

Jamie stepped back from the car. When she did, she saw Blondie—a half a block away—running toward her. Her mind was racing. *Need to lead them away from here. Need to get Richard some help.*

She began walking away. She wanted Henninger and his goon to follow. She needed to take them away from Richard.

Blondie got in the car with Henninger. Jamie heard the door slam. The tires squealed as he pulled out to chase Jamie. She began to sprint again. She ran one block and turned right. The car's headlights hit her just as she turned the corner. *I can't outrun this car.* At her right was a house with a low wrought iron fence and thick shrubs. She vaulted the fence and crouched behind the shrubs, clutching the pouch in her belly. The car screeched around the corner and then slowed down. The vehicle crawled by Jamie's hiding place, so close that she could see Henninger's face as he looked out the open window of the car.

She waited until the vehicle was well down the street before she stood up. *What to do Jamie? What to do?* She realized she was not far from the Italian restaurant where she and Richard had eaten just two nights previously. *Was that only two days ago? Maybe there is a phone booth near the restaurant.*

Five minutes later she was speaking to the operator in a phone booth just down the street from Salvatore's. "Operator, this is an emergency. I would like to report a crime—"

A half dozen patrol cars were at the Moreland Center—their blue lights flashing—were on the scene when Jamie came back. *Are you okay Richard? Please be alive Richard. Mr. Johnson! I forgot about Mr. Johnson!*

She walked briskly toward her car. When she got there, she saw Johnson in the back seat asleep. When she opened the door, he rose up. "I flashed the headlights," he said.

Jamie looked at him. His eyes seemed vacant. He repeated himself, "I flashed the headlights." Jamie realized it would do no good to try to explain to him what happened in the Moreland Center. But she had to think. *What do I do now?*

Emergency personnel wheeled a stretcher out of the building. *Please Richard. Please be alive.* An ambulance—Memorial Hospital written on it—backed up to the entrance and the back doors opened and the stretcher was rolled in. The ambulance pulled away, its siren wailing and the orange lights flashing.

The pouch. Must think about the pouch. What do I do with this pouch?

FORTY-FOUR

IN JAMIE'S DREAM, the blonde brute was beating Richard with the steel pipe—over and over—thud … thud … thud. The beating was relentless—thud … thud … thud.

Jamie began to wake up. A genuine sound replaced the sound in her dream. Thud … thud … thud … the sound of someone banging on the door. Her head began to clear. *I'm in a motel room. Someone is knocking on the door.*

The clock beside the bed said 7:55. *Mr. Johnson. Mr. Johnson is at the door.*

The events of the night before came back to her. After Richard had been taken away in the ambulance, she found Mr. Johnson in her car. "Flashed the lights like he told me," he repeated several times. Jamie found a motel near the hospital. It was after 1 A.M. when she and Johnson got in their rooms.

Thud … thud … thud—the knock on the door continued.

Jamie put on her robe. "Come in, Mr. Johnson," she said as she opened the door.

"I brought you some coffee," he said.

"Thank you." She took the styrofoam cup. "I could use some coffee right now."

354

"It was free. They have a pot in the lobby and they give it away to anybody who's staying in the motel." He sat down in the only chair in the room and sipped his coffee. He looked older, Jamie thought, than he had when she first met him only a few days ago. *What have I done to him? What have I done to Richard?*

"I still can't come up with those two names," he said. "Bothers me. I said I wouldn't forget those men."

"Mr. Johnson, I need to show you something." She pulled the pouch from under the mattress where she had put it the night before. "These are Henninger's records—the real records. He had his army records falsified. He paid the director of Moreland Center to keep his secret. These records will show how he betrayed 2nd platoon. This tells the truth about Henninger."

Johnson took the pouch but looked at it with little interest. He had known the truth about Henninger for forty years—all the paper records in the world would not add to what he knew to be true about Harrison Henninger. He put the pouch on the bed. He seemed very tired.

"I don't know what to do with these papers," Jamie said. "Richard could tell me what to do, but he's in the hospital. I don't know what to do."

"Sergeant Patterson was a good man," Johnson said suddenly.

He's thinking about the war. That's what he's thinking about. The memories of the war are coming back to him.

"We got ambushed," he went on without looking up. "It was only a couple of weeks before Henninger betrayed us, not long after I joined K Company. We came into a French village—right near the German border. They told us the Germans had abandoned that village, but they hadn't. They were still there. The machine gun fire caught us by surprise. A couple of guys were hit in that first spray—and it just kept coming. The street was covered by machine gun fire. The whole company, including our platoon, got scattered into several buildings—seeking cover. In that situation you have to be careful. You are just as likely to get shot by one of your own guys as by the Germans. Me and another guy, Mobley was his name, we sat on the first floor of a little house—underneath the kitchen table—for an hour or so. We heard the sounds of someone running in the street and the 'zip, zip, zip' of several dozen rounds from the German machine gun. Our door opened and we heard 'K Company, 2nd platoon, come to me.' It was Sergeant Patterson. The other platoon leaders were holed up, sitting on their rear ends, waiting for things to cool off, but Sergeant Patterson was making sure his men were okay. He didn't have to do that. He could have gotten himself killed. But the men in his platoon were *his* men and he took care of us. He was a good soldier—a good man."

"Was that when you climbed the drainpipe?" Jamie asked.

He nodded but dismissed the question. "Sometimes," he said, his eyes looking at something a thousand miles away, "Sometimes the memories come back very plainly—the smell of those wet wool uniforms that hadn't been washed in weeks, the faces of those men who forced themselves to smile when there wasn't anything to smile about, the sound of their voices when they talked about their families back in the states—sometimes those things come back plainly."

He paused for a moment. "But they're all gone now. All the men of 2nd platoon are gone now. Henninger killed them. All those men are dead now. They never got a chance to come home and live a normal life. I should've done something."

Jamie leaned over and kissed the elderly man on the forehead. "Mr. Johnson, give me a few minutes to get dressed. I will knock on your door when I'm ready." He nodded, picked up his empty styrofoam cup and left the room.

The parking deck at Memorial Hospital had six floors and there were no parking places except on the top floor. Mr. Johnson had said nothing as they drove into town. Jamie had looked over at him several times, but he seemed to be in a world of his own. She parked the car and went around to the passenger side and opened the door. Mr. Johnson got out of the car but said nothing. Jamie was glad he was not asking any questions because she did not have any answers. She stopped for a moment outside the entrance. Around the hospital a commercial area had grown up—fast-food restaurants and a couple of strip malls. And the hospital, eight floors of it, loomed above all. Above her a large sign announced MEMORIAL HOSPITAL.

What am I going to do when I go inside? Oh, Richard. Please be okay. Please, God, let him be okay.

She looked at Mr. Johnson who stood beside her. He looked tired. *He deserves to look tired,* Jamie thought. He's an elderly man whose house has been burned, who has been torn away from the only life he has ever known, who escaped an attempt to murder him—and who was up last night until the early hours of the morning—and his mind, she knew, was now on the events forty years before. And he seemed to be slipping away from reality.

Jamie looked at the hospital sign again. *Now what? Now what are you going to do—now that you are here?* Jamie had no answers to the questions swirling in her mind.

"Mr. Johnson, let's go inside."

He nodded. "Still can't come up with those two guys' names," he said. "Worries me."

She led him to a sitting area in the lobby. Several clusters of families were gathered there—all wearing the expressions people wear in hospitals, awkward smiles that covered their apprehensions.

She led Johnson to a seat. He sat down obediently, saying nothing. Jamie sat beside him and looked around. An information booth, a semi-circular structure, sat in the middle of the lobby. Jamie watched as a middle-aged couple approached the desk and asked about a patient. Jamie could hear the conversation. The young woman at the desk flipped through a notebook and then pointed the couple toward the elevators. "You'll find him in room 326," she said.

Jamie patted Mr. Johnson on the knee. "I'll be right back," He nodded.

"Good morning," the young woman at the desk said cheerfully, a bright smile on her round face. "Can I help you find a patient?"

"Perhaps so," Jamie answered, putting on a sheepish smile, "but I'm a little embarrassed to ask. You see, I'm not sure I'm at the right hospital. I came to see my great-aunt. She's having surgery. I believe it's her gallbladder."

"Well, let's see if we can find your great-aunt," the woman answered, maintaining a cheerful smile. "What's her last name?"

"Robinson," Jamie answered.

"First name?"

"Jackie." *Where did that come from?* Jamie asked herself.

"Her name is Jackie Robinson?" the young lady asked, a strange expression on her face. "Like the baseball player?"

"Well," Jamie answered. "It's actually Jacquelyn Robinson, but we always called her 'Aunt Jackie'."

"Oh, I see—but I'm afraid I don't see a Robinson on the list. She must be at one of the other hospitals."

"You don't think they might have misspelled her name?" Jamie asked. "That has happened before. Instead of Robinson, it might be Robertson."

"No, there's no Robertson either. There is a Roberts, but that's the spy they brought in last night."

"A spy?" Jamie responded. "A spy was brought in last night?"

The young woman leaned her round face forward. "A handsome spy, according to Arlene, who works the night shift. Arlene has been working here a lot longer than I have. She told me about him. Tall and handsome, she said. He was on a stretcher, she said, but she went around to take a look at him. Yeah, she said he was a really handsome spy—but I think she reads too many novels while she's working the night shift. She has tried to get me to work the night shift sometimes, but I have sleeping problems—"

"Was he—the spy—hurt badly?"

"Head trauma," the woman replied. You know, he's the one who killed his boss over at that building where they keep all the military records. Arlene thinks they keep a lot more information over there than just army records, but again, Arlene reads a lot of mystery novels."

"But the spy—is he going to be okay?"

The woman nodded. "According to Arlene—she talked to the shift nurse last night—they think he will come out of it … not that it would do him any good, according to Arlene, since he killed his boss—"

Jamie interrupted. "It must be awfully exciting to work in a place like this," Jamie interrupted. "I guess you get a lot of spies and people like that who are brought in here."

"Well, I don't know if we get a *lot* of spies. But we sometimes get other criminals—drug pushers, robbers, who have injuries."

"You probably have to have a special place to keep them in the hospital while they're recuperating—on the top floor I suppose."

The woman laughed. "Oh no, not the top floor. That's the maternity ward. We wouldn't put them on the floor of the maternity ward!"

Jamie forced a laugh. "Oh yes, that *would* be odd."

"Top floor! ..." the woman repeated, still enjoying the joke, "... a spy right in there with the mothers and new babies! That would be interesting. No, they always—according to Arlene—put the criminals on the 4th floor—at the end of the hall, where the guard can keep a watch on them."

A woman with two children—one in her arms and one tugging at her skirt—approached the information desk. Jamie stepped back from the desk. *Richard, I need to talk with you. I need to know what to do with the information about Henninger. But how can I get into your room?* She looked over at Mr. Johnson who sat quietly with the same faraway expression on his face.

As she stood beside the young woman at the information desk, Jamie noticed the woman's hospital

I.D. card clipped on her sweater which was lying on the desk. *Do I dare!* Before Jamie had time to answer her own question, she had picked up the I.D. card and slipped it in her pocket—just as the woman said goodbye to the young mother.

"Now, about your aunt—let me call the other hospitals—"

"Oh, that won't be necessary," Jamie answered. "I'm sure we will find her. Thank you for your help."

"But—" the young woman said, but Jamie had already walked away.

"Mr. Johnson, I need to go across the street for a moment. Can you wait here?"

He looked at her as if he were having trouble processing the question, but he nodded. She patted his shoulder. "I won't be long."

"It's for my sister," Jamie told the sales clerk. She was standing in a shop in the strip mall that sold uniforms for medical personnel. She held up a nurse's uniform from the rack. "Her birthday is tomorrow. She's the nurse in the family. Not me, I knew anything that involved blood was not for me." *Why are you blabbering so, Jamie? And when did you get so proficient at making up stuff?*

"What size does your sister wear?" the clerk asked.

"We're almost the same size," Jamie replied. "She's a year older, but most people think we're twins. Do you have one I can try on?"

When did lying become so natural to me?

She emerged from the dressing room a moment later. "I think this one will be fine," she said. "And I think I will just wear it. It will be a joke when I give it to my sister." The clerk had an odd expression on her face but said nothing. "Oh, and one more thing. Could I borrow some scissors and some tape?"

Back in the dressing room she cut the photo from her Duke University I.D. and taped it over the hospital I.D. which said *Evelyn Washburn.* She looked at it carefully. *Would not survive serious scrutiny, but it should work.*

When she returned to the hospital lobby, Mr. Johnson was still in his chair, still deep in his thoughts when Jamie returned. Evelyn Washburn—the real Evelyn Washburn—was giving directions to a family at the information desk. *She hasn't missed her I.D. That's good.*

Looking down a hallway that ran toward the administrative offices, Jamie saw a wheelchair in the hall. She took a deep breath. She walked down the hall toward the wheelchair. She looked around. No one seemed to be looking in her direction. She released the brake on the wheelchair and pushed.

Screech! Screech! One of the wheels on the wheelchair shrieked in protest.

"Hey!" a voice behind her startled her.

She turned slightly, careful that her I.D. was not visible. A hospital orderly pushing a cart full of bed linens, spoke to her. "If you're going to use that thing, squirt something on that wheel. It squeaks like hell."

"Yeah, I will do that," she replied, keeping the I.D. card from his line of sight. "Thank you." She started away. *Screech. Screech.*

"Hey," the orderly called again. Jamie stopped. Her heart was pounding.

"Yes," she answered.

"Are you new here?"

"Brand new."

"I thought so. Welcome to Memorial." He walked away, pushing the cart of linens.

The orderly was right. The wheelchair did squeak like hell. With each revolution, the front left wheel emitted a grating, abrasive sound that carried throughout the lobby. Every eye watched her as she traversed the lobby. Conversations stopped and magazines were dropped as Jamie went by, but she smiled apologetically as she passed by those in the lobby and tried to ignore the attention.

"Mr. Johnson," she whispered. "Would you mind getting into this wheelchair? He looked at her as if he had been interrupted in his thoughts, but he complied, not saying anything, and he did not seem to notice that Jamie was now in a nurse's uniform.

The abrasive noise of the front left wheel of the wheelchair was somewhat diminished with the weight of a passenger, but the sound was still noticeable—and she had to pass the information desk and Evelyn Washburn to get to the elevator. She turned her head away from the information desk and pushed the wheelchair briskly. Fortunately, Evelyn Washburn had someone at the desk asking for information and did not seem to notice when Jamie and Mr. Johnson passed by. Jamie punched the elevator button and the door opened immediately.

"I still can't come up with those two names," Johnson said as the elevator door closed. "Only nineteen of us in St. Lautern—half what a platoon should have had—and I promised myself I would not forget those names. One of the guys," he went on, "was from New Mexico. I remember that because someone in the platoon said he was from Arizona. That irritated him so much that everyone in the platoon began calling him 'Arizona'—just to needle him . . . but I can't come up with his name. The other guy, I think, was from Michigan, but I'm not sure."

Jamie looked at the man in the wheelchair. *Poor Mr. Johnson. I'm afraid we are losing you.*

The door opened on the 4th floor and Jamie pushed the wheelchair out, trying to do so with confidence— as if she knew where she was going. The nurses' station was to her left, so she turned right. A sign at the head of a hallway said **Rooms 401-420.** She looked down the hallway. *No guard. Can't be the hallway for Richard. Ugh. I will have to go by the nurses' station to get to the other hallway.*

She headed in that direction, the screeching wheel announcing her movement. She approached the nurses' station.

"Nurse," a voice came from the station. Jamie stopped. Her heart was pounding.

"Yes," she answered, without looking up.

"There's some lubricant in the maintenance closet if you want to spray that wheel."

"Yes, I will do that," Jamie answered. She headed toward the hall. She saw the guard at the end of the hall. She took a deep breath and pushed the wheelchair down the hall. She saw the guard look up as he heard the squeaking wheel. She came closer. The guard moved to the center of the hallway and faced toward Jamie.

"Taking Mr. Johnson for a ride," she said to the guard, smiling. He looked at her—running his eyes all over her. "He gets a little antsy in his room," Jamie went on. The guard, a young man in his twenties, whose uniform did not seem to fit him very well, kept up his examination of Jamie. "Is there a criminal on the hall?" she asked when she got close.

"A suspect," the guard corrected, his eyes still moving up and down Jamie. "Innocent until proven guilty. That's the law."

"Oh, yes, I guess you are right. Not that I know much about the law, but I do remember that from my high school social studies class." She gave him her most engaging smile and moved a step closer. "You must know the law really well. Have you been a policeman for very long?"

"Well, I'm not really a policeman—not right now at least. I'm with the security company, but I'm taking night classes at the technical college, and I plan to put in an application to the D.C. force. Once I get that degree I should be wearing the uniform by the end of the year."

"Wow," Jamie replied. "I'm sure that will be exciting, but aren't you worried about the danger?"

"Part of the job," he said, putting both hands on his belt. "Just part of the job."

"What about this crim—suspect? Do you know what he is accused of?"

"Murder."

"Murder?!"

"And espionage."

"He's a spy?!"

The guard looked up the hall. "I'm telling you more than I should—but you're a nurse—" He leaned over and looked at her I.D. "Evelyn. Right?"

"That's right."

"I'm Marvin," he said, smiling. "It's good to meet you, Evelyn. Anyhow, this guy," he nodded toward the hospital room, "we think murdered his boss over at Moreland Center—that place where they keep all the military records. You may have seen it on the morning news. Then, if you can believe it, last night, hardly twenty-four hours after he killed his boss—I should say 'accused' of killing his boss—he's back in the building and someone whacks him on the head."

"Amazing," Jamie said.

"Yeah, but if you ask me, it's more than just a simple murder case. I think there is some espionage involved."

"Really? Espionage?" Jamie answered. "But this spy … suspected spy," she nodded toward the room. "Is he going to be okay?"

"The doc thinks so. His arm is broken, but the real injury is to his head. He's got one huge headache, for sure—and when the detectives were here this morning, they couldn't get anything out of the guy. The doc told them it would be a day or two before the guy's head clears up enough to answer questions."

"Fascinating!" Jamie said. "A murder case and a spy case—and you are part of the investigation, even before you are officially on the force."

"Well, I don't know—"

"Do you think," Jamie asked, "that I could peek in and see the suspect? That would be something I could tell all my girlfriends! Think how jealous they will be!"

"I don't know—"

Jamie wasn't very practiced at giving an entreating expression, but she did her best.

"Well," Marvin said after a moment, "you *are* a nurse. My instructions are to admit only appropriate medical and investigative personnel—and I think you are *very* appropriate."

The come-on in the comment was evident and Jamie did her best to give a responsive smile. "Mr. Johnson," she said as she leaned down. "I will be only a moment. Just wait here."

The shades in the room were pulled, and it took a moment for her eyes to adjust to the darkness. The shapeless white clump on the bed slowly became Richard. His right arm was in a cast and a bandage swath went around his head. His left arm was connected to an intravenous tube. She edged a little closer to the bed. She had a strong impulse to lean over and kiss him … *Richard, you are going to be okay. I just know you are going to be okay. We are going to figure this out. I wish you could tell me what to do with these documents.*

"Evelyn," Marvin called. "That's long enough."

She took one last look at Richard before she left the room. "Hey, Evelyn," Marvin said, "you mentioned your girlfriends. You know, I've got some buddies. Where do you usually hang out in the evenings?"

"At the library mostly."

"The Library? Is it in this part of town? I don't recognize the name. Is that a new joint?"

"Actually, it's been around a long time."

"Give me your address and I will pick you up. You can tell me how to get there after I pick you up"

"Uh, you can get my address at the Information Desk."

"How about 7pm?"

"Uh. Sure. That's great, but I need to get Mr. Johnson back to his room. And look, I see the lady with the food cart coming down the hallway. It's lunchtime. Mr. Johnson doesn't need to miss his lunch." She smiled again at Marvin and started up the hallway, pushing Mr. Johnson.

She was halfway down the hallway when she saw him coming.

Blondie!

Blondie was walking toward her. But he was no longer blonde. His goatee had been shaved and his hair was dyed black—but there was no mistaking his bulk, which filled up the hallway.

Jamie crouched beside the wheelchair using Mr. Johnson as a shield. She acted as if she were working on the squeaking wheel. The big man came closer. He wore a dark suit and a black tie. His thick arms swung at an odd angle as he walked. *Why are you here? This does not make sense!* Jamie kept her head down as he came near. His big feet passed her, only inches away. The lady pushing the food cart looked at her oddly as she crouched beside the wheelchair.

She remained in her squatting position but moved to a place where she could see the big man go down the hallway. She could barely see Marvin at the end of the hall for the hulking figure going away from her. When he got to the end of the hall, he pulled out a wallet and showed it to Marvin. *He's posing as an FBI agent!*

"Mr. Johnson!" Jamie's voice was not loud, but it was urgent. She shook his leg and spoke directly to him. "Mr. Johnson, I need your help. I need you to act like you are sick—like you are having an attack. Do you understand?"

Johnson looked like he had just been awakened—but he gave a slight nod of comprehension—and then he slumped over and fell out of the wheelchair.

"Emergency!" Jamie shouted. "Emergency! Help!"

Two nurses started down the hall from their station. At the other end of the hall, Jamie saw Marvin take a few steps in her direction, leaving the big man behind. He paused for just a moment and then went into Richard's room. Behind her, several medical personnel came to Mr. Johnson's wheelchair. Jamie ran down the hallway and entered the room just behind the huge man. The room was still dark, but she could see the big man's silhouette as he stepped toward Richard's bed. "Excuse me," she said, trying to make her voice gravelly. "I need to check this patient's IV." Her heart was thumping, and her throat was dry, so the effort was effective.

The big man grunted and stepped back. Something was in his hand—a syringe! He put it on the table behind a water pitcher and then stepped away with his back to Jamie. "Need to check this IV," she repeated. She fumbled with the IV apparatus and thumped the tube—she had seen a nurse on television do that, but the big man was not looking in her direction. He stood by the window. "This won't take long," she said in her gravelly voice and the big man grunted. She looked at

Richard, unconscious on the bed. *Oh Richard. What can I do?*

Jamie took a quiet step away from the bed and picked up the syringe on the table, being careful not to rattle any of the items on the table. She took the syringe in both hands and without hesitation took a quick step toward the big man and jabbed the syringe in his buttocks, squeezing the syringe with all her strength.

"Aaahh!" he screamed. As he did, he grabbed the window blinds, pulling them down. The blinds crashed to the floor and light poured into the room. The big man looked down. The syringe was embedded in his buttocks, just dangling. Jamie could see the contortion in his face—both pain and fear—as he pulled the syringe from his body. He looked up. He saw Jamie. "You!" he said. He started toward her.

Jamie ran out the door into the hall. The food cart was between her and Mr. Johnson, but she could see that two nurses and an orderly were attending to Mr. Johnson. Marvin stood beside them. "Marvin!" she called, just as the big man burst into the hallway. She ran toward Marvin. "That man is not an FBI agent," she said to Marvin.

The big man started up the hallway—but his legs wobbled. He moved like a drunk man. He still held the syringe in his hand. He took two unsteady steps. He tried to say something, but the words were garbled. He looked at Jamie. A guttural snarl came from his throat. He started toward her, but his knees buckled. He stumbled and as he fell, he grabbed the food cart. His huge body hit the floor with a massive "thump" and the food cart—and its contents—spilled over his inert body, the metal serving bowls clanging as they rolled into the hallway.

"Back-up needed on 4th floor Memorial," Marvin said into the radio on his shoulder. "Back-up needed on 4th floor Memorial."

"That man," Jamie told Marvin, "is not an FBI agent. He was trying to kill Rich—uh, the patient you were guarding."

Marvin looked at her in complete confusion.

Jamie looked down. The giant man was sprawled in the hallway. The two nurses were now attending to him. Chicken quarters, green beans, mashed potatoes and Jello, were spread all over the floor. The big man had landed face up—eyes and mouth open—and a serving of green beans and Jello had ended up on his face, making him look ludicrous.

The radio on Marvin's shoulder squawked and he stepped down the hall to answer the call. Jamie looked over at Mr. Johnson, who was now standing and looking at the odd scene in the hospital hallway. She stepped around the huge figure in the hallway, trying to avoid the spilled food. The big man's mouth was open, and his tongue hung out of his mouth. Jamie could not help but think how stupid he looked with his mouth wide open. She took Mr. Johnson's hand. "Let's go," she whispered. He nodded in agreement, and they walked quietly away. As they came to the elevator, two security guards appeared and ran toward the scene in the hallway. As they arrived in the lobby a pair of D.C. policemen were on their way to the elevator. Outside she could see the blue lights of patrol cars flashing in the parking area.

She removed her photo from the hospital I.D. and went to the information desk and gave it to Evelyn Washburn. "You must have dropped this," Jamie said. Evelyn Washburn had a confused look on her face when she saw Jamie in a nurse's uniform. "Aren't you—?" but Jamie had walked away with Mr. Johnson. However, she had gone only a few steps when she came back to the information desk. "By the way, I have arranged a date for you tonight with Marvin, the security officer on the 4th floor. He will pick you up at 7:00."

"But—" Evelyn started.

"Sorry, I have to go." She took Johnson's arm, and they went out the front door.

FORTY-FIVE

THERE YOU ARE again.

Henry sat on a park bench in Lincoln Park, a half-eaten hot-dog in a paper wrapper beside him, looking at the statue in the center of the park. The strap of his valise hung across his shoulder. Around him a few opportunistic sparrows and pigeons gathered, waiting for the chance to grab crumbs. Behind him a little girl squealed as she slid down the playground slide. The oaks and maples around the edge of the park helped buffer the sound of the traffic on East Capitol Street. Henry was looking at the statue of Abraham Lincoln— the *other* statue of Lincoln—the one in the park named after him, not the more famous one on the mall. Lincoln wore his characteristic frock coat, leaning over to extend the Emancipation Proclamation to a slave.

Honest Abe. The one who always did the right thing. The one who always demonstrated integrity. The one we were taught to honor and admire.

Henry had decided to walk to RFK stadium to meet with Henninger. The appointment was not until 5:00, but he had nothing else to do, so he decided to walk. It was not a short walk, but it was a glorious May afternoon. The sun filtered through the greening trees and the light breeze dislodged the little "helicopters" from the maples and they spun down around Henry on the bench. Two young mothers pushing baby strollers walked by, chatting with each other.

Henry looked at the statue again. At least this statue of Lincoln did not look at him directly like the other statue seemed to do—but that did not make Henry feel less incriminated. He was still reminded of Lincoln's nobility—his doing the difficult, but right thing—issuing the Emancipation Proclamation.

Where is the nobility now? Where is the honesty now? Where is the righteousness now? Have we lost it all?

Abraham Lincoln, or at least his statue, did not answer any of Henry's questions. He just kept extending freedom to the slave below him.

Henry took the remaining part of the hot dog and threw it to the birds. He stood and cinched the valise over his shoulder.

Might as well go to the stadium early. I have nothing else to do.

FORTY-SIX

WHAT ABOUT THE pouch—these documents? What should I do? Do I return to campus? Campus?! I'm supposed to run a race in two days. How can I think about a race right now? And what about Mr. Johnson? What do I do with him?

The pouch with the Henninger documents lay beside Jamie's travel bag in the back of Jamie's car. She had brought the car down to the shopping area adjacent to the hospital, where she had watched as a half dozen police cars had their blue lights flashing at the hospital's entrance. She had been standing there more than an hour, undecided about what she should do next. She looked at Mr. Johnson. He had not spoken since they left the hospital lobby. He seemed even more detached—withdrawn into his own world. As for Richard, Jamie realized there was nothing she could do for him right now. He was safe—and he was receiving the medical attention he needed.

But what about the documents in the pouch? How can I get them to someone who will expose Henninger?

She was working these questions around in her mind when she heard the car door open. Mr. Johnson stepped out. "The names came to me."

"Excuse me," Jamie said.

His voice was stronger than Jamie had heard before. "Trevino and Haltom. The names came to me—the other two guys in the platoon. Trevino was the guy from New Mexico. Haltom was the other one—from Michigan. They just came to me. I promised myself I would not forget the names of all the guys in the platoon, but I had forgotten those two. I've been trying to come up with those names—Trevino and Haltom. They were the two I couldn't remember."

A great wave of emotion came over Jamie as she looked at Mr. Johnson—sorrow, pity, admiration and respect were all part of what she felt. *This man has suffered.* She wanted to hug him. She wanted to cry on his shoulder. She wanted to tell him that everything would work out—but she was not sure everything would work out. She had no reason to believe that.

Mr. Johnson saw a newspaper rack on the curb beside them. He walked over to it and bent down to read. A huge picture of Harrison Henninger was framed by a bold headline: **At the Gates—Henninger's 'Assault' Reaches Washington.**

Jamie came over to the newspaper rack to read over Johnson's shoulder:

> **Harrison Henninger's well-publicized "Assault on Washington" has reached its culmination—the nation's capital. The California billionaire will provide the keynote address at a rally on his behalf this evening at RFK stadium—the only venue in the nation's capital capable of handling the expected crowd. The major question—both in the city and throughout the**

country—is whether Mr. Henninger will officially announce his candidacy for president, or will he throw his support to one of the traditional candidates—and if so, which one?

"Do you know," Johnson asked Jamie "where RFK Stadium is?"

"Well, yes, it's not far from here, but—"

"I want to go there," Mr. Johnson said. His voice was different. It was suddenly stronger.

"I'm not sure that is a good idea, Mr. Johnson. Don't you think—"

"You can take me, or I will get there myself." The firmness in his voice surprised Jamie. He looked at Jamie, waiting for an answer.

FORTY-SEVEN

THURSDAY, MAY 17, 4:05 P.M.

HARRISON HENNINGER COULD never understand a patriot.

What a bunch of bull! He looked out the window of his limousine at hundreds of American flags—some arrayed on poles, others across the stadium, others— the small ones—stuck in the ground alongside the sidewalk, and still others were carried by those arriving early for the event.

Dozens of media vehicles and even more chartered buses were filling the parking lot. Getting off the buses were clusters of veterans, many of them wearing their old service caps. *Pathetic. These people are pathetic. They had one moment of glory, and they want to keep it alive. Pathetic. They just gather here to remind each other how brave they were forty years ago. They should remind themselves instead of how stupid they were.*

Harrison Henninger congratulated himself again, as he had for forty years—that he was not a patriot and that he was not stupid—not stupid enough to try to be a hero in the war. "Heroes get killed, son," his father had told him when he was drafted. It was good advice. "Take care of yourself. Nobody else will." That was what his father told him, and he had lived by that rule— both while he was in the war and ever since.

"Give 'em hell, Mr. Henninger," the parking lot attendant said as he passed through the VIP gate. Henninger did not reply.

This country is made up of gullible idiots—from the president down to the parking lot attendants. I'm tired of smiling. I'm tired of patriots. I'm tired of veterans—of slapping their backs and laughing at their jokes. And I'm tired of reporters and cameras. In just a few hours I will be through with them all. He looked at his watch. *That researcher from Moreland should be dead by now—just like his boss. If Dotson hadn't panicked he would still be alive. The bastard—he thought he would outsmart me—keeping a copy of those records he said he destroyed. I'm glad he's dead. It serves him right—the little pot-collecting loser.*

Henninger looked at his watch again. *Just enough time to meet with that pipsqueak errand boy for the president. He had better have those papers in order. I can change this speech in a moment.* He pulled out the folder with his speech and smiled as he read, "... tribute to the great heroes who wore the uniform of our country ... who sacrificed to gain our freedoms ..." *There won't be a dry eye in the audience. Hell, I may cry myself—just for effect.*

In his speech he would refer to "hours of agonizing soul-searching and prayer". He would not declare his decision in the first part of the speech. That would come later—after all the patriotic platitudes. *Let that mealy-mouthed excuse for a president squirm! I wish I could see him sitting in the Oval Office watching my speech, wondering if he will be sitting there next year—knowing it all depends on what I say in this speech. I hope he has to change his underwear when I finish. And when I finish—when I have those papers signed—I can quit this idiotic political crap and within six months, that puppet commission will be in place. A year later I will have majority interest in every significant enterprise in the Pacific Rim. A year after that I will have Europe, and then—I will be a billion times richer than the other billionaires.*

FORTY-EIGHT

IT WAS STILL more than two hours until the program was scheduled to begin, but already, when Jamie and Mr. Johnson arrived, the parking lot was half full. The buses, parked in orderly diagonal rows, looked like toys in a child's play set. Many of them had banners on the side denoting which VFW post to which they belonged. Several dozen attendants wearing orange vests were directing cars to the parking places.

"Mr. Johnson," Jamie said as they came to the entrance of the parking lot, "I still am not sure this is a good idea—"

"I'm glad I remembered those names," Johnson said, ignoring Jamie's concern. The strength of his voice surprised Jamie. He looked across the parking lot toward the stadium. "Trevino and Haltom. Those are the names I couldn't remember. But now I have them all. Templeton was from Tennessee, Jones from Kentucky, McKinley and Toomey were both from Pennsylvania. Toomey was the oldest of six. He wrote a letter every night to his brothers and his sisters. Admundson was from Minnesota—a big guy. He was the arm-wrestling champion for the company. Brooks was from Kansas, the son of a pharmacist—he planned to become a pharmacist after the war. I remember them all—Patterson, our sergeant, then Templeton, Jones, Brooks, McKinley, Toomey, Richardson, Simpson, Walker, Browning, McMurtry, Blevins, Armstrong, Childers, Davis, Hawkins, Trevino and Haltom—and Langston, Iowa Langston.

Jamie looked at Johnson in amazement. He seemed like a man who had awakened from a coma. His countenance had changed. His eyes seemed alert.

"Let's go inside," he said.

FORTY-NINE

THURSDAY, MAY 17, 5:15 P.M.

HENRY PURSLEY SAT in a windowless room in the interior of the stadium. The concrete block walls were a soft cream color. A green chalkboard, partially erased, the remnants of a football diagram—with x's and o's and arrows—filled a portion of the chalkboard. A small table sat in the corner and a dozen or so plastic chairs with aluminum legs filled the space of the room.

Get accustomed to small windowless rooms, Henry. You are destined to spend some time in one.

Henry held the papers in his lap. He looked at the president's signature. He realized the extraordinary nature of those documents. *Harrison Henninger will have the authority to control much of the world's economy—and he will have the assurance of a presidential pardon for any crime he commits.*

The fluorescent lamps hummed above Henry as he waited. He had waited an hour and a half—the folder with the documents with the president's signature in his lap. He had the odd sensation that the documents were burning his legs, so he put the papers in the chair beside him. When he did, a jolt went through his shoulder. *That was worse than usual.*

Henry jumped in his seat when Henninger barged in. Henninger said nothing. He put out his hand for the documents. Henry opened the valise, took out the folder and handed it to Henninger, who took a few minutes to read the two documents, squinting his eyes as he read.

Henninger grunted something that Henry took as an acknowledgement the papers were in order.

"The president asked if you would give some assurance—"

"Tell that miserable, spineless S.O.B. the only assurance he will get from me is that I will plant my foot squarely in his backside if he tries to doublecross me like he did four years ago. Put these papers back in the briefcase."

Henry did as he was instructed and gave the valise to Henninger.

"Is that purple heart on the stage?"

Henry nodded.

"Good. Now, you will have to excuse me. I have to make a speech. Try not to cry when you hear it. Here—here's a complimentary ticket." He threw a blue piece of paper on the floor. "You can sit on the front row."

Harrison Henninger smiled, took the valise and left the room.

FIFTY

THURSDAY, MAY 17, 6:05 P.M.

JAMIE FOLLOWED MR. Johnson as he walked briskly toward the stadium. The antennae of the television trucks—perhaps thirty of them, Jamie estimated—pointed toward the sky. Workers scurried around the trucks, managing cables and cameras while the newscasters practiced their scripts.

Jamie overheard one of the newscasters rehearsing his opening: "Will Harrison Henninger announce his candidacy for president tonight? Or will he throw his support to the president? Or to the president's challenger? That is the question—"

Nearby clusters of VFW men gathered, laughing at some jokes. Some of them used canes and a few had walkers.

"Mr. Johnson—"

"There's the entrance," he said, his voice insistent. He began walking briskly toward the RFK sign.

Where did you get this new energy, Mr. Johnson? And where are you taking us?

The two of them entered the stadium. Mr. Johnson looked around the concourse as if to get his bearings. Jamie looked at him carefully. He seemed to be much more alert—more purposeful—than the last two days. He headed toward a sign that said **Lower Level—A&B**

and Jamie followed. She continued to follow him as he walked down the steps toward the field. Much of the field was covered with rows of chairs. The chairs faced a stage with a huge banner over it: **Harrison Henninger.**

When Johnson reached the bottom row, he crawled over the iron railing to the field level. Jamie was surprised at how nimble he was. "Hey!" the usher protested to Jamie. "He can't go down there. That's reserved seating."

"I'm sorry," she said. "I will bring him back." The nurse's uniform was helpful in this situation, but she was having trouble catching up to Johnson. He passed a group of men with their VFW vests, Jamie following close behind. "Now, that's the kind of nurse I need," one of the veterans laughed and the others joined in.

Henry entered the arena, showed his ticket to the usher, and, after removing his suit coat, he folded it neatly over the back of the folding chair. He took his seat on the front row of chairs—on the aisle. Technicians and cameramen were testing their systems directly in front of him—at the base of the stage and on the stage itself. A row of veterans in wheelchairs were seated across the aisle. After a moment Harrison Henninger came on the stage with the event organizers. He had the valise—the one Henry had given him only a few minutes earlier—under his arm. Henry shuddered as he thought about the documents inside that valise. *Those documents could bring down a sitting president—and put me in prison.*

The crowd applauded as they recognized Henninger when he came on the stage. He waved as he walked toward the podium. Beside the podium was a small table and on it a glossy wooden box. *That must be the purple heart,* Henry realized. Henninger put the valise on the table beside the box. He held up his famous holster and put it on the table beside the valise. Even louder applause came from the audience. "Give 'em hell, Harrison" came from dozens of places in the stadium. It was still thirty minutes until the speech, but the event organizers were going through the details with the speaker and checking the sound system.

A wave of depression came over Henry. The depression, he realized, was not only about his situation; it was also about the corruption and hypocrisy taking place. A man who was not a patriot was about to give a patriotic speech—a speech in which he would call himself a hero—which would impugn the dignity of the thousands and thousands of legitimate heroes—

Give it up, Henry. There is nothing you can do.

Someone went by him—so quickly it was noticeable. The man passed by so closely that Henry could have touched him had he reached out. Henry looked up. He was an older man, but he walked briskly. Immediately behind him was a nurse, who apparently was trying to catch up with the man. *I wonder why a man that healthy needs a nurse.*

A line of veterans had formed at the edge of the stage—waiting to get their VFW caps signed by Henninger. The organizers had given Henninger a chair on the stage near the podium where he sat autographing the caps. On the table where he sat was the box with the purple heart and the valise that Henry Pursley had given him moments before—and his famous 38 caliber handgun. The microphone on the podium was live, but Henninger said nothing although the microphone picked up some chatter of the veterans.

Mr. Johnson stopped in front of the stage. He took a moment to appraise the situation. Beside him was the row of veterans in wheelchairs. He snatched the cap from the head of the one nearest him. "Hey!" the man said.

"I'm sorry," Jamie said to the veteran. "I will get your cap back." She followed Johnson up on the stage. Henninger was signing the caps quickly, scribbling HH on each one, without acknowledging the veterans, looking around as if to say, "How long do I have to do this?"

Jamie watched as Mr. Johnson got in line behind a half-dozen or so veterans, waiting his turn. She started to say something to him, to question him, but he gave her a look that told her to stay away. The line grew shorter as the men in front of Mr. Johnson got their caps signed. Johnson's turn came. He stood in front of Harrison Henninger. Henninger put his hand out expecting to receive a cap, but Johnson just stood there.

The cap was not offered. When no cap was placed in his hand Henninger looked up, impatience in his face.

Jamie stood only a few feet away. She wasn't sure what she should do. She heard Mr. Johnson speak. His voice was clear and low: "Lieutenant Henninger. Has anyone saluted you recently?" Henninger looked up, confused. Mr. Johnson slowly brought his middle finger to his own forehead, stretched it toward Henninger and then slowly returned it to his side, recreating the motion he had made forty years earlier. "Private E.W. Johnson, 2nd platoon, K Company, 108th regiment, 3rd Army ... saluting you again, just like I did at St. Lautern forty years ago."

Henninger's face twitched. His expression showed confusion ... then terror. He looked from side to side for help.

"I brought you a souvenir," Johnson continued. "It's from St. Lautern." Johnson reached in his pocket and pulled out the two 38 caliber cartridges, showing them in his open hand. "These came from your gun. These are the bullets you killed Iowa with."

Jamie heard the echo of Mr. Johnson's voice through the speaker system in the stadium. The stadium had gone absolutely quiet. All conversations had ceased. No one moved. Every person in the arena could hear the words from the stage. A palpable tension pervaded the stadium. The veterans and the technicians left the stage.

Johnson tossed the two empty cartridges onto the table in front of Henninger. They trickled out onto the stage floor, making a dull tinkling sound—a sound audible throughout the quiet stadium. Henninger looked around for help. He stood. "Help! This man is crazy! Somebody—"

He was not able to finish his sentence. The quickness and agility of Mr. Johnson's action surprised Jamie. He grabbed the gun—still in its holster—from the table, hit Henninger across the head with it with such ferocity that Henninger's legs crumpled, and he fell to the stage floor, knocking over the table with the box with the purple heart and the valise. Johnson rolled Henninger on his back and jumped on top of him, pulling the gun from the holster.

Henninger thrashed, trying to escape. Johnson hit him fiercely across the face with the gun, leaving a trail of blood across Henninger's nose and forehead. He screamed in pain, but his legs went still.

"Lieutenant Henninger," Johnson screamed in Henninger's ear. "I heard you wanted a purple heart. You're about to earn it." He put the barrel of the gun into Henninger's neck. "Is this gun really loaded? You say it is. From the look on your face, I think it is. That's good to know."

Jamie was the only one left on the stage with the two men. She could see the white circle of skin on Henninger's neck where the gun barrel was pressed. She stepped toward the two men on the floor. "Mr. Johnson—"

"Back away, Jamie. I've waited forty years for this." Jamie was amazed at the tone of his voice. It was not the voice of the old man who had been in a fog for the last two days. This was a different voice. This voice carried the timbre of a warrior, of a man who knew combat, of a soldier who had fought a war. It was not a confused or tentative voice. It was not the voice of an elderly veteran. It was the voice of a young soldier—a soldier who knew the horrors of warfare, and he was not seeking Jamie's advice—or anyone else's. Private Earl Wayne Johnson, a United States Army infantryman, knew exactly what he needed to do—and he was doing it. Jamie stepped back. As she did, she noticed that several of the tv cameras had moved closer and were capturing the events on the stage.

Henninger's face showed his terror. He looked around, desperately looking for help. Two security guards came cautiously to the edge of the stage, their guns drawn. "Are you hoping someone will shoot me?" Johnson asked Henninger, pressing his face closer. "Let me tell you what I saw once. One of the guys in our platoon shot a German in the head and that German must have fired a hundred rounds from his machine gun—sprayed the whole street—before he went to his knees, still firing, before he fell down dead. If someone shoots me, I will go to God with the memory of putting a couple of rounds into your miserable head, splashing your brains all over this stage—so you may want to tell those men to put their guns down."

Henninger whimpered. "Put your guns down." The security guards complied.

"Nineteen men—every man in 2nd platoon—you betrayed. They're all dead—except me—because of you. Patterson, Templeton, Jones, Brooks, Hawkins, Childers, McKinley, Toomey, Admundson, McMurtry, Browning, Davis, Simpson, Blevins, Armstrong, Walker, Patterson, Trevino, Haltom, … and Langston. You killed the others by abandoning them. You killed Langston yourself. You killed him with this gun."

Johnson raised his head slightly, still straddling Henninger. "Jamie, bring me that microphone." She went to the podium and took the microphone from its holder. It screeched through the loudspeakers in an otherwise silent stadium. "Put it down here near Lieutenant Henninger's mouth. He is about to confess to his murders." She did as she was instructed, placing the microphone directly in front of his mouth. Under the bright lights the blood from Henninger's face glistened.

Johnson used the gun barrel to turn Henninger's face toward his own. He put the microphone on Henninger's chest. The sound of the 'click' when Johnson pulled the slide of the handgun went through the stadium. "Now, Lieutenant Henninger, I want you to tell everyone how you betrayed 2nd platoon—how you intentionally left us across the river so that the Germans would overrun us—and how you killed Langston yourself, the next day. Tell everyone you betrayed 2nd platoon; you betrayed your countrymen. Tell everyone about that—and speak clearly."

Henninger turned his head from side to side, his eyes desperate and pitiful, looking for help. He ran his tongue over his lips. His jaw quivered.

Jamie screamed when she heard the explosion. She forced herself to look at Henninger. The top half of his left ear had been blown off. Blood was streaming from the wound, and Henninger was crying pathetically.

Johnson's face was contorted, and his teeth were clenched as he put his face into Henninger's. He screamed into Henninger's bloody ear, his voice loud enough to be heard throughout the stadium. "Tell them you betrayed your countrymen! Tell them you betrayed 2nd platoon! Do it now or I will—"

"I betrayed them! I betrayed them!" Henninger said, crying and pleading.

Johnson put the barrel of the gun in Henninger's nostril. "Say 'second platoon!' Say 'my countrymen!,' you miserable sunnavabitch or I will—"

"I betrayed second platoon! I betrayed my countrymen!" Henninger bawled, his chest heaving.

Johnson's body relaxed slightly. He stood up and took a deep breath and engaged the safety on the handgun. He picked up the case holding the purple heart and slowly opened it. "Here," he said, as he tossed the medal on Henninger's quivering body. "Here's your purple heart. I guess you've earned it now." He threw the handgun across the stage. He looked at Jamie and nodded slightly as if to say "mission accomplished".

For a moment, before the security guards came and put Johnson in handcuffs, the only sound in the stadium was the moaning and crying of Harrison Henninger, picked up by the stadium sound system as well as the microphones and cameras of several dozen news outlets.

FIFTY-ONE

NEVER IN THE history of women's athletics had there been so much media interest in a women's track meet. Eugene, Oregon was filled with both electronic and print media representatives. Ticket sales were up—well beyond any previous year. All hotel rooms in a 60 mile radius were occupied. This unprecedented interest in the NCAA national championships was accounted for by the presence of one particular athlete—Jamie Patterson of Duke University.

Jamie Patterson, two weeks earlier, had won the Atlantic Coast Conference 800 meter event, setting a conference record in the event—and was considered the favorite for the national championship. But it was not entirely her athletic accomplishment that had created the unusual media buzz—it was related to her connection to the events on the stage—two weeks earlier—at RFK Stadium, where Harrison Henninger confessed before a national audience his guilt in betraying his fellow soldiers forty years previously. Her picture—in the nurse's uniform standing on the stage a few feet away from E.W. Johnson and Harrison Henninger—appeared on the front page of practically every newspaper in the United States, and on most of the major daily newspapers around the world. "The

Mystery Nurse" the headlines read as reporters tried to determine who this enigmatic character was.

The sportswriters in North Carolina were the first to figure it out. The Sunday version of the Asheville Times had this:

> **We will leave it to others to explain the picture of Jamie Patterson on the front page of our newspaper. National news is not our beat. We will confine ourselves to explaining why her picture is on the cover page of the Sports section. Yesterday Jamie Patterson broke the ACC record for the 800 meters, running the fastest time in the NCAA this season. In two weeks, she will participate in the NCAA championships in Eugene, Oregon, where she will be one of the favorites and where she will seek to confirm her position on the U.S. Olympic team …**

The past two weeks had been a blur for Jamie. She had arrived back on campus—with a special presidential escort—on Friday before the conference championships the next day. She didn't really know what to expect of herself in her race, but just before she went to the starter's blocks, the team manager handed her a telegram. **You have won one race already. Win another one.—Richard**. She folded the telegram and put it in the waistband of her running shorts. When the starter's gun sounded, she found an emotional and physical release she had never known before.

One of the sportswriters said about the race:

Jamie Patterson ran with an intensity I have never seen. When she crossed the finish line well ahead of her competitors, it looked as if she could have kept running forever.

Sports Illustrated wrote: **At Duke University Jamie Patterson is known as a student of the ancient Greeks—particularly Greek athletics. She, no doubt, is aware that the Greeks called the places of competition the agonia, the place of agony. However, yesterday she contradicted that ancient description because she ran her race—at a record pace—with a smile on her face, turning the so-called "place of agony" into a "place of exhilaration" instead.**

On the Monday after the track meet, Jamie had returned to Washington—again with a special presidential escort. She testified before the FBI and then was received by the president in the Oval Office—along with E.W. Johnson, who by the president's orders was being held in protective custody, and who, in the photos later taken in the Oval Office, looked very irritated. She hugged him while the official White House photographer clicked away. One of those photos—of her embracing Johnson with President Cavanaugh standing just behind them—would appear the next day on the front page of the newspapers.

Those newspapers were filled with stories about Harrison Henninger as the details began to emerge about his past. His bodyguard, the muscle-bound giant, survived the injection—although the doctor said it would have killed two ordinary men. His bulk and the fact that he received immediate medical attention saved him. He, like his boss, was in a federal holding facility, where they were under constant interrogation.

"Is there anything I can do for you?" the president had asked Jamie.

Her request surprised the president. "Well, that is an odd request," he said. "But ... I'm the president of the United States. Surely I can make the arrangements."

Thirty minutes later Jamie sat in the back of a black Secret Service limo with a paper sack in her lap, as she was being driven toward Memorial Hospital. The purple construction paper and the scissors she had requested were in the sack. She took the scissors from the bag and began cutting. She finished her project just as the limo arrived at the hospital.

Evelyn Washburn was on duty at the information desk when Jamie went inside. Jamie started to apologize, but Evelyn cut her off. "No, please do not apologize. I understand now. You did what you had to do. You are a hero! What excitement! And besides, I have another date with Marvin. He's taking me to the hockey game this weekend."

Marvin was not on duty at Richard's room on the 4th floor. That duty had been assumed by two Secret Service agents. But they were expecting Jamie. The White House had made the arrangements.

Jamie stepped quietly into the room. In the dim light she could see Richard on the hospital bed. His head was bandaged, and his arm was in a cast and sling, His eyes were closed. Jamie spoke softly: "I brought you something," Richard opened his eyes. He managed a smile. "You won the race. Congratulations."

"Thank you for the encouragement," Jamie said. "I received your telegram just before the race—and speaking of encouragement, I heard you are improving rapidly and should be out of here in a few days."

"The men in my family are known for hardheadedness. That's what saved me."

"Speaking of the men in your family, I believe both your grandfather and your father were purple heart recipients." She reached in the sack she brought. She pulled out a piece of purple construction paper cut into the shape of a heart. She took a safety pin from the sack and pinned the piece of paper on his pajama collar. "The tradition continues," she said, standing erect and giving him a salute. "The third generation of Roberts men has his purple heart. Congratulations."

"Thank you," Richard said, a smile coming to his face.

Jamie leaned over and kissed him. "About this cast," she said, "when I see you next, whenever that is,

I do not want to see any female signatures on it. Understood?"

"Yes ma'am. Understood."

Jamie's father had flown to Oregon to watch the meet. Since Jamie's coach had made her "off-limits" to the media, he was inundated with requests for interviews. Jamie was both amused and gratified to watch her father talk with all the reporters. The story about his father, Jamie's grandfather, and his World War II platoon was soon in all the U.S. newspapers and Jamie was glad her grandfather—and his fellow soldiers and their families—were getting this long-delayed acknowledgement.

That story continued to dominate the newspapers and Jamie was amused when she saw the photo of the president visiting Richard in the hospital. The article explained that the president now understood that Richard was a "legitimate American hero" and that all charges against him—at the president's direction—had been dismissed.

Just before her race, while Jamie was limbering up on the track and her father was talking to reporters in the bleachers, she looked toward the stadium gate—Richard! She could not believe it. Flanked by two secret service men, with a patch on his head and his arm in a cast, Richard was entering the stadium. She ran in that direction and the media, seeing the commotion, left her father and followed her.

"Richard!" she exclaimed as she embraced him. "What—?"

"I tried to get in without being noticed—"

"But—"

"The president came to see me in the hospital," he explained. "As he was leaving, he asked me if there was anything he could do for me. "I thought 'What the heck. I might as well ask.' I told him I had always wanted to attend the NCAA track and field championships—and here I am."

"And how is your head? And your arm?"

"Both will be okay, however—" he held up his arm. "I have no signatures on my cast."

"I need a pen," Jamie answered.

"I just happened to have one," Richard said, smiling, as he pulled a marker from his pocket. Two dozen cameras clicked as she signed Richard's cast and as she kissed him on the cheek.

Her father had come over to the cluster of media people surrounding Jamie and Richard. "Dad, I want you to meet someone … this is Richard."

Jamie made that statement in such a way that it carried some communication, some message, that no one but her father could have understood. Her father shook Richard's hand with the comprehension that Jamie was not just saying, "This is a young man named Richard, but *This is Richard.*"

"Listen," she said. "You two can get better acquainted. You both have something in common." She smiled at them mischievously. "You both like history. But I have a race to run. I will talk with both of you later."

The Durham newspaper's Sports section, the next day, started the article this way:

They didn't have a chance—Jamie Patterson's competitors that is. Had they seen the smile on her face when she approached the starter's block, they perhaps should have given up. They just didn't have a chance ...

FIFTY-TWO

TUESDAY, JUNE 12

THE PRESIDENT OF the United States has tremendous powers—but those powers have limits, as President Wilson Cavanaugh and Brent Arens, his chief of staff, were to learn. Earl Wayne Johnson was *not* returning to Washington for any additional ceremonies, no matter how many appeals they made—and he wasn't going to accept the Silver Star that had been offered. No amount of pleading would change his mind.

Even though the administration had allocated funds to rebuild Johnson's house and a mobile home had been placed on the lot temporarily, and even though he had been welcomed back into the community of Jenkins Ridge, Earl Wayne Johnson wanted nothing further to do with the government or the media. Much had changed during the last few weeks, but Earl Wayne Johnson's irascibility had not. He still had his shotgun near the front door and more than once during the past few weeks he had fired several blasts over the heads of reporters that had pulled into his driveway.

They quit coming.

FIFTY-THREE

HENRY PURSLEY WAS flying in coach—but he didn't mind. And he was not flying alone. Myra, Amy, and Allison were with him. Not only did he not mind these circumstances, he was close to ecstatic in his coach seat. He reached over and took Myra's hand and squeezed it. She put her paperback novel in her lap and smiled at him in acknowledgement. Across the aisle, Amy and Allison both wore headsets and were flipping through magazines.

The flight would take them to San Francisco and then to Campo del Sur—and this was not a visit. They were moving back to California. It had been less than three weeks since the sensational events at RFK Stadium that had shaken the United States and the world. Henry had been as close to those actual events as anyone, and when E.W. Johnson finally stood over the whimpering figure of Harrison Henninger and threw the gun across the stage, from his front row seat Henry watched as the security guards handcuffed Johnson and medical personnel came to attend to Henninger. Immediately behind them came a flurry of cameramen and reporters—anxious to get close to the action.

All this activity was well-recorded on multiple video cameras—which were focused on the figure of Harrison Henninger curled up on the stage whimpering and crying. And although it was never noticed by the public—if one looked carefully at the edge of the screen during the commotion on the stage—one would have seen the figure of a man walking slowly in the background, coming near the table that had been overturned, reaching down and picking up a briefcase, Harrison Henninger's briefcase, and walking slowly out of the frame. "That's my boy!" the president had said when that portion of the video was shown in the Oval Office and both Arens and Olmstead nodded toward Henry in their mutual approval. The president became absolutely giddy. "That's my boy!" he repeated, pumping Henry's hand vigorously. "You saved us! Yes, that was really quick thinking on your part, Henry. You got the briefcase." The president took Henninger's briefcase from his desk and held it up to the others. "Do you think we should return this to its owner?" the president asked, his face in a wide grin. "Well, I guess there's no need." He held the briefcase upside down and shook it. "Well, what about that! It appears the documents have gone missing, haven't they? What a shame! And aren't we glad the smoke alarms in the Oval Office are not very sensitive!" He pointed to some gray ash in the trash can beside his desk. "And James," the president continued, "I can't believe you were so careless with that cigarette lighter—allowing those documents with my signature to get burned up."

Yes, the president was giddy—and he had reason to be. The most recent polls—confirmed by Elliott Congrove—showed him winning the upcoming election in a landslide.

"Henry, that was quick thinking on your part—really quick thinking!" The president kept pacing around his desk. He picked up the phone on his desk and rang his receptionist. "Bring a bottle of that 25-year-old Kentucky bourbon in here," he said. "And bring four glasses. We're about to have a celebration."

Henry had never drunk bourbon before—but he drank two and a half glasses that afternoon, and while he could remember the general atmosphere of that hour in the Oval Office—acute delirium—he could not remember much of what was said. And of certain events that afternoon—when he tried to recall them later—he was not sure they actually happened. *Do I remember that Olmstead and Arens had their arms around each other's shoulders? Or did I imagine that? Did the president actually take a handful of the ashes from the wastebasket and blow them around the Oval Office?*

Henry waited until the next week for the president to release him from his duties with the administration. The president made all the expected objections—but both realized there was no further need for Henry's services. Even so, the president told him there would be a cabinet level position available for him in the next term—but Henry was weary of Washington D.C. He felt like his life had been given back to him and he did not want to spend that life in Washington. He had accepted the position of city manager for Campo del Sur. The job would pay less than half what he had been making, but he had been approached about some consulting services which had the potential of providing additional income and Myra was talking again about opening a gift shop. They would be fine. He was sure of that.

Henry looked at Myra and then at the girls. Yes, they would be fine—and all the nightmares about going to prison were over and—

"Henry, you're rubbing your shoulder. Is it bothering you again?"

Henry smiled. "Actually, no. I was rubbing it because I'm surprised how good it feels. It hasn't felt this good in months." He rolled his shoulder as he looked at Myra. He had a somewhat silly look on his face, Myra thought.

She shook her head and went back to her novel. Myra was sure she would never understand her husband.

ACKNOWLEDGEMENTS

Mike Davis read the early draft and offered valuable suggestions. Jenny Ramsey and Star Good read the later drafts and both were meticulous and conscientious in their appraisal of the story. Lynne, my wife, brought her experience as a former English teacher to the project and had to endure my moodiness when the writing wasn't going well.

The story touches on the subject of PTSD in World War II (although that name for the syndrome was not created until the VietNam war era.) A valuable treatment of that largely neglected topic is *Soldier from the War Returning*, by Thomas Childers. Every American should read it.

ABOUT THE AUTHOR

D. Charles King is the author of the highly regarded biblical novel, *I am Malchus*. His father's service in World War II has made him a life-long student of that conflict. He and his wife make their home in Charleston, South Carolina

Made in the USA
Middletown, DE
27 May 2024